CANADA'S THIRD OPTION

3655
24

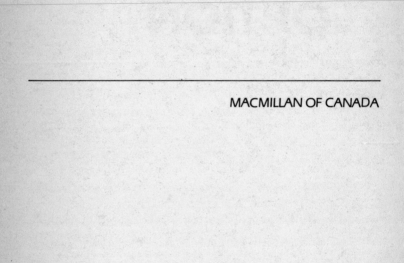

MACMILLAN OF CANADA

CANADA'S THIRD OPTION

EDITED BY

S. D. BERKOWITZ & ROBERT K. LOGAN

Canadian Cataloguing in Publication Data

Main entry under title:
Canada's third option

ISBN 0-7705-1589-4 pa.

1. Nationalism—Canada—Addresses, essays, lectures.
2. Canada—Politics and government—1963-
— Addresses, essays, lectures.*
I. Berkowitz, Stephen D., 1943-   II. Logan, Robert K.,
1939-

FC98.C35   971.06'44   C78-001299-2
F1027.C35

Printed in Canada for
The Macmillan Company of Canada Limited
70 Bond Street, Toronto, Ontario
M5B 1X3

TO OUR PARENTS AND TO
COLIN AND SHAWN AND DAVID AND RENEE,
who will have to live with
the decisions we are making now.

CONTENTS

ACKNOWLEDGMENTS

The editors would like to acknowledge both the help and encouragement of the large number of people who made this volume possible. Ann Marie Jones, Sophia Knapik, Ursula Gutenberg, Derek Mansfield, and other members of the staff, and Professor J. A. Sawyer, Director, of the Institute for Policy Analysis, University of Toronto, facilitated many aspects of the project. Alexise Stinson and Dianne Westheafer who rapidly and accurately typed most of the manuscript deserve our thanks.

Drs. A. and C. Baines, Brenda Billingsley, June Corman, Dr. A. Stein, Murray Shukyn, and many others who helped us to review articles provided us with the benefit of their sound and sober judgments for which we are grateful. We would also like to thank Virgil Duff, Roy Trueman, Jerry White, and Margaret Woollard of Macmillan of Canada for providing their timely and detailed editorial assistance which was invaluable in bringing the project to a successful conclusion. Finally, we owe a debt of gratitude to all of those who contributed to this volume, and to our families and friends for the patience with which they bore the disruptions of their own lives caused by the pressures to complete the task.

CANADA'S THIRD OPTION

CHAPTER ONE

INTRODUCTION

UNTIL RENÉ LÉVESQUE'S Parti Québécois government was elected on November 15, 1976, it was possible for Canadians to avoid thinking about problems of national unity. This is a luxury we no longer enjoy. Like it or not, the "Québec Question" will not go away by itself. Underlying it, giving it force, and shaping its historical course is a whole series of fundamental problems and issues. So even if we answer the "Québec Question" in some short-term fashion—even if, for instance, Quebeckers emphatically reject independence or "sovereignty association"—the centrifugal tendencies which it represents will be likely to appear again in some other form.

Both the Atlantic and the Prairie provinces, for instance, have their own historic objections to the way in which central Canada—and the federal government which they see as largely representing it—has been running things. And in both of these regions there are those who seriously consider alternatives to remaining within Confederation. The great historical irony of Canada's second century might very well be that while Ottawa and Ontario are preoccupied with finding short-term "solutions" to the Québec Question, Alberta, Saskatchewan, or Newfoundland will decide to leave.

For over a decade it has been clear to many socially concerned scholars that Canada is in deep trouble. Social, physical, and natural scientists in particular, though normally cautious by both inclination and training, have been speaking out on public issues with increasing frequency and in unprecedented ways.

For many people outside universities—or outside the circles within government which deal with academics on a day-to-day basis—this new faculty activism must have seemed strange. The Canadian university system has always been far more staid and conservative than the less-elite and much larger American

S. D. BERKOWITZ & ROBERT K. LOGAN

system. But suddenly, as if by way of imitation, Canadian academics seemed to get caught up in the spirit of the times; faculty members began to air their views in the popular press, to hold public forums, and to join committees. Everywhere one turned, it seemed, there were university professors issuing statements about the growing political disaffection in Québec, protesting the deterioration in our educational system, decrying the pollution of our natural environment, exposing structural flaws in the economy, reporting the breakdown of our social-welfare system, or witnessing to the collapse, in key areas, of federal-provincial co-operation. Furthermore, faculty activism continued even when student sit-ins, anti-war rallies, and the picketing of foreign embassies declined.

In retrospect, this is not so surprising. While the 1960s were pre-eminently an activist era—and while faculty shared many of their students' concerns—in both genesis and substance much of this scholarly agitation was and is deeply rooted. During the last decade, fundamental flaws in Canadian economic planning, education, science, and manpower policy, resource planning, ethnic and group relations (to name but a few) have surfaced in our research. These factors, in turn, are reflected in a growing foreign domination of our economy, declining estimates of our energy reserves, a deteriorating balance of payments, the emergence of permanently depressed regions in the country, lack of adequate training of students for university work, an increasing exodus of high technology, and, probably most seriously, a noticeably higher level of inter-group tension, racism, and semi-organized racial violence.

Much of the research upon which these observations were based was not, initially, reported in the public press in detail. But it gradually became clear to "Canada-watchers" that these destructive tendencies in our society were *not* isolated from one another but were connected and were reinforcing each other.

The evidence suggests that many of these trends have reached a point where they cannot easily be reversed or substantially curtailed. Moreover, if we try to intervene in timid and incomplete ways in the processes underlying them, it is likely that we will make things worse. In sum, many experts feel that we are now faced with a major *systemic* crisis.

Governments, both provincial and federal, seem for the most part singularly unable to understand or deal with this situation. Commissions are struck, reports written and published, task forces established, policy changes recommended, laws passed and proclaimed, and programs begun—but still nothing seems to change very much. Rarely are government bureaucracies able to carry things through with verve and enthusiasm. Inequities and inconsistencies in administration are all too common and have led to widespread cynicism about the efficacy of government.

Given this context, it is not surprising that the most deeply rooted and serious of these problems—political disaffection in Québec—has finally reached critical proportions. Although the evidence at present is far from complete, it is undoubtedly true that the rejection of the Bourassa government and the election of a Péquiste majority to replace it constitutes some kind of "protest vote". But we should not conclude from this that the November 15th election was simply a manifestation of "voter frustration"; nor can we delude ourselves that it simply reflected a rejection of the provincial Liberals—that it was not, in fact, an endorsement of separatism. The roots of Québécois discontent, we submit, lie in a persistent and pervasive regionalism in Canada which is based in our geography and enshrined in our constitution. It has pitted Québec against Ottawa, and moved Alberta, Saskatchewan, and Manitoba against her as well. It has turned the Atlantic provinces against both Québec and Ontario, and is both the product and a source of much of our unemployment, conflict among language groups, and differences in standards of living. And while, under more favourable circumstances, strong regional identification might have been the wellspring of much of our strength as a nation, in the present context it acts to exacerbate and amplify all the other problems we are facing. In the sense that it is the focal point for each of the other issues related to Canadian unity, this regionalism is the key to our present constitutional and social crisis.

During the last two or three years, the realization of this fact has grown. Whereas, a year or so ago, only a small minority of Canadian intellectuals were pointing out the similarities in the complaints voiced by Québec and the West, this observation is now a commonplace. Canadians have at last come to realize that the so-called "unity question" is not confined to the narrow issue of language rights—nor even to broader notions of cultural and economic development in French and English Canada.

Nevertheless we think that, as a rule, the average citizen does not yet fully recognize the truly general character of the crisis which besets us, and which, as a result, demands far-reaching solutions.

THREE ASPECTS OF UNITY

As we see it, Canada's current problem is multi-faceted. Each of these facets poses so significant a threat to national unity that, if ignored, it will undercut any solutions we may find to the others. As a result, any successful resolution of the unity question must be multi-pronged.

The first of these facets is reflected in a set of general constitutional questions. Under the British North America Act, Canada was set up as a federal state of semi-autonomous economic zones and governments bound loosely together by a thin line of infrastructure. The building of the Canadian Pacific Railway, the construction of telegraph and telephone links, and the subsequent creation of Trans Canada Airlines (now Air Canada) were all intended to strengthen these ties. But, given the sheer magnitude of our geography and the thinness of our population, this east-west axis has always been artificial in comparison, say, to the connections linking any particular region to an adjacent area in the United States. This pattern of infrastructure, in turn, has fostered a highly segmented and uneven development within Canada and has worked against the formulation of a clear set of national social and economic priorities. Often, the local and regional patterns of development in American regions contiguous with ours have been far more significant to us than what has been going on in other parts of Canada.

Given the continuation of such pressures in the future, it is almost inevitable that a loose federal state of the form we now have will be difficult to keep together. Thus, if we are to preserve Canada, we must find ways to offset these centrifugal tendencies —possibly with constitutional arrangements which will induce a greater consistency among the policies pursued by each of our regional governments. At the same time, we cannot ignore the regional basis of our economy and society, as a highly centralized federal state might, but must, instead, find some means for integrating our diverse regions with one another which both respects their integrity and precludes the overwhelming domination of the country by any one of them. By contrast, our present

constitution simply leaves the development of our national political economy to chance. One unfortunate consequence of this
has been the hegemony of that province—Ontario—which is
adjacent to the American midwestern industrial belt.

The second area requiring close scrutiny is the cultural one.
No nation-state can long endure on the basis of purely mechanical political and economic arrangements: there must be some
sort of common purpose beyond simple economic self-interest
which binds a nation together and provides a rationale for its
existence. Québécois seem to have more of this sense of being a
meaningful collectivity than "English" Canadians, but even this
"common ethos" is largely illusory: *neither* the "English" nor
the "French" are replacing themselves in the population. The
urbanization and industrialization which had, earlier, led to a
drop in the WASP birthrate has, since the Second World War,
overtaken the Québécois as well. And while these low birthrates
are, theoretically, quite normal and understandable, they have
intensified social and political conflict in Québec because each
group understands that it must control both immigration and
the education of immigrant children in order to dominate the
province linguistically. Ironically, of course, language is *not* culture and, given continued low birthrates, both Francophone
Québécois and Anglophone Québécois will have "lost the cultural battle" in the long run.

The point is, of course, that any culture—whether "English" or "French"—which must seek to perpetuate itself by
controlling the immigration and language of education of others
is not functioning properly. The desire to continue a culture
must be manifest in a willingness to oversee the socialization and
upbringing of children. Otherwise, that culture—especially in its
subtle non-verbal and attitudinal aspects—will die. To survive it
must be rooted in a sense of historical personhood which cannot
simply be conveyed through the learning of a language.

Come what may, then—and despite the liveliness of the
arts in Québec—traditional French-Canadian culture and traditional English-Canadian culture in Québec are doomed as things
stand now. Neither is operating in a vacuum: interacting with
and gradually eroding both of them is American culture which,
like the eighteenth-century missionary, is closely associated with
the flag of trade. Given the continued economic dependence of
our regions on the United States, French- and English-Canadian
culture—both inside and outside Québec—will eventually dis-

appear in the great American solvent. This will transform the English-speaking Canadian into a kind of funny "northern American" and lead to the substantial assimilation of the remaining French Canadians—or to their continued survival as part of an endangered species like, for example, the Cajuns in Louisiana.

We submit that the only reasonable way to avoid this eventuality is for both groups to forge a *new* identity for themselves —an amalgam of *both* English-Canadian and French-Canadian cultures. Such a cultural pattern would be strong enough to assimilate new immigrants *to* it and flexible enough to incorporate elements of the culture of other immigrants and of native peoples as well. This change, however, can only come about if we are able to go beyond the narrow sectarian interests of race, ethnicity, or language to recognition of the common fact that we occupy a unique geo-political space and must forge our identity in relation to it. This realization must be accompanied, as well, by a determination on the part of governments to establish and maintain policies which support cultural synthesis.

The third and final dimension of the unity question which we must face is implicit in the other two—but it must be dealt with in its own terms: that is, the socio-economic aspect of national integration. As we said earlier, the overwhelming fact of life in Canada is that its economic institutions are dominated and its cultural and governmental processes deeply compromised by American penetration of our national life. This is the source not only of a high degree of regional disparity, but also of our distorted labour markets, our structural and seasonal unemployment, and a generally poor quality of life in many parts of our country.

More and more during the last two decades these larger social and economic forces, rooted in our external dependence, have nearly wrecked our system of higher education by intensifying strains and tensions within it. In a largely self-enclosed economy and society, the educational system tends to train roughly as many specialists as the labour market can accommodate. The introduction of new technology promotes—with some time lag —new demands for specialists, which the educational system then fills. Wealth which is generated within the country stays within it and, as capital, provides the basis for introducing new technology and creating new jobs. Adjustments among these elements are comparatively gradual, and much the same process goes on whether a given economy is largely state-managed or private.

In Canada, by contrast, shifts in rates of economic growth are abrupt, discontinuous, and localized within regions because a large part of our national wealth flows out of this country in the form of dividends and natural resources, and flows back into it in the form of investment. Further, during neither part of this cycle are decisions made on the basis of what is good for Canada as a whole: they follow the exigencies of the market, interest rates, tax policies, and so on. At least half the time, these decisions are shaped by external rather than internal considerations.

In the manufacturing sector, for instance, this has meant that a large but indeterminate proportion of the high-technology goods that Canada consumes is fabricated in the United States, imported into this country, "repackaged" (where necessary), and distributed. In a period when market forces, tax policies, and government incentives favour production abroad, this results in a restriction of high-technology-related job opportunities. When these forces favour production in this country, jobs cascade into the economy generating shortfalls in manpower.

The point is that because these decisions are based, in many cases, on external constraints, they generate a "roller-coaster" effect: we are either desperately searching for people to fill jobs, or looking for jobs for people.

In terms of over-all regional growth and development, these same shifts in investment patterns produce either rapid growth or severe decline. Ontario's Golden Horseshoe—recently booming—is now suffering from high unemployment. Saskatchewan, which lost almost 30,000 in population between 1961 and 1971, now has an unemployment rate that is less than half of Ontario's, and Alberta is booming. The flow of net migration is now towards both these provinces.

Faced with either unemployment or migration, people living within regions in cyclical decline—especially the younger, more mobile, and better-educated parts of the population— move elsewhere. This phenomenon, which is known as "outmigration in the fertile age period", has led to really bizarre age pyramids in some Canadian provinces. Institutions dependent upon younger people—schools, for instance—then must constrict in response to reduced demand; and things begin to build on one another. In the process, families are separated, and cultural patterns broken. During the "boom" part of the same cycle, all sorts of shortages—in building materials or classroom space, for instance—develop, housing gets very expensive, and tensions mount between newcomers and established residents. Tax levels go up to provide new services, and many indicators of social stress rise.

The over-all effect of this economic dependence, then, is to produce disorganization and social instability. Coupled with our geography and population patterns, dependence has, over time, generated a series of regional economies and societies which it has been the thankless task of the federal government to try to co-ordinate. Within this context of regionalism, conflicts are inevitable. But when this sort of tension is aggravated by ethnic, language, and cultural differences, it is highly likely to result in open strife such as we are now experiencing.

We believe, in short, that the interrelatedness of our current problems is significant and that only by understanding how they are linked can we cope with the Québec Question. We must come to understand that the "Canadian unity question" is not an isolated issue, but that it embraces all the other pressing problems, issues, and conflicts we now encounter—from science policy on the one hand, to the role of the CBC on the other. All these issues are deeply intertwined and can only be dealt with together.

This is difficult to grasp at first. The whole thrust of our education—encouraging us, as it does, to separate ideas into tidy compartments—weighs against doing this. But if Canada is to emerge from her unity crisis with a long-lasting and realistic settlement, we Canadians must reject our old ways of thinking.

To change an entire society overnight is of course not possible, or even desirable. On the contrary, we suggest that some problems are more central than others—and that some are more amenable to direct and practical solutions than others. But we must attack aspects of each of our major problems at the same time in order to have a reasonable chance of success.

To those unfamiliar with the trans-disciplinary way of formulating and attacking problems implicit in our approach here, some aspects of the way we proceed from problem formulation to solutions—or partial solutions—may be new. On the face of it, for instance, there is only a distant and tenuous relationship among youth unemployment, science policy, and the structure of our communications network. But much of our youth unemployment today is a product of the sluggish economic growth which generates too few new opportunities for those seeking to enter the labour force. This, in its turn, is related to Canada's dependence on other countries for high-technology goods. As a consequence, then, of our science policy—or, more properly, lack of science policy—new technologies which could have been the basis for new markets, new capital growth, and new jobs have not been developed here. While we waited around for these technologies to be implemented for us, we lost the opportunity to exploit them ourselves. In the process, job opportunities for engineers and technicians, draftsmen, accountants, managers, salesmen, craftsmen, production-line workers, and advertising executives have been lost as well.

To take another example, the structure of our communications network both reflects and perpetuates our key problems. At present, the lion's share of our English and French programming originates in Toronto and Montreal, respectively. Production studios, film-editing facilities, actors, newscasters, costume-rental agencies, and producers and directors are also concentrated in these two centres. Young, media-minded Canadians from other regions must then leave the areas where they grew up, migrate to Toronto or Montreal, and compete with Ontarians and Québécois for limited opportunities for jobs and training. This drains other regions of talent and generates unemployment or underemployment in the metropoles.

Through a judicious application of existing technology, however—and here, once again, we see the importance of science policy—it would be possible to decentralize the production of broadcasting, present a wider range of programming, significantly expand opportunities for young people in broadcasting, and do this at less cost than it takes to operate our present overcentralized system. A not insignificant by-product of such an effort would be increased Canadian content in our programming and better coverage for the richness and diversity of our regional cultures. Out of this should come a decrease of regional jealousies and, in time, a stronger and more integrated sense of national identity and purpose.

In the present collection, we have tried to make the points of leverage in the current crisis clear: first, by identifying the most important problems and issues which underlie the current Canadian unity crisis; second, by showing the immediate relevance of each of these, both to the current debate over constitutional forms and to each other; and third, by proposing specific changes in policies which we take to be detrimental to national unity and providing a context in terms of which our own proposed policy directions can be understood.

This is no small task. In fact, it is impossible to do this both comprehensively and in detail. Still, time is running out for the Canadian experiment, and impossible things must be attempted. Furthermore, the current debate over Québec's status within Confederation is rapidly focusing on issues—language and cultural priorities and minority rights—which are neither fruitful nor, ultimately, resolvable in their own terms. Beyond this, as the debate has progressed, the options for Canada seem to have dwindled—to a dressed-up version of the status quo on the one hand, and independence or sovereignty association on the other. Neither alternative promises a positive and enduring resolution of the deeply rooted conflicts which have given rise to our present *impasse*. In the long term, the results of any Québec plebiscite, either for or against independence, are probably irrelevant: governments will still have to face the forces which have brought us to this juncture.

THE THIRD OPTION

In this book we intend to enlarge the current debate by offering, as our title suggests, a "third option": to reject both the *indépendentiste* and anti-*indépendentiste* alternatives, to reconsider our national goals, and to suggest how best to carry these forward. In some cases, this may involve borrowing heavily from the past—trying to preserve those traditions which are useful and instructive for the future. In others, it will involve striking out boldly in wholly new directions. In all cases, however, it must go beyond trying to fill new bottles with old wine: partial solutions and the establishment of some superficial consensus will only postpone the reckoning and further complicate our problems.

Our goal is not to present the reader with a book "about" national unity in the limited sense of a monograph on the BNA Act or a collection of articles on French separatism. Instead, we hope to induce the reader to enter into a dialogue with us about how to think about Canadian unity. Put another way, we try to go back to more fundamental and antecedent questions. What are the basic constitutional forms and institutional arrangements which will allow for sustained and enlarged social and cultural development in the northern tier of this continent? What type of economy will facilitate this? How and to what extent can and should this economy be strengthened or restructured through state participation? What would constitute a healthy relationship between local and regional economic, social, and cultural patterns and "national" policies? What sort of social-welfare and incomes policies are consistent with our larger social, economic, and cultural goals and, again, how can these best be implemented? How can we protect our environment and conserve our natural resources, and what policies should we adopt to ensure ourselves an adequate supply of energy from fossil fuels, renewable energy sources, and nuclear energy? What is an optional population size for Canada and who should be concerned with its regulation? And so on.

The essays which follow are an attempt to refine these questions by collecting together the thinking of a number of people—whose opinions are sometimes shared by the editors and sometimes not—who have both academic training and practical experience in dealing with policy questions of this kind. Because of their backgrounds and expertise in their fields, their views constitute a rough "barometer" of informed and engaged opinion in the areas they treat. Many contributors, moreover, have been actively involved in the debates surrounding various aspects of Canadian public policy for a number of years. In this sense, their arguments may have a wider application than those of narrow disciplinary specialists.

By selecting contributors in this fashion—by drawing for this collection on the work of activist intellectuals—we hope to undercut the myth that the central issues involved in the Canadian unity debate are the proper and exclusive domain of experts in constitutional law, finance, economics, sociology, or whatever. There are, of course, technical questions in each of these areas which bear on national policy, and we try to present many of them. But the national unity debate is not really bounded or defined by objective questions: it encompasses a range of preferences in political strategies, social patterns, and lifestyles which cannot be neatly categorized or measured in their entirety. We hope, however, that by showing the reader some of the consequences of the various choices we face, we can help him or her to choose among them in an informed way.

For this reason, we have organized this collection around a

series of themes which we feel underlie this debate.

In Part One, "The Constitutional Questions", we deal with those issues—such as the basis of Confederation, the legal status of a "referendum" on separation, historical claims by the federal and provincial governments to represent popular consensus—which are most closely associated with the Canadian unity debate in the mass media. In the first section of Part One, "Background for the Debate", the Honourable Jean Chrétien and the Honourable Claude Morin—speaking both as Francophones and as politicians—lay out the broad constitutional positions adopted by their respective governments. Both spokesmen are careful to leave some room for compromise, but both assume some general agreement among their listeners on underlying issues. Neither—and this we think is typical of the current constitutional discussions—takes on these issues directly.

Senator Eugene Forsey, in his article "Get It Right, Get It Right", sharpens this debate by describing the limitations of a "referendum" for resolving constitutional issues. If Forsey is right, and we have no doubt that he is, a plebiscite alone—no matter how decisive its outcome—cannot resolve the question of Québec's status.

In the second section of Part One, "The Constitutional Context", Anthony Scott and John Harney scrutinize those aspects of Canadian federalism which are central to the debate over separation. For Scott, the key question concerns the kind and scope of decisions which can or should be made by a central government or by provincial or regional governments. Too much of the current discussion, he feels, has been directed towards jurisdictional or symbolic aspects of the centralization or decentralization of powers in a federal system, and not enough towards the different functional or economic consequences of various plans for a division of powers. Here Scott introduces a pragmatic note which is a recurrent motif in this book. The real test of any scheme or set of schemes for redrawing constitutional boundaries, reallocating tax power, rearranging our system of social welfare, or whatever, should be the extent to which a given set of arrangements promotes, *in practice*, the aims for which it was designed. No "plan", no matter how apparently sound, should be regarded as sacrosanct until it shows signs of proving its worth.

Adopting a more general approach, John Harney argues that our current constitutional arrangements are and have been unworkable for some time. He proposes, in their stead, a "true confederation" with built-in constitutional recognition of both the common and the distinct interests and cultural aspirations of Anglophone, Francophone, and native peoples. This is an especially interesting paper because it brings to light a number of constitutional issues—native peoples' rights, for instance—which are not normally associated with public discussions of national unity, but which, none the less, must be taken into account if any new constitutional form for Canada is going to work.

Beginning in Part Two, we lay out a series of discussions of those cultural, social, and economic problems we see as posing immediate threats to national unity. Part Two focuses on the most obvious of these: the cultural and language conflicts undergirding the "Québec Question".

Milton Acorn begins this Part with a brief poem/essay which expresses the view that the time is long past when English Canadians could lay some moral claim to Québec. English Canada, he says, has already sold itself into economic and cultural bondage to the United States—and has, thus, forfeited the right to play a role in determining Québec's future.

Many Canadians, in the arts in particular, seem to share this view. Québécois language rights, they argue, were enshrined in the BNA Act, but very little of substance was done to protect them in practice for almost 100 years. Economically and culturally, Québec was treated as a colony of English Canada—which, in turn, was allowed to become a colony of the United States. This "double colonization", they argue, is the ultimate source and proximate cause of Québec separatism.

Perhaps the best-known recent attempts to reverse these trends were the series of federal language policies which grew out of the Bilingualism and Biculturalism Commission of the early 1960s. Two of the members of this commission, Royce Frith and Davidson Dunton, contribute the next two articles in this section. Frith confines himself almost exclusively to the most significant outcome of this commission: the Official Languages Act of 1969. Although Frith recognizes a number of deficiencies in the programs brought into being by the Act, he maintains that the ideas underlying them were correct and that, on balance, the programs were effective. Dunton, however, maintains that English Canada failed to adopt the recommendations of the commission. Ontario should have declared itself bilingual, and courts in Ontario should have become accessible in French. In addition, Manitoba—which had a special responsibility because of its large French-speaking minority—has not gone far enough in developing facilities for it. Slowness to implement necessary changes in the recent past now means that English Canadians must go even further than the commissioners originally recommended towards recognizing these rights as a sign of English Canada's good faith.

Gregory Baum and Marshall McLuhan and Barrington Nevitt contribute the concluding articles in Part Two. Their pieces focus on the cultural differences which aggravate the conflict between English and French Canada. Baum contends that these cultural differences extend beyond simple preferences to a wholly distinct "world view" which is rooted not only in inherited differences between English and French "culture" in the abstract, but in historic differences in the experience of these groups in North America. Because of this structural basis for conflict, Baum argues, nothing short of some constitutional accommodation between the two cultures will preserve Canadian unity.

McLuhan and Nevitt take a different tack. The cultural conflicts in Canada, they say, are simply one manifestation of larger patterns of cultural disintegration and change going on throughout western society. This larger context, they argue, is frequently obscured by the more obvious and visible events ("figure") which we experience through mass media. Only by recognizing that the cultural confrontation between "WASP" and "Québécois" is part of this pattern—which has been intensified by the peculiar ability of electronic media to meld past and present events into one—will we be able to understand the emotive and non-rational dimensions of this confrontation. McLuhan and Nevitt argue that a reconciliation of Canada's two solitudes is dependent on understanding and dealing with this dimension in new and creative ways.

In Part Three, "Threats to Unity: The Problems of Regionalism and the Economy", we broaden our discussion to include the structural causes of the constitutional and cultural conflicts which Scott, Baum, and McLuhan and Nevitt identified. The organization of our economy and the role of the state in it, strategies of development and their impact on regional inequality, health care, and means of ensuring our energy supply while effectively managing our natural resources and environment are given close consideration.

This Part has the broadest scope of any in the book. At the same time, it is the most highly integrated. It is also likely to be the most controversial because it exposes the heart of political conflict in Canada: disagreements over the role the state ought to play in regulating and maintaining various aspects of our lives.

The answers provided by the authors whose articles appear in this Part, however, defy classification in conventional, political terms. S. D. Berkowitz and June Corman, for instance, argue that the dynamics of Canadian development have always necessitated a large role for the state in managing our economy. The real choice facing us, then, is not one between "free enterprise" and "state management", but between various models or scenarios for state management. This is a view which a number of Canadian economic planners of various political hues—most notably, perhaps, Walter Gordon—have advanced over the years. Berkowitz and Corman carry this argument one step further by explicitly examining various models of "state economy" and outlining their advantages and disadvantages. Given the constraints under which Canada is now operating, we have little practical choice but to move towards a model—what they call a "state-centred" economy—in which governments explicitly plan labour supply and manage certain key sectors of the economy.

Larry Felt continues this line of argument by suggesting that regional underdevelopment—and deteriorating standards of living in some regions of this country—are a by-product of the inappropriate models of development and social welfare followed by both provincial and federal governments. Some provincial governments—and here he is thinking specifically of Atlantic Canada—have been historically fascinated by ambitious development projects which fail, in the long run, because local markets are not sufficiently developed to sustain them. These schemes, Felt argues, have been aided and encouraged by unrealistic federal-grants programs like those administered by the Department of Regional Economic Expansion (DREE), and by unwieldy transfer payments schemes. In their stead, he proposes a single guaranteed annual income (GAIN) program to maintain reasonable standards of living while encouraging local industry and markets.

This theme of the necessity for centralized planning but *decentralized* responsibility for carrying out programs informs the article on our health-care system, "The Community-Centre

Alternative", by Jan Dukszta and Teresa Berkowitz. The mechanisms for funding health care across Canada are quite similar,
but radical differences in the quality of care are apparent among
different regions and between northern and southern areas
within them. Moreover, the fiscal basis of provincial medical
schemes is now in jeopardy because of poorly articulated
planning at the federal and provincial levels, and because of
changes in the age structure of our population. The effects of
these changes are most likely to have an immediate impact in
those regions with serious outmigration due to falling levels of
employment. Instead of the present system, Dukszta and Berkowitz argue for a single, national health-care system with clear
assignment of fiscal and planning responsibility at the federal,
provincial, district, and community levels.

Leonard Waverman and John Kinzel, who contribute the
last two articles in this Part, show how conflicting provincial and
federal policies in the resource sector have hampered all efforts
to ensure that our mineral reserves are developed in the public
interest. Waverman lays much of the blame for this on "warring
political jurisdictions" which have ensured that "the prices consumers pay [for energy] bear little relation to the long-run costs
of the various energy sources they use". Canadian energy policy
has been more consistent—and therefore more successful—
than U.S. initiatives in this field, but, as Waverman shows, the
annual federal-provincial showdowns to set the price of oil (the
"*Real* Calgary Stampede") still leave future energy supplies very
much at risk.

Kinzel suggests that an important and, in some cases, in-
dispensable tool for ensuring a more rational policy is a program
of "selective public ownership". Had such a policy been in force
in 1972, he argues, it would not have been nearly so easy for the
foreign-dominated oil industry to "lull . . . Canadians to sleep by
telling them they had enough oil and gas for centuries to come"
while our known energy reserves were rapidly dwindling. Ottawa's reaction to provincial moves along these lines, Kinzel argues,has been to "assert its centralist power", thus hampering
provincial attempts to create rational resource-development
plans. Unlike many of the authors in this volume, Kinzel sees the
roots of federal-provincial conflicts in this area not in the BNA
Act, but in Ottawa's unwillingness to share power.

In Part Four, "Threats to Unity: The Social Issues", the
thrust of the argument is that Canada's failure to live up to its

social commitments is not, as some would have it, the result of some tragic flaw in our national character, but of structural patterns which originate in Canada's colonial past and institutional dependency.

Lorne Tepperman points to one such pattern enshrined in our legal system. Criminal justice in Canada has reflected our society's overweening faith in expertise. Rather than try to foster a broad popular understanding of the purposes and workings of the law, Canadian legal elites continue to clothe their activities in obscure language and mysterious ritual. We acquiesce in our own mystification because of a widespread lack of confidence in our ability to shape our own destiny—a lack attributable, in part, to historic patterns of cultural and economic dependence— first on Britain and then on the United States. As a result, our legal institutions are authoritarian, conservative, and repressive. They have not adjusted to changing social circumstances, or to increased knowledge about the sources and consequences of crime, or to advances in legal theory. Instead, they continue to uphold narrow class and establishment interests—rather than those of the society as a whole. If we are to break this pattern— and Tepperman is doubtful that we can—we must, among other things, develop a sense of our unique legal requirements and of our potential as social innovators. This awareness, in turn, must be reflected in mechanisms which provide for greater direct popular participation in shaping legal institutions and practices.

This same abdication of social responsibility, Ernest Chang argues, is the source of many of the failings in our system of health care. The bill for health is rapidly rising because our methods of providing health care have been almost exclusively determined by medical practitioners wedded to capital-intensive and technology-intensive medicine. While the costs of this system have increased dramatically, the benefits (measured in terms of decreased morbidity and mortality) have been slight. By contrast, the causes of many of our diseases—the stress of urban living and environmental and industrial pollution—flourish unchecked. But our medical profession—committed as it is to "free enterprise medicine" and curative rather than preventive health care—still largely ignores the societal and environmental context of illness. Chang argues for the creation of a *truly* public system of public health which springs from a view of health as part of a broad *social* policy and not just the professional bailiwick of medical specialists. It is up to us to de-mystify medicine and subject it to closer public scrutiny.

A similar drastic restructuring of education is called for in the next piece. Robert K. Logan and Gale Moore look at the state of our current practice in education and find that our system is pursuing goals which are largely outdated. Schools have failed to recognize that the institutions—extended families, small communities, and strong churches—which have traditionally carried much of the burden for the education of children outside the home are increasingly threatened in an urban-industrial society. But schools are unwilling or unable to fill the resultant void in the area of moral education. In addition, Canadian schools have traditionally focused on teaching narrow analytic skills rather than those broader, pattern-recognizing capabilities which are necessary for grasping interconnections among events and processes. Only by shaping its educational practice in the light of contemporary realities can our educational system perform its proper function in our society.

Edward Harvey, in "Education for What?", then provides a context for assessing this larger question of educational goals. The 1960s were a period of unprecedented growth in our educational system—in terms of both enrolments and costs. Unqualified optimism characterized most estimates of what the educational system could be expected to provide. In the 1970s, declining enrolments in some areas and recognition of the long-term economic implications of high levels of spending dampened this enthusiasm, and education is entering upon a period of constraint. Harvey suggests that we should now re-examine a number of fundamental issues. Given declining demand for university graduates, what should the goals of our system be? We can, for example, use our educated manpower more effectively by increasing our research and development activity; but we must also recognize the "intangible" benefits of education—how it can be used to extend our opportunities and horizons, and its potential impact upon the quality of life.

The last two articles in this Part—"Environment, Resources, and Confederation", by F. Kenneth Hare, and "A Long-term Policy for Federal Funding of Scientific Research", by Robert K. Logan—focus on the pressing nature of this need for rational planning and systematic utilization of our talents and resources. Hare sees Québec separatism as a clear and present danger to our ability to understand and manage the environment. At present, he says, Canada—with a population of twenty-three million—is barely able to marshal the financial resources necessary to meet its minimum commitment to doing this. Québec (with a commensurately smaller population) and Canada-without-Québec would both find it well-nigh impossible to do so.

Logan underscores this by noting that total federal expenditures on scientific activities are not even keeping pace with inflation. As things stand now, Canada invests a smaller proportion of its GNP in scientific research than most western countries. If we continue to allow our energy and resources to be drained by a perpetual political crisis, we will not be able to sustain activities like scientific research which are essential if we are to meet economic challenges in world markets. We are, in effect, mortgaging our future in order to pay the cost of our present political conflicts. Logan urges us to reassess our priorities and direct our spending on scientific research to areas which show the greatest promise of generating economic spin-offs in the near future. This, coupled with the systematic development of basic research in "centres of excellence", will strike a better balance in science policy than the one which we have at present.

Under the best of circumstances, bringing about the sorts of change envisaged in these chapters would be difficult. Given that our current dilemma springs, in many instances, from an absence of effective mechanisms for establishing popular consensus and implementing policy, it is probably foolhardy to expect our current mechanisms to work any better under the pressure of the moment than they have in the past.

The final Part of this book proposes ways of defining and dealing with Canada's problems which go beyond crude polarities, and simple mechanical solutions. Two essays—one by Senator Maurice Lamontagne and one by Robert K. Logan—are designed to jog the reader into conceiving of our old problems in new ways. Lamontagne, a scientist, suggests that a precondition for establishing or re-establishing national unity is some general agreement on national goals. These, in turn, must be highly articulated with one another because the underlying phenomena they address are closely intertwined. In order to formulate these goals, he suggests the creation of a new institution, "Horizons Canada", whose task it would be to orchestrate discussions and debates across the country. These encounters would initially involve key decision makers, but should eventually include a substantial number of active and involved citizens.

Lamontagne hopes by this means to break down many of the stereotyped and hidebound reactions to issues which inhere in our current decision-making structure.

Speaking as a physicist in "Québec and Canada, Quantum States? The Ins and Outs of Confederation", Logan argues by analogy that the notion that Québec must be either "in" or "out" of Confederation reflects a Newtonian model of the universe. But, in modern quantum physics it is impossible in principle to determine the location of an elementary particle without specifying in advance the *purpose* for which the determination is made. Every elementary particle, then, is "in" an atom for some purposes and "out" of it for others. If we refuse to accept a mechanistic or Newtonian view of Confederation, we could create a broad range of opportunities for the constituent parts of a restructured Canada to be "in" Confederation for some purposes and "out" of it for others. For instance, it might be desirable for Québec to be "in" Confederation in terms of energy policy, but "out" of it in terms of cultural ties which it might want to establish with the French-speaking countries. Canada might, then, become a leader in developing a flexible form of union to supersede the mechanistic forms of nation-states which are under pressure all over the world to accommodate to cultural and ethnic minorities.

In the final essay, "Towards a New Unity Through Diversity: Canada's Third Option", we try to provide a framework which integrates and clarifies many of the goals and policy proposals suggested by ourselves and by other contributors. We hope, ultimately, to enlarge the context for current discussions of the Québec Question and other issues related to national unity. If, by writing and assembling this book, we have helped to set in motion a series of actions which will move these discussions beyond the destructive and unproductive "push and pull" of much of the current debate, we will have succeeded. If, moreover, we have made the reader see possibilities in the present which will help him or her to imagine a new future for Canada, then perhaps we can surmount our present crises and move on, stronger and more self-consciously, towards that destiny which Canada has every right to expect.

PART ONE

THE CONSTITUTIONAL QUESTIONS

CANADA IS NOW FACING a series of tests which will determine, for the immediate future at least, whether or not she will continue to exist as a nation-state. The immediate cause of our crisis is the election of an officially separatist government in Québec. But this particular crisis has been long in the making, and Canada's current trauma is also simply further evidence of a deep and unqualified failure in her political and social institutions. The Parti Québécois government, after all, did not come to power in Québec in the midst of general prosperity and heightened social well-being: November 15 followed in the wake of deep recession, high unemployment, and perennial scandals and charges of wrongdoing in Québec City. Moreover, these phenomena have not been confined to the province of Québec, but have been visible in greater or lesser degrees across the country, and in Ottawa, for some time. We should be, therefore, not so much shocked that the people of Québec have decided to open the door to profound changes in their form of government, as surprised that other provinces have not opted for the same course.

The battle lines between René Lévesque's government and Ottawa are usually defined in constitutional terms. Does Québec, we are asked, have the *right* to leave Confederation? Is the BNA Act—despite the fact that it is simply an enactment of the British Parliament—a solemn bargain struck between provinces which cannot be dissolved except by general consent? Or is it a fundamental law which can be withdrawn whenever the *people* of a province feel it is in their best interests to do so?

The answers to these questions are by no means clear. And, if we extend our legalistic speculations further, the issues become more, not less, complex. Can, for instance, the federal government unilaterally abrogate its treaty commitments to Québec's Indians and the customary rights of the Innuit by passing these over to some successor government? What guarantees can the federal government exact from any independent government in Québec to ensure that minority rights, recognized in law and by custom in the rest of Canada, would be respected by the successor power if separation occurred? How, moreover, could it enforce these guarantees?

Beyond these strictly legal issues lies a host of broadly constitutional questions which are outside the purview of law, *per se*. Does the federal government, for instance, have the moral right to force Québec, by one means or another, to remain in Confederation if the vast majority of her citizens decide to leave? How can this intent be unequivocally established? And what accommodation should be made for parts of Québec—the Lower Townships, for instance—which might not want to remain part of Québec if it left Confederation? The answers to these questions are even less clear—and, perhaps, even unanswerable in conventional terms.

These issues, of course, do not even begin to exhaust those broad constitutional ones which would arise if separation were clearly in the offing. In this Part we try to present the reader with only the most general and basic of the constitutional issues surrounding the Québec Question—leaving the task of a more detailed analysis of these to experts in the field of constitutional law. Moreover, since we suspect that a resolution of the legal and para-legal issues involved will not come about through arguments in the courts or through the overwhelming acceptance of scholarly argument on the subject but through political and social compromise and consultation, we have tried in this chapter to focus on those aspects of constitutional issues most closely linked to the social problems which will be crucial to any final solution.

Any number of scenarios could be devised now to represent possible forms and future states for some sort of Canadian union. In the first section of this Part, two of the leading protagonists in the public debate over the Québec Question—Jean Chrétien and Claude Morin—argue for, on the one hand, an organic continuation of the status quo and, on the other, a sovereignty association between Québec and the rest of Canada. These two brief pieces were not specifically prepared for this volume, but were delivered as political speeches. They are included here because they summarize so ably the positions *vis-à-vis* the Québec Question and Canadian unity currently adopted by their respective governments and form the context in terms of which the debate over the future form of Confederation is taking place. The assumptions and imagery of the two ministers reflect the radical differences between their respective visions of Canada: Chrétien talks in terms of a pluralistic, multicultural, and multi-ethnic society; Morin of a binational state, deeply divided over questions of national self-determination and cultural rights. Both "scenarios" are, as things now stand, unlikely ones. We propose neither to support nor to reject these proposals in their entirety. But we hope that their inclusion will stimulate new ways of thinking about future forms of a Canadian union and help us find one which we may bring into being together.

As Senator Forsey reminds us in his unmistakable and vigorous way, it will ultimately be up to *parliamentary* bodies in Ottawa and the provinces to decide what force to give to any decision taken in any other public forum. Anthony Scott and John Harney analyse the larger framework in terms of which any proposal must be tested. Both pieces are rich in insights into the sorts of practical issues which these bodies will have to deal with in the months to come.

CHAPTER TWO

A: BACKGROUND FOR THE DEBATE: TWO IMAGES OF CANADA

ADDRESS

... I have often spoken of my country as extending from the
Atlantic to the Pacific and from Windsor to the North Pole ....
A land of freedom and of tolerance.

IT HAS BEEN SAID that man does not live by bread alone;
so today, despite the fact that I am speaking to a conference on food, I shall address you about other matters.

All of us here are Quebeckers and Canadians and proud of
being both. And so I want to talk a bit about Canada, the type of
nation we have become over the years, and the options that are
open to us for the future.

I have often spoken of my country as extending from the
Atlantic to the Pacific and from Windsor to the North Pole. I
have spoken of Canada as a tapestry woven of two founding
peoples and many different cultures ... all of whom have maintained their individuality and as such have contributed to the
uniqueness of our land. And like a tapestry, when you start
unweaving it the whole thing comes apart; it does not improve
with separation.

In my years in federal politics, I have had the good fortune
to come to know this country very well and I have learned that
its greatness is found in its immense diversity. And I have learned
that above all else, Canada is a land of freedom and of tolerance
... virtues that are rare in today's world.

There is no such thing as a monolithic English Canada or

* Speech delivered on May 2, 1977 to L'Association des détaillants au
alimentation du Québec, in Montreal. Published here in modified form by kind
permission of the author.

JEAN CHRÉTIEN

monolithic French Canada or monolithic ethnic Canada. There
is one Canada of different people with different interests. Despite what some people say, Québec is not monolithic; neither is
English-speaking Canada. The people of the Prairies, of B.C., of
the Atlantic provinces, of Ontario also have their differences just
as the people of La Mauricie, of the Saguenay, of Gaspé, of
Montreal, and of Québec City are not all alike.

Parts of Québec have much more in common with areas
outside of Québec than they do with other parts of Québec;
similarly, parts of the West or the Atlantic provinces may have
more in common with Québec than with Ontario.

But put all of it together and you have a people who have
developed in the last 110 years from colony to nation; from
isolated rural communities to one of the most advanced nations
of the world.

In his autobiography, Bruce Hutchison reminds us that:

> The modern Canadian who deplores the regionalism of his coun-
> try cannot imagine how insular, prejudiced, and hermetic were
> Canada's regions half a century ago, or how their inhabitants
> enjoyed a life not yet informed, sophisticated, or improved, since
> they had tasted nothing better.[1]

We have come a long way as Canadians and, by and large, we
have progressed in peace and tolerance, something of which we
should be very proud but not complacent. For peace and tolerance are virtues one must work for; they can disappear quickly.

Of course, our development as a nation has not been without its problems. French-speaking Canadians have had to struggle to overcome obstacles, prejudice, and discrimination. In recent weeks, those who are pre-occupied with the past have reminded us of the conquest. As I have said, it is of no use to
re-fight old battles. Had we been here in 1759, one of us would
have wakened Montcalm when Wolfe came in the night. But we
were not there!

We have been reminded of the fact that in the early years of
Confederation, Ontario and Manitoba took away rights of
French Canadians. Those who are so pre-occupied with the
injustices of the past have found a remedy which I believe is
intolerable. That is, the creation of injustice in the present by
removing liberties enjoyed by one million of our fellow Quebeckers whose native tongue is not French. I will discuss this

narrow-minded approach in a moment. But first, I want to talk about a broad-minded approach.

In 1960, Québec woke up to the challenges of North American life in the second half of the twentieth century. The Quiet Revolution was a time of testing, of experimenting, of ferment in all fields. We as French-speaking Canadians discovered that our vocation was industrial as much as agricultural; that we could prosper by looking out instead of in. We discovered that we could meet the challenges that faced us. Within Québec, we experienced tremendous pride in the building of a new society where to be French speaking was no longer a disadvantage.

At the same time as the Quiet Revolution was taking place in Québec, there was a similar phenomenon occurring in Canada as a whole. Despite the fact that our nationalists have blinded themselves to the results, they are spectacular. Not only had French-speaking Canadians formed a modern society in Québec, they had joined Canadian society and, for the first time, had taken their full place in the federal government.

During the past fifteen years, countless French-speaking Canadians from Québec have gone to Ottawa to carve out a place for themselves in politics and in the public service. Those of us who have gone to Ottawa have not gone as traitors or as sell-outs, but as proud Quebeckers with something to offer our fellow Canadians. We have tried to contribute to the best of our ability to the building of a Canadian society that not only recognizes the Québec reality but that welcomes it as a dynamic force in our country. We believe that we can work for Québec in Ottawa. And, by and large, I believe that we have succeeded.

I do not pretend that all the obstacles have been overcome, nor that there have been no setbacks—the air traffic control issue was a serious setback—but I do declare that the face of Canada has been changed in the last fifteen years by those French-speaking Canadians who have served in Ottawa. Not only have we occupied a large place in the government of our country, but we can take some pride in the job that we have done. We have proven that we belong; our progress is now irreversible.

In the past, as French-speaking Canadians, we refused to face up to the Canadian challenge. The emergence of a modern Québec in 1960 enabled us to meet the Canadian challenge. And we have proven that that challenge can be met.

In the linguistic field alone, there has been a social revolution in Canada in the last few years. Let me mention a few high points:

1. the passing of the Official Languages Act in 1969;
2. the extension of French-language radio and television across the country. There are now, through the CBC, 92 French-language television stations and 137 radio stations across Canada. Ten years ago, this was an impossible dream;
3. the tremendous increase in Francophone participation in senior levels of the federal public service. In 1970, 14 per cent of senior executives were Francophones; today the figure is 21 per cent, an improvement of 50 per cent;
4. the federal language-of-work policy for Québec which, as President of the Treasury Board, I announced in August 1975. This policy states that French is the principal language of work for federal public servants in Québec, outside of the National Capital Region, except inasmuch as service to the public requires the use of the official language of the client.

At the provincial level over the last ten years, significant progress has been made—often slow and far from completely satisfactory, but none the less progress, towards a more open and tolerant society. And always it has been progress towards repairing the injustices of the past in a broad-minded manner. We may be critical of the speed, and I am, but we cannot criticize the direction.

Let me mention some of the measures that have been taken in law. There has been the passage of the Official Languages Act in New Brunswick. In both Ontario and Manitoba, important steps have been taken to improve the place of French in their school systems. In 1970, Manitoba repealed legislation establishing English as the only language of instruction in schools and in its place added French to stand side-by-side with English if parents so desired. English and French are now in law the official languages of instruction in Manitoba's schools. It took seventy-five years to correct a terrible injustice, but it has been corrected.

In Ontario, in 1968, legislation was passed creating for the first time a full-fledged program for French-speaking students. This system has been improved in amendments over the last nine years.

In practice, there are many difficulties. The intent of the

new laws has not been completely fulfilled; all the rough edges have not been smoothed out; but the progress has been substantial if we compare today's situation to that of ten years ago.

In all provinces, there is a significant demand by English parents for French immersion courses for their children. Furthermore, there is a growing demand for the school systems to produce graduates with a good knowledge of the French language.

And let me tell you that whenever I travel outside of Québec I feel most welcome. And I am told over and over again that Quebeckers are most welcome and that Québec is an integral part of Canada and must remain so. And I am told to take that message back home, and I do so here today.

This is the record of a tremendous success story in Canada in the field of linguistic progress over the last decade. It is a record that is conveniently ignored by those so overcome with intolerance and narrow-mindedness that they can only find the black spots in our history. What nation has a history with no black spots?

I, too, believe that French must be the principal language of work in Québec. And I took action in this regard in establishing the language-of-work policy for federal public servants in Québec. I too believe that French must have a prominent place in the boardrooms of our companies. But I do not believe that the stature of French can be enhanced by attitudes of intolerance bordering on hatred.

Québec was for too long a closed and inward-looking society. I do not want to return to those days. I do not understand why the Parti Québécois government is afraid of the open society created by the Quiet Revolution; I do not understand why it insists on looking inward. How ironic it is for those of us who knew René Lévesque in the early 1960s that he should be quoted in Charlottetown as saying that his government is the logical heir to the autonomist tradition started by Duplessis. To think of Maurice Duplessis as the hero of René Lévesque!

As a French-speaking Quebecker, I do not want to be closed in a ghetto when the world is getting more open. I do not want the government of Québec to tell my children and your children that unilingualism is advantageous when many of the members of the government were trained in leading English or American universities.

Indeed, I might remind some of our nationalists who are so

in favour of unilingualism for others that a survey taken at the end of last year on behalf of the Montreal Catholic School Commission showed that 65.5 per cent of parents would prefer to send their children to a bilingual school.

I do not want to see the French language promoted merely by the removal of rights of others in the name of the collective good. When rights begin to be eroded in the name of the collectivity, the process is often difficult to stop. And while I do not want to be alarmist, I am afraid of actions which to some smack of totalitarianism. In my mind, the most dangerous aspect of the White Paper on language, and Bill 101 (formerly Bill-1), is the insistence that everything emanates from the state. We must not allow the state to become all-powerful.

There is one other point I would like to make about the attitude of those who want to make Québec an independent country. It is the intellectual dishonesty that is becoming more and more apparent every day.

When Rodrigue Tremblay, Bernard Landry, and Claude Morin were caught making errors in the billions of dollars in their interpretation of the Public Accounts of Québec—$4.2 billion in indirect taxes and hundreds of millions per year in services—the best Mr. Tremblay could do in reply was to suggest that I had no training in accounting. I do not; but the public servants who work for me at Statistics Canada have superb training in accounting! If Mr. Tremblay's statement is the result of his fifteen years of deep study then I suggest he has failed his examination!

When Rodrigue Tremblay or René Lévesque suggest that Québec is in a similar position to the 100 countries who have gained independence since the Second World War, I tell him as a Quebecker that we need not be compared to Zaire, Uganda, Upper Volta, Togo, and so on.

When Camille Laurin attempts to mislead Quebeckers by citing extracts from the Gendron Commission in a very selective way, I say that he is being intellectually dishonest. For example, Claude Ryan in Le Devoir on April 4 found that studies for the Gendron Commission established that Francophone workers deal in French 87 per cent of their time at work. When the White Paper said that 82 per cent of communication in business is done in English in Québec, it forgot to state that it was referring to communications by English-speaking businessmen! I am glad that Dr. Laurin has agreed to correct his technical error in future editions of the White Paper.

This type of intellectual dishonesty is unacceptable coming from those who were elected to give honest government. It is the behaviour of people who are willing to go to any lengths to prove an untenable case.

In conclusion, let me say the following.

To the Parti Québécois challenge of closing the doors and creating a narrow, reactionary, inward-looking society, I respond with the challenge to throw open the doors and grasp the opportunity that is Canada. Unlike those who prefer to compete in a small arena, I prefer the big leagues.

To those who offer us withdrawal as the solution, I suggest we participate—that we participate in a country rich in its diversity; rich in tolerance; rich in its freedom; and last, but not least, rich in its natural resources and rich in its standard of living. This material richness may be matched by a bourgeois Péquiste ambassador somewhere in a Cadillac, but it may not be matched by the average Quebecker in an independent Québec.

Let us be proud to be Canadians and let us resolve to fight wherever we can be most useful to preserve Canada and to pass our Canadian heritage on to our children.

NOTE

1 Bruce Hutchison, *The Far Side of the Street* (Toronto, 1976), p. 65.

CHAPTER THREE

ADDRESS

... we are operating within the framework of the federal system as it now exists in Canada. Let there be no doubt however that the [Parti Québécois] government is still committed to its fundamental platform.... This commitment stems...from the realization...that this constitutional framework has entrenched Québec in a permanent minority status.

IN CANADA TODAY, understanding of fundamental issues is being blurred by deep emotional reactions. This creates a climate of suspicion and misunderstanding of the objectives of our government. For this reason, I consider it necessary to bring to you my interpretation of the present political situation in Québec, as well as my answers to some of the questions that may have arisen since the November 15 election.

First, whatever explanation has been given for the victory of the Parti Québécois in the last general election, no one can deny that this result came about through the operation of a democratic process that is central and fundamental to the Parti Québécois—a basic foundation of its existence as well as its purpose.

After years, if not generations, during which politics in Québec were marred by authoritarian as well as paternalistic leadership, the Parti Québécois was established with the purpose of bringing about a fundamental change in political values and social ethics within the Québec community. From this point of view, the Parti Québécois is a direct and natural by-product of the Quiet Revolution. Not only is the democratic process a basic justification for its existence, but it is also its main principle of government. Whatever steps are to be taken in the pursuance of its goals, we feel that they must be taken in accordance with the

* Speech delivered on June 3, 1977 to the Annual Joint Meeting of the British Columbia and Alberta Bar Association, Jasper, Alberta. Published here in modified form by kind permission of the author.

CLAUDE MORIN

will of our people. We have committed ourselves to consultation of all Quebeckers on their political future.

This is why, in the coming months, we are going to adopt a law making it possible to hold a referendum—that is, a public consultation—on Québec's future. This consultation will take place during our present political mandate. It will be the first time in Québec's history that our population will have had such a direct say in its own affairs.

Second, I would like to emphasize that the party now in power in Québec, while a new party, is not the sudden and precarious outcome of a political accident. On the contrary, it has deep roots going back far into our history. In a sense, our party is the logical end result of generations of efforts pointing to a greater degree of political autonomy for Quebeckers. We are these days, but with means more adapted to our problems, simply trying to succeed in a collective task that has always been in the mind and in the heart of our community. We want to be masters in our own house and, at the same time, to keep good and positive relations with our neighbours. When one studies, even superficially, the evolution of Québec over the years, one is struck by this constant quest and deep purpose.

Third, then, the commitment towards political sovereignty for Québec is and will remain a basic component of the platform of the Parti Québécois. It is the *raison d'être* of this party. It is what it stands for since its beginning. To suggest, in those circumstances, that our victory was realized through misrepresentation or that the party in government should act like any other provincial government is to set aside the essential part of its platform, notwithstanding the fact that the previous government fought the PQ on the grounds that "a vote for the PQ is a vote for the separation of Québec from the rest of Canada".

True, the victory of the Parti Québécois cannot be attributed entirely to the support it has generated for its aim of bringing about political sovereignty for Québec.

Any change of government, as you very well know, is a mixture of many ingredients. In the minds of the Québec electorate, there was certainly a growing dissatisfaction with the previous administration. That dissatisfaction, however, resulted in good part from the positions taken by this administration concerning the place of Québec in the Canadian federation and its relations with the federal government. For generations, people in Québec have been sensitive to those issues because they are very closely related to the existence, survival, and aspirations of the Francophone community itself. The least we can say is that Quebeckers wanted a change to happen and that the Parti Québécois represented this change.

Our government is thus clearly committed to change in the political institutions of Canada. At the same time, we have stated many times that we do not, at the present time, have the mandate to achieve political sovereignty for Québec, not because Quebeckers have turned down this option, but mainly because we chose not to ask for that mandate during the last electoral campaign. We decided instead, as I said a few moments ago, to put the issue to a referendum which will be held before the next general election.

In the meantime, we are operating within the framework of the federal system as it now exists in Canada. Let there be no doubt, however, that the government is still committed to its fundamental platform. This commitment stems not only from the realization by a growing number of Quebeckers that this constitutional framework has entrenched Québec in a permanent minority status and that the operation of the system has rendered more and more difficult the realization of our collective goals for cultural and economic emancipation, but also from the fact that the government of Québec is in a better position than any other government to fulfil those collective goals.

Fourth, we have economic problems that can only be solved through an imaginative and firm approach. Economically, Québec has been losing ground in comparison with the rest of Canada in all areas, whether it be growth rates, per-capita income, or per-capita spending and investment. On the other hand, although French Canadians comprise 80 per cent of the population of Québec, they occupy only a very minor position in the industrial development of their own community.

Studies have shown that we control just 5 per cent of the mineral resources sector of our economy, about 22 per cent of the manufacturing sector, and about 30 per cent of all service industries. In 1974 a study carried out by the International Institute for Quantitative Economics showed that Francophones in Québec hold about 30 per cent of all positions with an annual income in the $15,000 range. What these studies of the state of the Québec economy and many more both current and from past years indicate is that the French-Canadian community is being held in a minority position in its own province.

Perhaps the French-Canadian community has not shown the vitality and interest in business and other economic issues that it should have; and perhaps also the old system of education did not provide the proper training to equip generations of young French Canadians (except for a small privileged group who could afford it) to handle the economic levers of their community. But one must not disregard the fact that, over the years, policies of the federal government, whether they be stabilization, trade, or financial policies, have too often overlooked the fundamental needs of the Francophone community of Québec.

With endemic unemployment to alleviate, and with the problem of having to find suitable work opportunities for the growing number of university graduates that Québec has been turning out of its new education system at great cost, it is a major responsibility of our government to introduce radical changes in the policies conceived to solve those various problems. Québec has been investing a tremendous amount in building its education system during the past decade. At the present time, more than 30 per cent of annual government expenses go into supporting both the English and French education system in Québec. In fact, on a per-capita basis, Québec ranks among the leading countries of the world in this area.

Major investments have been made in education so as to cope with the needs of the present age and aspirations of our community. However, Québec finds itself in a position where it is more and more difficult for a French Canadian to live and be successful in his own language and in his own province.

Furthermore, we have the responsibility to ensure that, collectively, our community will benefit from economic growth and achieve its rightful share of the benefits of this growth.

My fifth comment deals with a point I want to stress. One may reasonably assume that in 1867 when the Canadian federation was established, French-speaking citizens of Québec accepted the new political regime because they were told that it would guarantee the autonomy of their private and public institutions in fields that they considered important at that time. In other words, Quebeckers felt that the new regime more or less granted them a form of self-government. At least, no one told them that a centralization of political power in Ottawa was not only possible, but regarded as a normal outcome of the federal system by their English-speaking counterparts.

As you realize, this means that a deep misunderstanding

presided over the birth of the present political structure of Canada. Quebeckers thought it would forever guarantee for them large possibilities of self-determination, while at the same time other Canadians understood that they could from then on look forward to the establishment of a very strong central government in Ottawa. All of which means that French Canadians and English Canadians decided to go along with the new regime but for motives which were different, if not, to some extent, contradictory. No wonder, then, that there are various interpretations of the meaning and direction of federalism, depending on the source of those interpretations. This may also explain why Québec has sometimes invoked the virtues of federalism to object to federal centralization, while, on the other hand, other Canadians have used them to foster an increase of federal powers.

Taking into account the political hopes that the establishment of the federal system may have created for Quebeckers in 1867, one has no difficulty in grasping why there has been, over the years, such widespread dissatisfaction with this regime in Québec. This dissatisfaction, of a political nature, has today culminated in a complete rejection of the whole system by large segments of our population.

Why is it so? Mainly because we feel, in Québec, that almost all the important political powers, almost all the significant governmental tools are, more and more, becoming federal instruments. We also feel, through experience, that the regime itself facilitates and even encourages that evolution, through the existence and the clever use of such federal powers as, for instance, control of taxation and spending and the "peace, order and good government" clause. This makes provincial administrations into regional branch offices of the Ottawa government. When one considers that the Québec government is the only major political instrument to be easily controlled by us, it becomes clear that the present tendencies are equivalent to a gradual lessening of our political power and significance, as Quebeckers. This, coupled with a stagnation in our birthrate and the integration of immigrants into the English-speaking community, makes it clear that, in our eyes, the federal system and the present rules of the game in Canada must absolutely be changed. For us, this is a necessity which at least partly explains why our party, created in 1968, has succeeded in taking power within only eight years.

My sixth point has to do with the recognition by the Parti Québécois of the necessity to maintain a yet-to-be-defined and negotiated framework of economic association with the rest of Canada.

Thus, we reject the idea of being branded "separatists", or accused falsely of pursuing the isolation of Québec from the rest of North America, or of "dismantling" Canada. I, personally, do not see why people both inside and outside Québec should deliberately refrain from acknowledging what has been part of the Parti Québécois platform since its early beginnings. I would say, even more, that the idea of association was an integral part of the earlier movement that led to the establishment of this party and which was precisely named the Sovereignty Association Movement (Mouvement Souveraineté–Association).

It is in the interest of all parties concerned, and for reasons which are not only economic, to maintain the basic elements of co-operation between the different entities which comprise Canada. It has been said that Québec, more than the rest of Canada, is dependent on the existence of protective tariffs for the maintenance of a substantial part of its industry; also that there can be no overwhelming reasons for the other provinces in Canada to support the new system. I do not think, personally, that it would be very rational, on economic or on political grounds, not to do the utmost to bring about an agreement with Québec for, in my view, everybody will lose if there is no arrangement.

It has also been argued that if the scenario calls for the establishment of a customs and monetary union between Québec and the rest of Canada there is then no need for political sovereignty since Canada is already in a customs and monetary union situation. I would only add to this that the question is not whether such a union should exist or not, but how the management of this union should permit fulfilment of the aspirations of the different communities taking part in it. The question is, therefore, who will have the power to manage it and how can it be managed in a way that will be satisfactory to both communities.

The time has not yet come to set out before our English-Canadian friends the various scenarios for making new arrangements based on our Sovereignty Association concept. But whatever the scenario, I certainly hope the emotional climate that is evident in the English-Canadian community whenever our government comes forth with new policies, will give way to a more rational and candid approach towards finding solutions to our different problems.

In making my seventh point, I would like to comment on the recent introduction of a White Paper and bill on the French language. It is a good case in point. The reaction from organized segments of the English community in Québec to the tabling of this legislation in the National Assembly was, as expected, very negative. And I can very well understand that feeling. It was more the psychological impact of the government's having to legislate on language, rather than the substance of the bill, that brought about this reaction. I could, of course, go at length into the details of this legislation to explain the different stipulations of it. How we never set out to make the French language the only spoken language in Québec. How we introduced safeguards so that the English-speaking community would go on benefiting from a public-school system which, incidentally, is in the only province which provides its minority group the access to its own school system. How also we provided for special temporary resident status whenever executives of foreign corporations move into Québec with their families. But what I resent personally very strongly are the acusations of short-sightedness that are being made throughout Canada and even in the United States, to say nothing of accusations of racism and intolerance. This hostile attitude does not take into account the fact that, even with this piece of legislation, benefits granted to the Anglophone community in Québec will remain considerable and much more extensive than those granted to Francophones outside Québec.

Finally, if you will allow me, I would like to stress what I would consider to be a "must" for Canada today. Due to the recent changes in Québec's political situation, due also to the tensions that those changes have underlined, it has become imperative that English-speaking Canada do a little homework of its own. So far, over the years, the constitutional impulse has come from Québec. I mean that whenever new political schemes were discussed in Canada, most of the time they originated in or because of Québec. This should come as no surprise, for Québec has been going through such a political transformation that it is quite normal to expect more creativity from us than from anyone else in Canada.

However, now that we are at last beginning to see where we want to go, the time has come for us to ask a very pertinent question: What does Canada want? It would be pointless to evade that question. We both know that the present federal structure of Canada cannot be preserved as if it were a museum piece. More and more people outside Québec believe that it needs to be brought up to date. This is the least we can say. Québec goes further of course. We want eventually to propose to you a new type of relations between Québec and Canada. This will be an important step in both your political life and ours. How does English-speaking Canada feel about what is taking place in Québec? What proposals does it have? Of course, we do not expect answers to be given today. We only hope that they will go beyond emotional reactions based on a wrong assessment of our true intentions.

In closing, I will quote from a statement I made in Ottawa, on December 6, 1976. This will explain what our present attitude is.

> The global attitude of the new Québec Government is at once *positive*, *realistic* and *serene*.
>
> *Positive*, because our objective is to solve the political problem which for all times has been posed in Québec, by attacking the root and the causes of this problem and not only its most obvious manifestations as was done in the past.
>
> *Realistic*, because we do not ignore that this solution of a political order, to be effective, must necessarily take into account the concrete geographic and economic context of Québec and of Canada.
>
> *Serene*, because we have no animosity whatsoever towards anyone and because we believe that the application of the major reform provided for in our programme, that is to say, political sovereignty coupled with economic association, shall engender between Québec and Canada possibilities of cooperation all the more fruitful because they will be based on mutual respect.

For the future, we are firmly convinced that a dialogue of much greater scope is essential for mutual understanding. We will undertake this dialogue in the coming months, in all good faith, without ulterior motives, with frankness, and in a constructive spirit. We expect the same attitude from our partners, and this for a very simple reason: the Canada and the Québec of tomorrow shall be built by our helping and respecting each other.

CHAPTER FOUR

B: THE CONSTITUTIONAL CONTEXT

GET IT RIGHT, GET IT RIGHT

NO PROVINCE has any legal right or power to secede from Canada. Secession would require an amendment to the British North America Act.

No such amendment could be passed by the Parliament of Canada under section 91, head 1, of the BNA Act. Any such legislation is excluded from the powers of Parliament by the exceptions in that head. Secession would, therefore, require an Act of the British Parliament.

Parliament in Britain would certainly pass any such amendment asked for by the Parliament of Canada. It would certainly not pass any such amendment except at the request of the Parliament of Canada. Since 1871, all amendments to the BNA Act passed by the British Parliament have been requested by both Houses of Parliament of Canada.

Since 1930, every such amendment directly affecting the provinces has been requested by the Parliament of Canada only after the unanimous consent of the provinces affected (the four western provinces in 1930, to the amendment returning their natural resources; all the provinces in the other case).

An amendment providing for the secession of Québec would manifestly directly affect all the provinces. It is therefore highly unlikely that the Parliament of Canada would pass the necessary Address of both Houses unless all the provinces consented (though it is possible that if only one small province objected Parliament would go ahead anyway).

* Appeared first in *The Financial Post*, December 4, 1976. Published here in modified form by kind permission of the author.

EUGENE FORSEY

The consent of the other provinces would almost certainly not be unconditional. The amendment would have to include provisions protecting what the other provinces considered their essential interests.

Parliament would therefore not pass any Address for the amendment except after negotiations between the government of Canada and the government of Québec, negotiations in which the governments of the other provinces would almost certainly insist on at least being consulted.

No government in Canada is likely to enter into such negotiations unless it is unmistakably clear that a majority of the population of Québec wants to have the province secede.

The only way to be sure of this is a plebiscite. A plebiscite asks the voters for their opinion on a particular subject (most of the provinces have had plebiscites on the liquor question).

The government then decides what action it will take in the light of the results of the vote. It is not bound to take any action. A very small majority, especially if there were a small turnout of voters, might cause it to stay its hand and take no action at all. (After the Dominion plebiscite of 1898 on prohibition and a Québec majority against it, the government took no action.)

Premier René Lévesque proposes to hold a plebiscite, probably this year. If it produces a clear majority for separation, presumably he will ask the government of Canada to negotiate on the terms of separation.

The federal government might decline to negotiate until it had submitted the question to the people of Canada in a general election in which it would presumably set before the electorate the terms on which it was prepared to settle. A national plebiscite would not be suitable for this purpose, since it would be virtually impossible to ask anything much more than: "Are you in favour of separation, yes or no?"

If Québec and Canada succeeded in negotiating a separation agreement, it might be necessary to submit that agreement to a plebiscite or plebiscites. People who might vote "yes" to the question "are you in favour of separation?" might not vote "yes" when they saw the terms of the agreement: they might not be willing to pay the price.

The terms of any separation agreement might constitute a stiff price. Canada and the Atlantic provinces might insist on a corridor across Québec for communications between those provinces and the central and western provinces. Canada and Ontario might insist on stringent safeguards for the St. Lawrence Seaway. The division of the national debt and the national assets might be a stumbling-block for one side or the other.

There might well be others. Lévesque has said he wants "association" with Canada, with control tariffs, monetary policy, and transcontinental transportation vested in joint boards, with, as I understand it, half the members from Québec, half from Canada. Canada is unlikely to agree to give Québec a veto on its tariff policy, or its monetary policy, or its transportation policy.

Lévesque, on reflection, may not be much enamoured of giving Canada a veto on Québec's tariff policy, Québec's monetary policy, or Québec's transportation policy. And if he modified his proposal to give Canada a majority on the joint boards, how much would be left of Québec's independence?

Altogether, the whole subject bristles with difficulties which do not appear at first glance. It cannot be reduced to a French-Canadian version of the old spiritual, with Quebeckers singing:

> Go down, René,
> Way down in Canada land.
> Tell old Trudeau
> To let our people go,

with the rest of us joining in some sort of chorus, let alone in the Hallelujah chorus that some besotted English-Canadian separatists might like to sing.

CHAPTER FIVE

AN ECONOMIC APPROACH TO THE FEDERAL STRUCTURE

THE SHORT RUN VERSUS THE LONG RUN

WE ARE CONSIDERING the future of Canada's federal structure of government. Many voices are heard. When we render them all down we are left with two arguments. The first argument is about what path Canada should follow now, in the short run; the second is about what kind of governmental structure Canada should be trying to build in the long run.

In my opinion, the first argument, immediate and urgent as it is, concerns means rather than ends. What strategy should be followed by the various governments and political actors this year? What should be said to the press? What stance should the Atlantic provinces and western Canada strike? These are all short-run problems. The second, remote and abstract by comparison with the fire and fury of the first, concerns the ends (that is, long-run goals). Those who are engaged in this debate are disputing the merits and demerits of alternative structures of government. On one side are ranged the enthusiasts for a more centralized structure; on the other the champions of a decentralized, dispersed pattern of government authority and power.

These two arguments are not independent of each other. If we can agree on our long-run goal, we must still make a decision about a transformation period. Should it be brief or protracted?

* Lecture delivered to the "Options Conference" on the future of the Canadian Confederation, University of Toronto, October 14-15, 1977. To be published in the *Proceedings* of the conference. Published here in modified form by kind permission of the author.

ANTHONY SCOTT

Should it build on a series of intergovernmental conferences, or place more emphasis on revolutionary, violent, or individualistic gestures and phrases? How will the manner and speed of transformation affect the attitudes of the various parts of the country to each other? If the immediate crisis is prolonged, citizens' tastes and attitudes to, for example, Québec's place in the ultimate structure may become harder or softer. Indeed, Keynes wrote that it is this short run, this transitional period, that really matters, "for in the long run we are all dead".

Nevertheless, in matters of government structure, the transformation period, no matter how important it may become in historical retrospect, has no force, unless it is seen by contemporaries as transition towards some new structure, or set of institutions. Some eventual shape of society must be the goal. The basic energy for short-run decisions and activities is drawn from men's resolutions to achieve (or to retain) some long-run steady state for government and society. The transitional strategy is the means, the chosen structure of government is the end.

The purpose of this essay is to say something helpful about the selection of the long-run ends to which our current discussion of the constitution may lead us. Ideally, we should compare a variety of attainable alternative government structures towards which we might wish to progress. Recognizing that some of these structures can never materialize because the sort of transition they require would be too painful or too protracted, we should nevertheless exercise the "constitutional" part of our imaginations to survey or review the choices open to us. We may then compare the net benefits of the preferred constitution with the net costs of the transitional steps we must take to reach it, and try to decide whether the end justifies the means.

My aim here is to stimulate discussion about the long run. What sort of "governmental structure" should we be working for—or, perhaps, trying to retain? I would like first to introduce the idea of an *economic* approach to the constitution (that is, to the structure of government) and then to develop and refine some questions which this approach raises.

THE CHOICE AMONG FEDERAL STRUCTURES

By "federal structure" I mean the pattern made by the levels of government which symbolize our nation, implement our choices, and provide our public goods and services.

You may find it helpful to think of the structure of our government as it would appear in a diagram of a federal pyramid.[1] At the top is a single block representing the single central government. Next down is a wider band of blocks, each representing the government of a state or province. These do not overlap, but have each their own territory. All of them lie within the territory of the central government. As we climb down to lower levels, we find local-government strata. There are many of these units, and to the architectural eye they look more like rubble than the foundation blocks of a great pyramid, for they differ greatly in size, sometimes overlap territorially, and do not have a uniform height from the ground. On inspection we do find that each of them lies within the territory of only one provincial government, but this is almost their only regularity.

This structure can be modified in a number of ways. The height of the pyramid can be changed by inserting or removing whole jurisdictional levels, or by doing this under only a part of the level above. The width and breadth of the pyramid can also be changed by replacing each block at one level with several blocks, thus, for example, changing from a federation with only a few constituent republics or provinces to one with many states, and so on to the French idea of a level with dozens, even hundreds, of *départements*.

If one looks around the world, one can find many types of pyramids. Yet to focus attention on the mere shape of this pyramid and the number of its levels is to run the danger of attributing importance to jurisdictional levels where in fact governments have little or no significance, but are mere hollow shells. What, then, are the criteria for an "important" level of government? We can suggest three: (i) how many citizens it has; (ii) what it stands for; and (iii) the character of the decisions it may make.

As an economist, I am inclined to give weight to the third of these: a governmental level's importance depends on the importance of the decisions which it can make. The other two criteria are also important, however, and I will consider them briefly.

The most frequently used criterion for size is population. This criterion however is both trivial and misleading. It is trivial because it must *always* tell us that the senior level, governing the whole country from the top of the pyramid, is more important than levels further down. History is replete with examples of top-level, high-population jurisdictions that are powerless. One need only reflect on the Emperors of China, Japan, and the Holy Roman Empire at certain periods, to find confirmation that smaller, subordinate, lower-level jurisdictions are those to which attention should be paid.

What it stands for, however, is another matter entirely. A government and its territory are symbols of all the history and all the aspirations of a society. Such concepts as legitimacy, sovereignty, and representativeness are preoccupations of those who consider the merits and demerits of a governmental structure. There are, of course, easily understood reasons for this. In international relations, especially in periods of war, it is the government that assumes the role of ethical and social and economic spokesman and representative for all its population, *vis-à-vis* the rest of the world. And in time of peace, the power to use compulsion to make policies, collect revenues, and provide services also endows a distinct territorial jurisdiction with a symbolic importance; such jurisdiction may attract like-minded immigrants, repel those who find its actions objectionable, and gradually become a home, a fortress, a bastion, an academy, or even a temple, for its own kind of people.

It seems to me that the Canadian debate about our structure of government has centred on this definition of government: what it stands for, who it speaks for, what rival jurisdictions may claim to speak for the same principles and people. Historians and political scientists have focused our attention on these questions, and on their consequences for our national political parties, pressure groups, and churches, almost to the exclusion of any other way of identifying the importance and role of the state.

This habit has had two unfortunate consequences. Both stem from a disregard for what politicians and bureaucrats do most of the time, which is to concern themselves with the whole range of decisions about the provision of public goods. Instead, elected territorial politicians are regarded as spokesmen for their regional populations, as tacticians, and as philosophers, fighting some kind of continuing interregional war. I do not claim that mayors, premiers, and prime ministers cannot or should not do these things; I do claim that their statements of what they stand for are usually not tested at the polls and not implementable with their constitutional power.

More serious is the second consequence of looking at a regional government as though its chief function were to act as some kind of regional symbol, leader, or spokesman. This is that it leads us to ignore the economic nature of the public sector. We must not lose track of the fact that by the structure of government is also meant the permanent assignment to the various levels of governments of powers and responsibilities to make decisions, provide goods and services, supply welfare transfers, levy taxes, borrow, and raise or lower barriers to the movement of capital, goods, and people between jurisdictions. This allocation of powers may have a most profound impact on what is actually done. Locally provided goods and services have a different cost and a different quality from nationally provided ones.

By approaching the matter in this way, we catch sight of the third criterion of the "importance" of a level of government: the amount of impact it has on the economy and on those aspects of the rest of society that can, at least approximately, be brought into relationship with the measuring rod of money.

Some may feel that the present crisis is one in which the dollar impact of a government's operations is not very important. However, as an economist I can speak more clearly if I use a benefit-and-cost approach to the structure of government. We are concerned here with the long run. Economic considerations may seem to be overshadowed today by religious, racial, linguistic, and legal passions, and Canadians may believe that our constitution has and will be the net result of all such emotional and political forces, playing on the structure of government in different periods. In other words, you may believe that our constitution is just the long-run result of a series of random short-run episodes. But our present structure of government also reflects a large number of economic judgments, and I suggest that we may profitably think about our present crisis in terms of the simple economics of the constitution towards which we would like to move.

THE DEGREE OF CENTRALIZATION— GENERAL ARGUMENTS

In this section I shall discuss the best-known arguments for and against a federal form of government. The Canadian federal structure was coolly and pragmatically modelled on previously constituted examples by working politicians and British public servants. It is often argued that, because already by the 1860s both separation of the Canadian colonies and Union had been tried without success, federation was the next candidate for a form of government. But federation is not a single form of style of government; it is a bundle of characteristics pulled together by theorists and practical men in different places to deal with different problems. What kind of federation should they adopt?

The negotiators from the Canadian colonies were obviously most aware of the American example. It too had been pulled together pragmatically, to meet the different demands of the states who previously had been little more than members of a confederation or alliance against the British; and by 1867 it had been somewhat modified by the slavery issue, territorial expansion, and the influence of industrial technology. It is easy to forget how much fundamental, long-run, economic reasoning about centralization and decentralization went into the original Philadelphia recipe. Athens and the Holy Roman Empire, the writings of Hume and the newly published Adam Smith, such French philosophers of the Enlightenment as Rousseau and Montesquieu were all consulted. Thus, in adapting the American model, the Canadians were in fact reacting to the earlier American constituent assembly's application of ideas from many European sources.

The Canadian governmental structure was also influenced by the nineteenth-century British experience. In the aftermath of the Napoleonic wars Britain had, around the world, been experimenting with new forms and patterns of control; military and mercantile authorities were giving place to independent colonies. Even more important was the century-long development of a tier of local government for Wales, Ireland, and Scotland. Great Britain was gradually rationalizing its disorderly mosaic of counties, boroughs, districts, provinces, regions, and authorities. Parliament had been progressively setting up new decentralized territories for the administration or provision of education, welfare, and housing. Many philosophers and politicians, from Wilberforce to John Stuart Mill, asked themselves whether these new bodies should be self-governing, on the American pattern, or under rigorous central control, as in France. There was much agreement that Parliament could not handle the great variety of local situations; but there was also gloomy agreement that unfettered local democracy, a counter to the unlimited power of the Victorian Parliament, was to be avoided at all costs. Mill agreed with Alexander Hamilton a century earlier, and with many

European writers, that the pool of talent of men and women suitable for leadership was too small for a decentralized government: thus centralization was seen as a means for economizing on the time and powers of the scarce governing elite. It is a fair conjecture that, when the Canadian Fathers of Confederation were negotiating in London on the future structure of Canadian government, their British hosts inserted many of the current British notions about the desirable and practicable extent of decentralization.

The arguments of those days are still in use today, and we can summarize them briefly. It is assumed that government is democratic and representative. And it is assumed that the essence of the argument is whether, at one jurisdictional level in the pyramid, it is better to have a few large, or many small, governments. Under either system, the same total group of citizens would be served, taxed, and regulated. This question produces almost the same answers as a similar one: is it better that most power and responsibility should be centralized in the single block at the top of the pyramid, or decentralized in many blocks at a lower level? Both ways of posing the question raise a further question: can we pinpoint the chief advantages of decentralization, and the chief advantages of centralization? As it happens, this is fairly straightforward. The advantages of decentralization all have to do with precisely satisfying individuals' demands and preferences by setting up small governmental units that can listen to their demands and attempt to satisfy only them. Ideally, the outcome is that diversity among citizens' demands is satisfied by diversity among actions of small governmental units.

That is the "demand" side. On the "supply" side, the factors entering into government provision of its policies seem always to reveal economies of scale. The costs of serving a large population are not much larger than those of serving a small population; hence, there are gains to be harvested from entrusting the provision of public goods and services, the work of bureaucrats and regulators, and the protection of police, military, and the courts, to the highest level of government. From this point of view, centralization is the escape route from the high taxes and second-rate services afforded by the tiny state or parish. Obviously, we must choose. We cannot have a government structure which is both centralized and decentralized—in which all territories and populations are both big and small. The centralization debate may lead to compromise, but there is really no happy mixture of the two forms: they pull in opposite directions. Let us examine their details briefly.

The decentralization argument really is an amalgam of many propositions and assertions about the relations between citizens and their politicians and bureaucrats. First, and most important, is the capacity of decentralized governments to escape from a uniformity of policy decided upon by a nation-wide majority. It can adopt policies that reflect varying regional tastes, preferences, industries, and geographies. The politicians of each jurisdiction can stay in office only by doing what local citizens demand, regardless of what is demanded and supplied elsewhere in the nation. Furthermore, if a nation that is divided among majority and minority parties (or interest groups) is cut up at random into small territorial jurisdictions, the total number of citizens who must suffer as minorities from the policies of majorities will decline; that is, the number of people who are left in disagreement with their local governments' decisions will decrease. This has been the great attraction of federalism in modern western and colonial history: decentralization has allowed regional jurisdictions to develop or retain their own policies not only as regards regulation, industrialization, labour conditions, debt, taxes, expenditures, and other aspects of economic policy, but also as regards education, religion, language, law, and citizenship.

There are still other benefits. Local or provincial government can be less impersonal, less remote, more responsive, more involved than national governments. John Stuart Mill advocated small and local governments because they could become the training ground of ordinary persons in citizenship and of more gifted persons in taking a role in national affairs. A more recent discovery has been that citizens' demands on local governments are reasonable and moderate because they associate the cost of whatever they demand with their own tax bill; whereas their demands on central governments are more irresponsible and carefree.

Nevertheless, common observation and history show, not the gradual adoption of communal or grass-roots democracy, but the amalgamation of local authorities and the union of provinces, states, and nations into today's sovereign nation-states. In many of them centralization of powers, taxation, and social policy have reached a very high level.

How are we to explain this? Granted, no economic model

is adequate to account for the unsettled, kaleidoscopic variety of governmental structures to be seen around the globe today. Nevertheless, widespread democratic consent to politicians' centralizing tendencies must have some common basis. The explanation in economic terms is simple. Many government activities can equally well serve many or few people, large regions or small, many businesses or few. The area where this principle is most readily seen is defence. A military shield costs the same and affords the same defence regardless of the number of people sheltering behind it. But the actual tax and human cost per citizen falls as the size of the state rises. The same is true of many other kinds of protection: dams and dykes for flood protection; lighthouses and dredging for safe navigation; police, coast-guards, and fire marshals for deterring criminals; parliaments and news media for obtaining and exchanging political information. All these *and most other* public goods are technically capable of extending their benefits far and wide without a proportionate increase in citizens' taxes.

The benefits of centralization may also extend to improvements in the quality of the environment, as for instance, in reducing the amount of industrial air pollution emitted from a single source. The new benefit can be enjoyed equally by all citizens, and neighbouring citizens who live outside the jurisdiction that is providing and paying for the government service may get a "free ride". They are not called upon to pay, even though they may enjoy the benefits just as much as those citizens who stump up the finances. Situations like this (all too familiar these days in city finance) have for centuries motivated kings and politicians to amalgamate their tiny states into cost-reducing super-states. In the jargon or lingo of economics, centralizing the structure of government both "internalizes" the financial costs of public services and "internalizes" the political decisions about what extent, quality, or type of service is to be provided into a single Parliament. Without "internalization" a state may suffer from "externalities". When a state is too small, both its services and its disservices spill over into neighbouring jurisdictions. These neighbours become either free riders or innocent victims of the policies of external governments. And the government that is causing or permitting the external spillovers cannot be deterred from harming its neighbours or rewarded for serving them better.

Thus, in economists' jargon, a government structure that is

made up of small units fails on two related but separate counts. First, it fails to profit from the economies of large-scale provision of public services: it under-utilizes the potential of its government. Second, because it is providing free services to neighbours who neither pay taxes nor vote, it tends to provide too few of these spillover services. The neighbours who now get a free ride would, if they were able to vote, support an expansion of the spillover services, even if they had to pay all the tax bill for the expansion. In short, setting up very small jurisdictions is uneconomic both because they must levy taxes that are too high for the services performed, and because each of them excludes neighbours who cannot exercise a financial demand for extended services. To most writers, the remedy for these two evils has long been obvious: turn over the provision of public services to larger governmental units. Centralize the provision of public goods and services, and internalize the decisions that affect neighbouring people and regions.

This centralization *vs.* decentralization dichotomy presents the structure-of-government question in terms that do not assist us to perceive our choices. First, it does not really allow of compromise, because even the extremes of the opposing tendencies can be justified. The argument for decentralization, based on fully recognizing the variety of demands existing in different regions, suggests no limits to how small a government might be. A district, a parish, even a family might be too large a unit to give full weight to the preferences and incomes of different citizens. Indeed, political and economic philosophers who wish to get away from government, and get as close to *laissez-faire* as modern society and population pressure will permit, have urged that the sub-structure of governments should be visualized like a series of "clubs"—small bodies like town meetings and village councils, each controlling as few persons as possible, and each giving citizens a market-like opportunity, through migration and moving, to select the club that offers the mixture of taxes and services that they prefer. By this criterion the province or state and most metropolitan areas are already too large!

The argument for full centralization also seems unfounded. Pointing as it does towards the large jurisdiction, the unitary state, and the abolition of spillovers between neighbouring units, it tells us that in order to avoid the damages of harmful spillovers and in order to reap the full economies of large-scale production of public goods and services, the government structure should be revised until there is only one super-jurisdiction.

The tension between these two principles is often left unresolved by writers and speechmakers. Instead of acknowledging their incompatibility, commentators comfortingly describe them as a source of "balance", leading us to have a structure of government in which the units at the various levels are "not too big, not too small, but just right".

To some political scientists, the tension or antagonism between the two principles is a matter for congratulation. This is because political scientists, and legal scholars too, if I may venture to paint their approaches in very broad strokes, do not see the role of government in terms of what it can do for the individual. They do *not* see it as providing public services for the citizen and the business, as the private firm does in the private sector. Instead, they see government in "symbolic" terms. They talk about "nation-building", as though that in itself were the goal of patterning a constitution. In my eyes, they walk into the problem backwards. They assume that there must be a nation, and a structure of government within it. That structure has then to be reshaped so that the various political units and levels within it can survive and flourish. The structure of government has to be reformed only to the extent that the various units are failing to achieve their own purposes—their *own* purposes— not the purposes and preferences of the citizens whom the economist thinks they exist to serve. Far too many of our political thinkers believe that the health of the governments in our federal mosaic is the objective of constitutional revision. They are concerned with shadowy aims like "province-building" or "nation-building". They think of the constituent provinces and the nation as though they were organic minds or spirits in search of goals, like the hippies of the 1960s who had lots of time to study their destination but no place to go. And they think of constitutional change in terms of reforming the pattern or pyramid of jurisdictional units, instead of better providing the public with services, goods, regulations, and protection.

AN ECONOMIC APPROACH

In the remainder of this essay I wish to discuss centralization and decentralization in what is sometimes called a "functional" way.

Instead of starting with the pyramid of governmental units, and reforming the constitution to make each of them more viable, we start with the citizens. Not for the first time, I suggest that governments are institutions that people create themselves for the purpose of resolving essentially collective issues about the provision of public services.

The centralization criterion told us, to begin with, that we should eschew the proliferation of small governments because we as citizens also wish to reap the benefits of large-scale production and enjoyment of public services. My point is that this "balancing" approach collapses once we recognize that the economies of scale in production of public services are independent of the size of the government that makes the decisions to provide and pay for them.

Let me offer two examples, over-simplified but suggestive. Take local fire services. Assume that the chief element in fire protection is the public provision of fire engines. Now we all know, from inspecting the mass-production facilities of General Motors, that there are giant economies of scale in the production of fire engines. But this economy of scale may benefit many different sizes of governmental unit. Production of fire engines is carried out in the private sector to serve many kinds of public jurisdiction, each of which reaps economies of scale from this production, regardless of its size and population.

Or take medical services. Assume that although a good public health system generally utilizes large treatment centres, hospitals, clinics, etc., the optimum size of territory which can be served by such units need not exactly "match" the jurisdiction of the government which supplies them. Decision making and financing concerning the services of the public medical units can then be divided among many smaller territorial units; you have all seen examples of that approach. Or, one huge political unit can easily include several parallel medical units.

By the same token, international military alliances are essentially very specialized and loose federations, or *con*federations. The alliance puts together whatever armada or chain of fortifications it needs for joint military action. NATO is just such an alliance. But there is no necessary connection between the size or level of each of the governments that participates in decisions about military policies and the militarily optimum size of the defence activity they have jointly caused to be produced.

In brief, there is no necessary connection between economies of scale in production of services and the level or jurisdictional scope of the government that provides them. Centralization may be a good thing, but it is not rationalized, explained, or furthered by reference to economies of scale in production.

Our own economic approach therefore requires identification of a different limiting factor, that will allow economies of scale and production and yet limit the proliferation of small units of government. What is it that keeps us from living in a world of many small governments, or even clubs? The answer is simple. What keeps government from becoming subdivided into family-size molecules is the unit cost of setting up *governments* and the costs of operating them. Thus our approach is an economic one. Freed from considerations of symbolism and public purpose, we need only investigate the more mundane question of how the citizen can get his government to provide (not produce, but provide) the services he demands at reasonable cost by means of economy in government organization, bureaucracy, political participation, and so forth.

Now this economic approach is, actually, compatible with an older "economic principle", which is embodied in sections 91 and 92 of the BNA Act and in many subsequent federal documents. There, the "national interest" and "local interests" are used as criteria to be played off against each other in the assignment of functions to provinces and to Canada. Railways and their regulation, for example, are assigned to Ottawa. The Fathers of Confederation knew that in Europe railways successfully cross national borders without any fuss. There is no imperative *technical* reason for having such international transportation problems under international jurisdiction; and there is no technical reason for the railways of Canada to be controlled by Ottawa. Or take criminal law. To Canadians it has always seemed mandatory that the prevention and control of crime must be regulated by the national criminal code. But in fact decisions about prosecution are made locally; in the United States, too, much criminal law making is also a local function. Or take Ottawa's regulation of combines in restraint of trade. In Europe they are experimenting with monopoly regulations which stretch across national boundaries, and in Canada, much of whatever successful use has been made of our combines law has been of a strictly local character. Indeed, the more one looks into the matter, the weaker the *technical* reasons for assigning functions to Ottawa become, if only because we can always find counter examples of federations where the functions are successfully *de*-centralized. If you think about each of the functions assigned to Ottawa, you will find either that they have a *strictly* national character (like those that deal with Canadian foreign affairs or the federal budget, or the transfer within the nation of money from rich Canadians to poor), or that they are functions that could, if necessary, be handled by smaller units like the provinces.

The same is true of the provinces. We all know of strictly local functions that are now sacred to provincial or municipal decision making. But we all know that, if necessary, Ottawa *could* deal with these same functions. In fact it does so now. Take fisheries, environmental matters, agriculture, port development and management, DREE, urban land use, and so forth, all under federal jurisdiction. In many cases Ottawa has in fact delegated some of the relevant decision making to local councils or given autonomy to its local officers. Often it makes special legislation to apply only to particular regions. This suggests that the provinces could handle those functions just as well as Ottawa, or that Ottawa, if it had the time and inclination, could legislate differently for the different regions.

If you think about each of the functions assigned to the provinces, you will find that they either have a strictly provincial character (like setting up the legislature or transferring monies from some part of the province to another) or that they are functions that could technically be performed from Ottawa.

What then lies behind the typical division of powers? If it is not technical, what is it? Our answer, as already intimated, is that it is the cost of the "transaction" of the "governmental organization" activities that would go with each structure of government.

Now we need a finer definition. We are no longer talking about over-all centralization. We are talking about the assignment of each of the different functions—to spend, to tax, to borrow, to regulate, and to redistribute—between the two or more levels of government. We are now analysing the pyramid of government in more detailed, "functional" terms. Centralization is *increased* when a function is re-assigned upward to a more senior level of government; it is decreased when some function is assigned to a lower level, or shared with it.

Every re-assignment of functions changes the total organization, operation, and set-up costs of government. It may be technically feasible to assign most functions (even welfare, redistribution, equalization, and stabilization) to any level of government. What differentiates the various assignments is that some ways of trying to make a government structure work are very costly, in the men, time, and materials making up organization costs, and some are more economical. The economist claims that in the past those who framed our constitution were aware of these costs, and that those who would build a constitution for tomorrow should, likewise, make them a major determinant of the assignment of powers.

For example, not only the Fathers of Confederation, but those who have later, by agreement or amendment, altered our constitution may be represented as arguing that, although railways *could* be controlled by each of the provinces (as in the Australian states), the *cost* of negotiation and co-ordination among provinces would be so high that citizens would gladly yield this power to the central government, where matters of safety, freight rates, gauge of tracks, etc. are all "internalized". Or take radio and TV. There is no reason why the allocation of radio waves among transmitters, and the allocation of time to commercial broadcasting stations should not be arranged in each province. Of course, there would then be interregional conflict. But "conflict" only means that there is a need for negotiation and co-ordination in order to arrive at some workable division of the radio-wave spectrum and the hours of the day. This co-ordination already works between adjoining small countries in Europe, and between the United States and Canada. It is a source of co-ordination and negotiation costs. But these costs need not be overwhelming, and they may well be less than the government-organization costs that would be involved in trying to settle such questions internally under a more unitary government. The prevailing practice of assigning most such spillover functions to the central government reflects to my mind a belief that the external co-ordinating and negotiating costs are often higher than the internal agreement and the information costs. That is why we find that, in the past, constitution builders have made many of the assignments that otherwise have no technical explanation.

For a final example, take the difficult subject of the co-ordination of provincial government spending in order to flatten out the business cycle. No one says that such co-ordination is impossible. But it would be so time consuming and so draining of the energy of eleven governments, that it is not seriously advocated or attempted. Once again, it is the costs of organization, not the technical feasibility, that is decisive.

Albert Breton and I have divided organization costs of government into four quite different sorts of activities. One pair we have already referred to: the costs that small units of government have in negotiating the co-ordination of their policies with those of their neighbours. These are common in urban situations, and also between national units. The larger the economies of scale in the production of some government services, and the larger the scope of environmental policies, the higher will be the expenditures that must be made on external co-ordination. As against these, each government has internal costs of government. These are associated with administration, information, agreement, enforcement, and the mere setting up of a government apparatus. When we decide that a function is to be assigned to a certain government level, we must forecast how it will affect the total external and internal organization costs of that government.

There is another pair of organization costs. These are borne directly by the citizen. Citizens incur costs when they vote to obtain a particular package of public services. The most visible cost is that of voting, but there are further costs of political action; all the activities which signal to government what bundles of policies the different groups of citizens demand are costly. Furthermore, disgusted citizens may take the final step in political action, and move out. The cost to them of moving is also an organization cost.

Costs from this pair of organization activities are related to the structure of government. When functions have been assigned to governments, levels of governments, or sizes of territory in an irrational way, citizens with very different tastes or preferences for public goods and services will be grouped together. The problem may be schooling, language, street-cleaning, religion, weights and measures—anything. Ways of assigning functions that will keep citizen discontent to a minimum, as revealed by the costs they incur in political action or moving to obtain a better bundle of services must, then, be found.

It should now be clear that the economic approach links well with traditional historical or journalistic accounts of the origins of federalism. Those accounts stress racial, religious, or linguistic differences. Our account stresses the diversity among citizen tastes. We may be talking about the same thing. Their account says that, if the differences are too great, the unitary state will fail and a federal structure will take its place.

I disagree. Many peoples of diverse tastes and incomes live together in the same jurisdictions in the government structures of many countries. But it is pertinent to ask when such strong preferences, such diversities, will be recognized in the allocation of functions so that each sub-group of the population can have the policies it desires. It is true that diversities of taste, preference, and need may and usually do increase the social cost incurred by citizens who feel impelled to move or to engage in other forms of political action and signalling. Whether the cost of maintaining an established form of government despite social pressures will exceed the costs of co-ordination and administration that might arise from a more decentralized structure must also be examined. That is the key to the economic approach to the constitution. We attempt to quantify the cost of the divisive forces in each jurisdiction, as they bear on both the costs borne by citizens and the internal administrative costs of governing. And we attempt to confront the total of these costs with the total organization costs that would arise if the division were dealt with by subdividing the country, or by assigning the functions to lower levels. These solutions could lead to lower costs of governing, higher costs of moving, and a far more costly array of organization for the co-ordination and partnership of small units in Balkan arrangement with each other.

There is nothing theoretical about this economic approach today. Every time the European Economic Community turns to the question of internalizing another function of government, the constitution makers with their critics must compare today's staggering costs of external diplomacy among the nine EEC members with the equally staggering costs of trying to agree on and administer a uniform European policy on such functions. Who can say which has the higher costs? Centralization is sometimes more expensive, sometimes less expensive, than decentralization. Or, consider the attempts in London to unscramble the United Kingdom omelette. Admittedly, there are many party-political and short-run reasons for and against devolving certain functions and taxes to Scotland. In the long run, however, the new constitution makers must also consider the social costs. Given a desire to have a certain uniformity on many policies, and a certain diversity on others, is there some structure of government that can manage both the increased internal domestic costs in London and the increased co-ordination costs between the semi-autonomous kingdoms? All government costs would seem to rise—will these be offset by falling political, signalling, and mobility costs of discontented individual Scots and Englishmen? This, we submit, is not an empty or useless question—it is an abstract but constructive way of organizing the considerations that must, *in the long run*, play a decisive role in deciding upon the future degree of centralization of the United Kingdom.

SOME OBJECTIONS ANSWERED

Let me begin this concluding section by summarizing matters thus far. In previous sections, I have distinguished between the long-run and short-run views of the structure of a nation's government. I have shown, so far as the long run is concerned, that the "degree of centralization" is a distinguishing characteristic of a country's existing structure of government, and that this does differ among federal countries and among different time-periods in the same country. I have argued, however, that the "degree of decentralization" of a country is not in itself a suitable subject for discussion or resolution, as it is merely the visible outcome of the crude forces of local decision making and centralization (such as the alleged economies of scale in the provision of public goods) pulling in opposite directions. Finally, I suggest that what matters is not the visible over-all extent of centralization or de-centralization, but the assignment of each and every function to a jurisdictional level in the national pyramid in such a way as to cut to the bone the total of organization, administration, co-ordination, signalling, and mobility costs of various assignments of functions. I suggest, too, that this "economic" approach is already implicit in the assignment embodied in sections 91 and 92 of the BNA Act—many of these assignments were made "as if" the Fathers of Confederation, the courts, and those who have made federal-provincial reassignments by agreement were motivated by a desire to minimize organization costs.

There will be plenty of objections to this view. Some will argue that it is not a helpful way to approach the long-run problem of the Canadian constitution. Others will argue that the theory destroys itself by internal contradictions.

As to whether it is helpful or relevant, you must be the judge. The fact that such issues as cablevision, the provincial ownership of airlines under federal regulation, agricultural policy, pipelines, and social policy with respect to family matters like abortion, divorce, desertion, and maintenance are all being continually revised with an eye to simplifying the problems of administration, co-ordination, and citizen compliance, suggests to me that Canadians *do* favour simple, rational, and low-cost ways of administering policies and so are implicitly acting as my economic approach suggests. Thus I believe it to be a helpful and relevant abstraction of the process of making and re-making the structure of government.

It may rightly be asked whether citizens ever are consulted about their preferred assignment of functions. My response is twofold. In the first place, I do not think that citizens care much about the structure of government, if that is defined in the precise assignment of particular functions and powers. What they want can be summarized in the following triad: policies they agree with, at a tax-price they can afford, provided by an overall structure that is not costly. Within these rules, they are largely indifferent and ignorant about which government is entrusted with what responsibility.

But who is responsible for seeing that a cost-minimizing structure is adopted? Recent Canadian authorities have argued that our politicians and top civil servants are unlikely to follow the authors of the American *Federalist Papers* in pointing the way to an economical assignment of powers. The attainment of an efficient assignment of functions among all levels of government is rarely a political goal. Bureaucrats and top advisors are more flexible in their motivation, but they too are more likely to seek power and status than to support the assignment of their responsibilities to other levels of government. Failing politicians and their civil servant advisors, which persons—or what mechanisms—can bring about the best allocation of powers? Pondering this question, I feel great sympathy for those who have argued that we ought now to look outside government for the members of a national constituent assembly. The economic approach I have outlined can save its members from wallowing in spirals of do-good platitudes. Like a jury, they would have a job to do: find the most economical assignment of functions. Obviously, leaders of ruling parties and their politicians and public servants and harassed officials must necessarily have a point of view that is too short run to take into account the minimization of organization costs in the long run. There is instead much to be said for the *ad hoc* council, assembly, or gathering. I do not feel strongly about its membership, except that it should be broadly and visibly representative of regions, parties, languages, and social classes. It is important that its members should be neither neophytes in political matters, nor in a position to gain personally from the structure on which their assembly finally agrees. Such a detached assembly may even be capable of defining justice and equity. Maybe so. I feel more confident that it could at least suggest long-run modifications to our constitution such that our mosaic of citizens with their variety of preferences can obtain the policies they desire with a minimum of government or voter organization costs.

Finally, I would like to address the almost cynical view that what matters, what really determines the assignment of functions, is the power of taxation. Whichever level gets the most prolific tax bases finds that all the other powers and duties are also given to it.

As historical generalization about the economy, this may be correct. The power of the purse, the power to pay, and to make grants may have seemed to explain everything else. Certainly many Royal Commissions have acted as though they felt the assignment of the power to tax must be the essence of constitution making.

I say that the assignment of tax bases, like the assignment of expenditure and regulatory functions, can be included in the economic approach I have advocated. Tax bases can be subdivided and shared, and, along with grants, abatements, and subsidies, can be entrenched in the constitutional assignment of functions. The rationale for matching powers and revenues should, once again, be to minimize organization and compliance costs.

No one can deny that money matters to the long-run structure of government. But the sources of revenue should not be treated differently from other powers and responsibilities. Both can be approached simultaneously from the organization-cost perspective.

Too often the assignment of functions is examined as though it were a game between contending jurisdictional levels. Let us try another metaphor. Let us imagine a deal in which powers are assigned like cards. Sources of revenue are dealt out in the same neutral fashion as spending responsibilities. The dealer is not one whose own career depends on how the assignment comes out. The object of the game is to achieve a distribution of functions that reduces to a minimum the cost of implementing them, not to make any particular card trumps, or any particular player the winner.

NOTE

1 One handy consequence of using "economic activity", rather than "size", or "symbolism", as a measure of the importance of the level of the governmental pyramid is that it allows us to hammer out a crude measure of the degree of centralization implicit in our present structure of government. Consider two pyramids, for three nations. In one, all the spending, taxation, and regulation is undertaken by the lowest level of government: the upper tiers are splendid but inactive. In the second, the top-most block undertakes all the expenditure, taxing, and regulating. In the third, the middle tier, the provinces, have the main economic impact. Albert Breton and I have evolved an index of centralization that would take into account the amount of government expenditure at each level. If all of it goes to the top, then that society has a structure of government with an index of 1.0; if all is done by the lowest-level jurisdictions, the index value is close to zero; and if most of the activity and spending is undertaken by the middle-level governments, the index takes on a value of close to one-half (0.5).

   We have applied this "index of centralization" to our own and to other federations. International comparisons are obviously difficult, because definitions of the role of government vary from place to place and from time to time. Nevertheless, our suggested index has proved itself by showing that Canada's degree of centralization is not unduly high compared to that of the United States and of Switzerland and that, like theirs, it has been declining since the 1930s and 1940s. (Figure 5:1, below.) For Canada alone we have also divided up the various kinds of government activity. In Figure 5:2 (below) we see from the lowest line that government expenditure on goods and services (excluding defence expenditure) has been almost constant, and highly decentralized, since 1926. Transfer payments, on the other hand, have become centralized (top line).

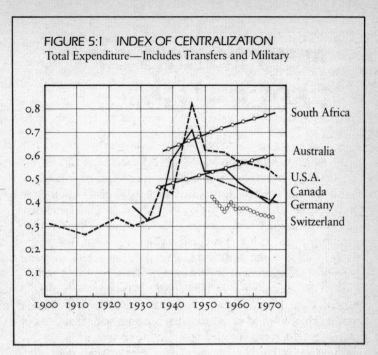

FIGURE 5:1 INDEX OF CENTRALIZATION
Total Expenditure—Includes Transfers and Military

South Africa
Australia
U.S.A.
Canada
Germany
Switzerland

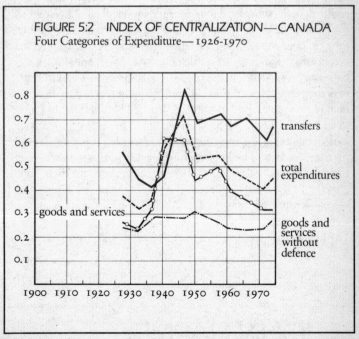

FIGURE 5:2 INDEX OF CENTRALIZATION—CANADA
Four Categories of Expenditure—1926-1970

transfers

total expenditures

goods and services

goods and services without defence

CHAPTER SIX

NEW FORMS OF FEDERALISM

MUCH HAS DEVELOPED since November 15th, 1976. The victory of the Parti Québécois took many Canadians by surprise. It revealed, among other things, the remarkable lack of preparation on the part of the leadership of English-speaking Canada to grasp the meaning of the event. Attempts were made to explain it away as a protest vote against the ineptitude of the Bourassa Liberal government. (If that had been the real reason, other provincial governments had better look to their mandates.) It dawned slowly on observers in English Canada that the PQ vote was not just a protest vote and that it actually stood *for* something. So, both socialists and non-socialists took refuge in the hope that the PQ was, after all, nothing much more than a social democratic party intent on righting some wrongs. Then, in mid-winter, René Lévesque told the Economic Club of New York that it was indeed his intent to take Québec out of Confederation. Because he had spoken his intentions on holy ground, the elites of English-speaking Canada believed him. After all, even politicians rarely lie in church. It was then that the agitation began; the man seemed to mean what he had been saying all along. Confronted by what should have been evident, English Canada responded by cautionary advice, endearments, offers of accommodation (always vague), a general promise to do and be better, considerable sentimentality, some brutish threats, much handwringing, and, now and then, some practical suggestions regarding the mending of our binational ways—from calls for decentralization to proposals for massive constitutional revision. Now the process is fully engaged. Groups, committees, seminars, conferences, conventions, and

* Prepared for this volume. An excerpt from this essay appeared in *The Gazette* (Montreal), December 15, 1977.

JOHN HARNEY

convocations will multiply our attempts to come to grips, to grasp the situation and plan courses of action. It is because I believe in the existence and resilience of English-Canadian culture, and its ultimate willingness to consider new ways of doing things, in this case new ways of living with French-speaking Canada, that I join the reconsideration of the forms of our collective existence and propose new forms of co-existence to satisfy the substance of our identities and projects.

A constitution is a written or unwritten set of ground rules (or a basic law, or a supreme law) by which a people or peoples agree to work out their being and desires. Whatever synonym we want to use for the word "constitution", we always emerge with a sense of law or principle which we respect as something beyond or superior to the laws, by-laws, and regulations which we develop to produce convenience, safety, order, and comfort in our daily lives. Constitutions stand behind, or act as the ground on which we make lesser legislative decisions.

Perhaps one of the great mistakes we make is to let constitutional law become the exclusive preserve of the expert—the statesman, the scholar, or, sadly, the lawyer—for if there is one kind of law that the average person can grasp and ought to have a share in forming, it is that of constitutions.

I like the terminological device the Germans chose to use after the Second World War. Political sensitivities in West Germany forbade the naming of the ground rules for the new German Federal Republic a "constitution" because the Republic was not "constituted" of all Germans (since a goodly number were living forcibly apart in East Germany). So what was produced was a "Basic Law". The term is a fortunate one. Though I cannot hope that it will replace the word "constitution", I want to give it some currency here by using it liberally throughout this essay.

I think we can all understand what is meant by a basic law. It is that law, that set of principles—few in number but large in import—which governs the long-term relationships of a people with itself, with its governing institutions, and with other peoples with whom it is associated. That is why there is, in everyone, a sense that such law should be hard to make, difficult to change, and almost impossible to repeal. Combined with this sense is the one which tells us that basic law needs the consent of more than mere majorities: majorities need to be overwhelming in order to make, change, or repeal basic law, not only so that minorities can be assured of a voice in the process, but in order that the process itself will be *deliberate*. We know and respect the knowledge that it is not and should not be easy to get most people to agree to a basic law which will likely be in force for a long time.

If overwhelming majorities are needed for the making of basic law, then it should be obvious that the people, as a whole, should be directly engaged in this process. Basic law should be prepared by a body which effectively represents the people and should require their approval, through the process of ratification, before it can come into force.

Though all of this is fairly obvious, it still needs to be said —particularly in this country where we have lost the habit of thinking clearly about constitutional matters, and particularly at a time when events are putting a heavy premium on clear thinking about fundamental relations.

Canada provides us with an irony. No student of federalism can avoid studying the Canadian experience, for it is one of the oldest and most articulated in the world. But few Canadians are students of federalism. In spite of the fact that Canadians live in one of the world's most unique federal experiments, most of us have only the faintest notion of the nature, origins, and workings of our system.

So, before we embark on an exploration of new forms of federalism, perhaps we had better clearly understand our current form of federalism. Once we have done that, we then can ask ourselves what we would like our federalism to do for us. After this, we can attempt to mold a type of federalism to suit our purposes.

If I seem to be talking here as if federalism were a device rather than an objective, I do so intentionally. Federalism is an aspect of our basic law which should serve our purposes. It is not an end in itself. Furthermore, it is important to stress that federalism can only be one part of our basic law, there being much more to a constitution than the relationships between peoples and sovereign institutions in a country. Basic law also has to do with the relationship of the state with its citizens, with citizens and their relationship with each other, and with the form, scope, and process of governing institutions.

Fortunately for our purposes here, only the last of these has any direct bearing on our present concern: we will be chiefly concerned here with methods and types of representation and the structure and source of government.

The popular press would have it that the country is now torn between "federalism" and "separatism". The term "federalism" finds parallels in "confederation" and "national unity". The manner in which the terms "federalism", "confederation", and "national unity" have been used more or less interchangeably in the present decade reflects our confusion, since a "confederation" is not the same as a "federation"—and neither of them is the same as a unitary state.

A *confederation* is an association of peoples or states in which the common or central authority is not independent of the constituent member peoples or states. Confederations come together for limited common purposes—such as defence, trade, or even common statehood—but the members of a confederation usually continue to exercise their sovereignties, usually do not have common citizenship, and seldom are directly taxed by the general authority or directly represented in its councils. There are several types of confederation, running from the loose association of a "league" (such as the League of Nations), to NATO, an association of states established for mutual defence against a threat perceived in common by the member states, to the European Economic Community, which is slowly leading to a confederate if not federated Europe through the process of mutual and common accord over trade and economic questions.

Leagues and treaty organizations aside, we can count very few proper confederations in modern history. The Confederate States sought to become a federation, and both the Swiss and the Canadian confederations are also mainly federal—and are indeed more unitary than confederal. But the notion of "confederation" may be of use to us in dealing with our situation in Canada; for it becomes apparent upon inspection that what many French-Canadian nationalists are seeking is some kind of confederal relation with English Canada.

Federations are more common than confederations. Depending on one's definitions, one can count from four to fourteen federations in the world. The classic and relatively permanent examples of this are Switzerland, the United States, Australia, and Canada. An expanded definition would include India, Nigeria, Malaysia, and West Germany. The classic examples, at any rate, indicate that federations consist of state structures involving at least two levels of government: a general or federal government, and regional, provincial, or state governments—both levels having independence in each of their fields of action.

They also have a shared citizenship, and direct taxation as well as direct representation. Put in the simplest terms, in a federation the citizen not only has a sense of "belonging" to the general state, but also has a direct share in making its laws, in directing its administration, and in shaping its objectives through representation in a common or general legislature. Perhaps even more important, his sense of belonging and participation makes him willing to be taxed by that central authority—surely the most enduring and practical if not the most noble test of allegiance.

A unitary state has no constituent parts. There is the state and its citizens. There may be local governments, but their power is usually clearly circumscribed by the central authority. France is a classic example of a highly centralized unitary state. It has no provinces or regional states, its local authorities are departments whose prefects are appointed centrally, and it has one capital, Paris, which until recently, did not even have a mayor.

Most of the world's nations are unitary states, operating under various degrees of administrative centralization or decentralization and jurisdictional devolution. The United Kingdom is an interesting example of a complex unitary state. It has only one major government based on the Crown and the Parliament at Westminster; there are no regional governments as we understand them, but there are strong local governments with considerable scope and authority—the city and county councils—and certain jurisdictional devolutions such as the autonomy of Scotland in matters of church and civil law and the delegated power of Stormont to attempt to govern from time to time the affairs of Northern Ireland. Complex as it may be, the United Kingdom is a unitary state because there is no authority within it that is co-ordinate, or independent, or not derived or delegated from the central power.

A further distinction has to be made here. No matter what the basic form of association may be—confederal, federal, or unitary—no state appears to be governable over time without local administration or municipal law. Such matters as sidewalks, streets, sewers, policing, fire prevention, parks, and traffic are usually the concerns of local authorities. Most of us understand that local administrations have to deal with necessities (we may or may not choose to have a navy, depending on our sense of security or our aggressiveness, but we cannot choose to do without sewers), and we are willing to help pay for these necessities. But apart from a certain sentimentality, we usually do not pay allegiance to our municipal structures.

This distinction is not as insigntificant as it may seem: the municipal aspect of governance manifests itself not only at the local level, but also at the provincial level (for example in highways and policing), and even at the federal level (in the post office and the penitentiary service). In other words, there are concerns which are largely controlled by physical necessity and allow relatively little latitude for the exercise of policy or party preference. We may fight over a flag or disagree about the ownership of natural resources, but we rarely come to strong words about the operation of storm sewers. Generally speaking, we operate on the principle that "municipal" concerns which are related to real-property physical installations are best regulated at the local level, but that our personal, civil, and national concerns are better dealt with at more general or "higher" levels of government.

Though I can hope that these distinctions may have reduced the confusion which attends the current debate about the nature and direction of our Canadian state somewhat, I cannot hope to eradicate it totally because it is inherent in our structures as well as in the way we talk about them. Canada is, like most other states, not a pure form of either confederation, federation, or unitary state. It is primarily a federal country, but with some marked unitary aspects. Its central administration is decentralized to some degree, and there are tensions within it straining towards confederacy. So whether we choose to say we should be more or less federal, more or less decentralized, more or less unified—or even more or less confederate, or "associate"—we remain more or less on topic, because the Canada that is (as well as the Canada that will be) has a degree of complexity that allows for discussion of all these aspects.

We are now ready to ask ourselves what we want our federalism to do for us. This, the simplest of the questions before us, will be the most difficult to answer, because there is no way that one person can adequately express all the wishes and hopes held by a people. Many of these wishes fail to intermesh; some are in fundamental conflict with one another. A wiser way to proceed is to ask ourselves who we are and to then try to extract from such an identification the range of possibilities each collectivity feels it must have, and will allow the others to have.

The Canadian identity can be approached in many ways. The approach I use here is more existential than analytical, and I will pay more attention to the present than to the past — although any understanding of a matter such as national being requires a strong sense of the past.

Let us begin by making the distinctions we need to have in hand. First, there are at least two Canadas. The people of one past are called and call themselves Canadiens, Canadiens-français, and Québécois. The people of the other call themselves Canadians, or English Canadians (in order to distinguish themselves from French Canadians), or Ukrainians, Italians, Greeks, or whatever, in order to distinguish themselves from the two major groups. Then there are the native Canadians — for example, the Innuit and the Dene (both names meaning "the people"). This is admittedly a rough and ready list, and it is based on language and country of ultimate origin. Some further distinctions could be made within it.

As well as distinctions based on language and country of origin, Canadians will claim a degree of regional allegiance. In terms of extent and intensity, we could list the regionalism of the West (with or without B.C.), the Atlantic provinces (with or without Newfoundland), B.C., and central Canada. How strong one's identification with a region or province can be is a matter for debate — but there is no doubting the existence of a felt sense of regional belonging in Canada. The regionalism of central Canada, particularly of Ontario, is peculiar in that it is not aware of itself *as* a regionalism: the strongest regionalism is that which is not aware of itself.

To call the self-awareness of Québec "regionalism" is to sell it too far short — although there is some regionality in the Québécois perspective. The Québécois sense of belonging to a nation far overwhelms the sense of being part of a region. The sense of place of the Québécois is that of a nation to land, or country. A proud Saskatchewanian can certainly relate to the prairie and have fond attachments to his province, but never will he call it "mon pays".

Even after some inspection, it can be seen that there are really only three "peoples" in Canada: the French-speaking, the English-speaking, and the native peoples. It can be further observed that the French speakers are as homogeneous as a people can be expected to be, that the English speakers are a mixed lot in national origins, and that the native people, whether Indian,

Métis, or Inuit, are beginning their voyage towards rediscovery of nationhood. I believe that, although all of these entities want to remain in association with each other, they nevertheless have a sense of their own distinctiveness and have concerns and objectives which they must work out for themselves. Within these dual objectives of association and autonomy, what are the particular traits and objectives of each people?

The French in Canada are a nation distinct from all others in language, history, and a sense of place. In the past, their collective will has been bent to the survival of their language, religion, and culture. In this they have to a large degree succeeded. Now they seek to flourish, and to do so they feel, most of them, that the laws of their national state must be endowed with certain powers to ensure the thriving of the French fact in North America.

None can doubt that the native peoples of Canada have the attributes of nationhood. They are now attempting to regain the instruments and institutions of nationhood, but more particularly, the existence and security of their culture and, perhaps most urgently, their sense of place through territorial claims.

Perhaps the most difficult of the tasks of national definition is that for English Canada. Although I can argue strongly that there is an English-Canadian nation because it has a sense of history, a strong culture, a common language, shared and cherished national institutions, a common view of law and government, and certain other less existential attributes, I have to admit that English Canada has resorted to "crutches" to shore up its sense of nationhood. The British connection was certainly real for a majority of English Canadians until well into this century. For many, Britain remained the homeland, the source of their culture and civilization, and indeed, the object of allegiance. The First Canadian Division was overwhelmingly a mustering of men who were living in Canada and who were born, or whose parents were born, in Britain. Canada did not even establish her own citizenship until 1945.

Another crutch was the obverse of this one: we were Canadian because we were not American. The tory-minded could, in their way, replace "life, liberty and the pursuit of happiness" with "peace, order and good government". Left-wingers could more easily attack capitalist monopoly on the grounds that it was foreign. The culturally unresolved or insecure could ignore spiritual inadequacy or sluggish imagination and blame it all on the crass overwhelming materialism of Yankee pop and Hollywood lucre.

Though some of us always managed to live our Canadian nationhood without either the British or the American prosthetics, most of us in English Canada had a sense of "difference" which was in part based on the fact that we were a binational, or bilingual, or bicultural country. Whether we liked them or not, the French were there, and they formed a considerable segment of our national concern and self-awareness. Repeating "what does Québec want?" was not as idle a question as it appeared to be for many of us in English Canada. Like the family with the unusual and sometimes difficult brother or aunt, we were aware of them, knew they gave us a sense of being, and, though we recognized that they could make life a little difficult, did not want to be without them.

This "crutch nationalism" has been and still is a significant aspect of English-Canadian nationhood. Our history, and especially the record of our electoral politics, gives vivid examples of the importance of these crutches as we argued about exchanging one for another. But though most of us now know that the British connection is an ever more tenuous one, and some of us are beginning to realize that a more existential nationalism based upon economic self-determination is more useful and realistic than cultural anti-Americanism, few of us can now disregard the psychic support which the presence of French Canada provides for us.

Abraham Rotstein once remarked that the English-Canadian image of Canada is geographical, or spatial, and thus explained why such terms as "breaking the country up" and "tearing the country apart" are so believable and emotive. No less a politician than Pierre Trudeau seems to be aware of this, and this is perhaps why his speeches on Canadian unity and against separatism are well larded with the terminology of physical separation and break-up. It is not by accident that the Canadian motto "from sea to sea" has come to mean so much to English Canadians. The French in Canada, perhaps because they were forced to repress their territorial urges, took on a temporal or historical view of their land. Their place is a time, and it is a time which goes back into the past, and remembers, as Dr. Laurin remembers.

Any attempt to state what we want our country to be has to take into account all this and more. But "more" will have to wait for another time and place. It is enough for now just to tackle the task of describing what it is that we want our country to be for us, and to work out the structural relationships among ourselves that will, at the least, remove impediments to the working out of our aspirations and perhaps even provide the ground on which a peaceful and generous future can rest.

Ironically, what we need in Canada, though we admittedly do not yet wish for it, is a confederation, properly so called. The Canadian community, which enfolds the peoples that live on the northern half of the North American continent, can survive into the future only if it permits of the fact as well as of the principle of full and open association among its constituent peoples, the English (Canadians), the French (Québécois), and the native peoples (Innuit, Dene, Métis). We English Canadians will have to accept that in a confederation there can be no question of majority—minority, and that only mutual accord obtains, that there is no large or small, but parity among all. The Québécois will perforce accept that the definition of "nation" has to include, even under its narrowest understanding, the native peoples. This *ménage à trois* may not come to be, for we do not know whether the native peoples would choose a nationhood of their own.

The principle of mutual accord is a simple and venerable one, but one which we Canadians will have to come to understand better if we are to build a new Canadian community upon it. It is a principle which we know well in private, professional, and associational affairs, but one which has not had much spoken currency in national affairs. Put negatively, it says that an association of persons or peoples can only undertake a measure or action or adopt a policy when all participants agree. It is not a working principle which is needed in a homogeneous, unitary state (for reasons which should be obvious), which is why we are unfamiliar with it at the political level. If the question is: "Who is to pay for our sewerage system?" we may wish to answer "those who use it most", or "everyone equally", or "those who can most afford it", but whichever of these answers is to be chosen we would insist that it be chosen on the basis of majority vote. In general, the questions before a confederation as such will not be of the "sewerage" type, elsewhere described as "municipal" questions. The questions before a confederation, in the main, will have to do with the relations between constituent member peoples and their choices for common action, not with the details of their internal lives.

Is the principle of mutual accord different from the principle of consensus? It is, for in the approach to consensus, participants work together to the point where a sense of the majority will is arrived at, whereas under mutual accord, each participant entity works out its position which it then brings to a process of open negotiation and contract-setting. If there is not assent, there has to be withdrawal into the constituent entities, where differences have to be considered in coming to a new approach to bargaining. The parallel between mutual accord in a confederation and collective bargaining is close but not perfect, since none of the parties can lay claim to residual or undefined rights; but it is close nevertheless, because both contain and depend upon the principle of contract. A contract is an explicit statement or document which can be amended at future negotiations and which can always be reopened upon term or the desire of one of the parties. Contract is a kind of law, of course, and in a confederation the contract between the parties is the ground, substance, and letter of the basic law governing their relationships. Under contract, under a confederation, there is, properly speaking, not unity but community. The idea of unity always contains within it the possibility of subordination and even assimilation. Community works on solidarity, and that provides for shared decision and action without the absorption of the constituent elements in the decision or action.

A confederation is unlikely to be between peoples only, for peoples have lands, *pays*. There is no doubt at all that the new confederal structures would involve allocation of territory and such allocation is more easily said than done. Perhaps of the three entities, the allocation of land to the native peoples will be the most difficult, though the allocation of territory to French and English will not be easy either. Let us start by tackling the former problem, since its solution will certainly contain guides to the solution of the latter.

It is virtually impossible to imagine a landless people, but not totally so, since the Jews maintained their peoplehood during two thousand years of dispersal. This situation was not desired by the Jews, and now most of Jewry takes status that some Jews are citizens of their own land, Israel. Though the material situation of the Montreal or New York Jew is not affected by the existence of Israel, we are not to gather from that that the continued existence of Israel as a free, independent, and secure national homeland is immaterial to him. It matters, for most Jews, a great deal. All know that they could, in principle, become actual citizens of that state. Some do become citizens, but most will live to enjoy the possibility in principle only. What matters to the individual Jew is that his people have a place, a land, and that he has a choice.

I think that a settlement of native land claims in Canada in such a way that some lands that are now part of Canada are ceded to the native peoples can serve the purpose of giving all native people a status, whether or not they will reside in those territories which will be theirs in the fullest sense of the word. Though I cannot imagine a circumstance in which all of the lands of the north are ceded for all purposes by the people of Canada to the native peoples, I can see the possibility that some of the land can be ceded for some purposes to them. Of course, the state which will establish itself to govern that land will be sovereign and so will take the form its citizens wish, but a condition of cession could be that the native state should offer citizenship or "membership" to native people who do not reside in the native state's lands but who wish to be citizen-members. A voluntary register of native people could be established, and this register would make up the citizenship-membership of the native peoples' state which would have not only a land, a place of its own to hold and govern as it sees fit, but which would extend beyond the borders of that land to include those natives living elsewhere in Canada who choose to be citizen-members of the native peoples' state.

I need not go into more detail about the possible arrangements here since my main purpose is to tackle the problem of nationhood and territory. The notion of an extra-territorial register seems to me to provide a valuable means to a solution of the native territory problem. Persons on the register would be governed by the state which they join, and in turn would have full voting rights in that state's national affairs. Those living outside the boundaries of the state would have their municipal existence with its rights and responsibilities in their place of residence. I have used here the compound term citizen-member because I do not want at this stage to preclude the possibility of citizenship pertaining to the Canadian community as a whole.

In his masterful campaign to convince Québécois and Canadians of the rightness of his sovereignty-association cause, René Lévesque has made two strategic decisions which at first glance appear brilliant, but which are major errors in the design of his campaign. The first was the decision to proceed to independence through a referendum; the fact is that the PQ most likely would have obtained only about 40 per cent of the popular vote in 1976 without the commitment to a referendum, and so would not now be in a position, given the crudity of the Canadian electoral system, to work directly towards independence and association with Canada. The second was to establish the campaign ground for independence as the actual territory of Québec. This was and is for the time being a masterful stroke. Thus Lévesque got around that age-old tactical problem of French-Canadian nationalists: how to mobilize a nation whose membership spilled over interprovincial and, even, international boundaries. Let us recall that the great drive behind the celebration of St. Jean Baptiste Day in the 1880s was the reunion with the homeland of the hundreds of thousands of French Canadians who were domiciled in the United States. In 1880, some twenty thousand were organized to come by special excursion tours from New Hampshire, Connecticut, and the other New England states in order to celebrate "la fête des Canadiens-français". By making its objective the "sovereignty" or independence of Québec, the PQ appears to have reduced the problem to manageable proportions, but in effect they have merely put off the reckoning. Should they be able to persuade an overwhelming majority of French-speaking Quebeckers to vote "oui" to independence in a referendum, an overwhelming French yes vote will still be needed to offset the overwhelming English and ethnic no vote in Québec, and should Québec proceed to independent status with or without association with Canada, the time would come, sooner or later, when elements within Québec would agitate for the "repatriement" of those French elements just over the Québec borders in Ontario and New Brunswick which are large and homogeneous enough to be considered natural if not legal extensions of French Québec. I leave aside here the very real problem of the unhappy, recalcitrant, English minorities in Montreal and western Québec, for I have said enough to demonstrate that there is a "territorial" aspect to the resolution of French-Canadian nationhood which will not disappear with the question of the independence of Québec. The present Québécois nationalism would give way to a still-viable Canadian nationalism which could not be contained, and certainly not satisfied, by the present territorial system.

The device of an extra-territorial register suggested above to deal in part with the native peoples' citizenship-membership in their national state may be of further use here to deal with the question of the French minorities outside Québec and the English minorities within it. Members of either group could individually and voluntarily enrol in their respective registers and be dealt with and behave as citizen-members of the state of their choice, regardless of their place of residence, which would be of civil and legal significance to them only in the municipal aspect of their existence.

Non-resident members of a constituent Canadian state would have their interests protected by the state of their choice, and by the surveillance of the common or general government of the Canadian community. Prime Minister Trudeau was in effect looking to some such principle when he suggested in his Matane remarks on the eve of St. Jean Baptiste Day this year (in 1977) that the federal government could take up the responsibility for the educational rights of minorities in all provinces. Unfortunately he does not seem to have looked to the ground rules—to the fact that the provinces have total jurisdiction in education—before proposing this massive change. But given a state of affairs in which Québec was assured of its sovereignty and chose to be somehow associated with the other parts of the Canadian community, and given the structuring of a common government in which the constituent parts have parity and wherein true contractual bargaining can take place, it is possible that the communal government might be responsible for the protection and promotion of minority rights.

But the major question of the internal organization of the constituent parts of the Canadian community still remains unanswered. In spite of the general presumptuousness of my approach in this article, I will not begin to presume what shape the internal organization of the native peoples' state should or could take. They have models to draw on, among them both parliamentary democracy and their own highly evolved traditions of consensus. I have, for example, hardly ever heard of a more sensitive, articulated, balanced, and respectful deliberative process than that evolved in the Huron confederacy.

I also expect that Québec will retain the form and substance of a unitary state. There is a great variety of regions within Québec—la Mauricie, la Gaspésie, Montréal, les Cantons de l'Est—but the homogeneity of the Québécois, and the strong sense of community they must maintain while surrounded by over two hundred million English-speaking North Americans, will not permit Québec the luxury of much jurisdictional devolution, even if such a course were desired, which it is not. (Incidentally, herein lies a major material argument for the particularity of Québec. Though it equals in population the provinces of Canada less Ontario, its internal regionality is not such as to give rise within it to any kind of federative approach, a desire which is actual as well as felt in the rest of Canada.)

What is still in question is the internal organization of English Canada. Will the English-speaking provinces of Canada work towards a more unitary structure for themselves in recognition of their shared culture and destiny? Or will they choose, from long habit and tradition, to continue with some form of federalism? I suggest that there is some impatience with provincial structures among English Canadians, and that a central government which could administer such things as the development of natural resources or education would appeal to them more than a cumbersome federation to express their regionality. What is important is not that this question be resolved now, but that we see that changes in our interregional relationships could be made without either a confrontation with Québec over provincial rights, or the collapse of the whole federal house of cards about our ears.

Having invented it, what do we call it? Proper naming is not just an afterthought, for in the names we choose for ourselves lie a grasping of our history and a reaching out for our future. I have written elsewhere that the Québécois used to be "Canadiens"; I think they would still wish to be if the name did not involve a denial of themselves. At the first St. Jean Baptiste Day celebration in 1834, young Georges-Etienne Cartier sang his composition "*O Canada, mon pays, mes amours*". By the St. Jean Baptiste Day of 1836 (no male chauvinists, they), they had remembered Josette and sang "*vive la Canadienne*". By 1880 Calixa Lavallée and Judge Routhier had published "O Canada". For many generations the English in Canada knew it as "that French anthem", and it took the "British subjects" until the 1940s to establish a Canadian citizenship, and a few more years yet to call themselves Canadians and replace "God Save the Queen" with "O Canada". Now they are Canadian with a vengeance, and wonder why the Québécois would be less so than they.

Perhaps the simplest thing to do would be to call the Canadian community "Canada", short for the Canadian community or the Confederation of Canada or the Union of Canada. Within it, there would be Québec, and a state for the native peoples (with a name of their choosing), and the United Provinces of Canada, each retaining its own and present name as long as its residents wished to. This Canada would be a true confederation of these constituent parts: Québec, the United Provinces, and the Native Peoples' State. Each resident would be a citizen-member of his or her own state, and would share a common citizenship with all other Canadians. Each state would be sovereign, but could choose, after a process of parity bargaining, to delegate to the common government certain responsibilities and functions which would enhance the mutual good and advantage of all.

What I have argued towards here is a new kind of Canadian confederation and the substantive and historical ground for it. The next few remarks are unsupported by argument, but may serve to anticipate questions and suggest a basis for further development of the proposal.

The Canadian community will need at least three capitals: a central capital, which might as well be Ottawa, since it is there, and it clearly now has the emotional as well as the monumental attributes of a capital; a capital for Québec, which I expect will be Québec City, and a capital for the United Provinces, which certainly must not be in Ontario, but which could alternate between Moose Jaw and Charlottetown (no one has much against either at the moment). This might go some way to alleviate western and eastern alienation, and would also recognize the desire for administrative and economic decentralization which is so strong in English Canada. The native peoples may not choose or need to have a capital at all.

The languages of the common government will, of course, be English and French, and hopefully for more than ceremonial purposes, a native tongue proposed by the native peoples. The language of Québec will be French; the language of the United Provinces, English; and again, *à leur choix* for the native peoples. English and French would, and Ukrainian, Italian, Greek (others if needed) could, be given the status of minority languages in both Québec and the United Provinces: the first two also having an effectively enhanced position in each state by virtue of their official status in the general government.

The Canadian community would have to have a deliberative and legislative body for those matters left to it or delegated to it by the constituent states. Whatever the method and form of representation, questions affecting the constituent states could be decided on a parity basis and with the consent of the affected states. The community would need, as well, a confederal court, and a common head of state, who could also serve as head of state of the constituent states of the Canadian community, although the integrative benefits of this approach could be outweighed by the exigencies of selecting a candidate to play such a role.

I would hope that the common government would be given the power to tax the citizens of each constituent state directly, and not only renew its operating funds, as the U.N. does, in the form of agreed-upon contributions from the member states. I would want there to be some sense of allegiance on the part of the citizen in each state, not only to his state, but to the Canadian community. Since allegiance presupposes knowledge and attention and concern, I can think of no better way to arouse concern and the paying of attention than taxation. There should never be taxation without representation, of course, but there is also no true representation without taxation. If I pay them, I want them to play my tune, some of the time at least, and will listen carefully, to see that they do.

PART TWO

THREATS TO UNITY: THE CULTURAL CRISIS

THE THREATS to Canada's continued existence are not confined to political or constitutional confrontations between governments. No nation-state ever disappears—except by force of arms—unless purely mechanical confrontations of this kind are interpreted and given meaning within a larger cultural context. In practise, this means that separatist movements almost always justify themselves in cultural terms.

Canada is no exception to this rule. From the beginning— even before the Plains of Abraham—cultural interpretations have been placed on almost every contest for power between English and French Canadians. When the Québécois speaks angrily of "les Anglais", his disdain extends beyond the group itself to a complex of cultural attitudes. What he is rejecting, in effect, is "the English way of doing things". Similarly, when the English Canadian reciprocates, he is not simply rejecting a concrete social or ethnic group. So when the diehards within each group talk of the "language issue", they seek to imply by this much more than language.

This conflict or confrontation between English and French Canadians, however, though important, is only the first of three crucial cultural issues which bear on our current national crisis. In the end, these other issues may be central factors in its outcome.

Canada today is very different from the Canada of 1867. In both Ontario and Québec, the principal source of new population over the last decade and a half has been immigration— much of it from outside of western Europe. With respect to origins, both the Ontario and the Québec populations are really multilingual and multicultural. This—and the fact that neither of our two "Founding Nations" has in principle a greater claim to this land than the indigenous peoples—has been largely ignored in the current debate. Both of these groups, however, have cultural rights to protect in the present situation and they are likely to become more militant in doing so as time goes on.

The third cultural dynamic is the tendency of all Canadian cultures to become absorbed into North American culture—to become, in short, Americanized. As things stand now, neither English-Canadian culture nor French-Canadian culture is likely to hold up very well in the face of the powerful influence of our neighbour to the south. American culture has made substantial inroads in Britain and France: why should we assume that it will not have a far more powerful effect here?

Those concerned about developing and extending Canadian culture have been badly split by the Québec Question. Milton Acorn, whose poem/essay appears in this Part, is among those who feel that English Canada has already largely given up the fight anyway. Others reject Québec separatism on political grounds, but do not connect their cultural sentiments to their political rationale. In an article in this Part, Gregory Baum does make this connection—but argues for constitutional accommodation to French-Canadian cultural rights in any case. Royce Frith and Davidson Dunton discuss the larger issue of the rights of non-British, non-French immigrants. Only Marshall McLuhan and Barrington Nevitt, of all the contributors, recognize a *fourth* cultural dynamic which has, after all, been at work in Canada fully as long as the others: the tendency, over time, to form a unique Canadian culture which is neither English nor French, which incorporates within it elements of both—but which respects the integrity of both at the same time. A simple comparison between local dialects in places with substantial French majorities or minorities and standard English or French should be enough to convince even the most sceptical that this factor is and has been at work as well. In some sense, however, this fourth dynamic is implicit in each of the articles in this chapter, in that, no matter what legislation governments may enact, cultural fusion seems to be one of the most obvious facts of our time.

CHAPTER SEVEN

"IF YOU WONT LIVE . . . "

If you wont live your own dreams I claim
All which belongs to this damned land I love;
Though all the souls you've expelled
From your blood's own warmth, hustle and shove
Into mine . . . 'Til each swimming cell has a name
Which should have been yours, and a mouth
To spit those bolts of truth you wont impel.

IF QUÉBEC LEAVES CONFEDERATION and slides into the maw of the United States, what is lost? The whole country is slipping into the maw of the United States; and it's through Confederation this vile devourment is being accomplished.

If Québec leaves Confederation, establishes her independence; while the rest of the country slides into the maw of the United States; then one country is saved from American Imperialism. Since Canada is going fast anyway, there's a net gain.

If Québec leaves Confederation, establishes her independence; and by her example inspires Canadians to strive for and win independence; then there is a double gain.

If, partly in consequence of Québec leaving Confederation, both Canada and Québec slide into the maw of the United States; nothing is really lost because that's the situation anyway. It's only a question of formality and degree.

Rise Canadians! To flip on your stomachs
Like snakes or multiple cords of a whip.
Squirm to the charmpipes of the U.S.A.
Letting your blood trip south, sip-a-drip—

* Appeared in *Jackpine Sonnets* (Toronto: Steel Rail Press, 1977). Published here by kind permission of the author.

MILTON ACORN

Content to live as worms in her excrement;
Loosing your resentment on Québec.
Pardon me if my decoded tongue
Wont obfuscate the cowardice you vent.

CHAPTER EIGHT

LANGUAGE RIGHTS AND PROGRAMS

THE WAY WE WERE

THE EXPLODING MAILBOXES of 1963 and the violence of October 1970—all hitherto uncharacteristic of Canadian politics—now seem far away. The crisis for the moment seems more characteristically Canadian, expressing itself in words rather than weapons. The symptoms change but the disease hangs on because we seem only to treat the symptoms instead of the cause, and a chronic inability to accept the realities of history and demography stubbornly resists treatment.

Our most substantial effort at diagnosis started with Prime Minister Pearson's establishment of the Royal Commission on Bilingualism and Biculturalism. Ten Canadians, of whom I was one, were appointed to the commission. The terms of reference, drafted by Senator Maurice Lamontagne, asked us to:

> inquire into and report upon the existing state of bilingualism and biculturalism in Canada and to recommend what steps should be taken to develop the Canadian Confederation on the basis of an equal partnership between the two founding races, taking into account the contribution made by the other ethnic groups to the cultural enrichment of Canada and the measures that should be taken to safeguard that contribution.

The commissioners came, not as politicians or social technicians, but as citizens, who, through research studies, public hearings, and in the light of their own backgrounds, could report as eye-witnesses on the Canadian condition in the areas of lan-

---

* Paper submitted to a Liberal Party Policy Conference workshop, Toronto, March 1977. Published here in modified form by kind permission of the author.

ROYCE FRITH

guage and culture. They came not as teachers but as students—
undertaking an inquiry, not launching a movement.

In February of 1965, after a cross-country series of informal regional meetings where people were invited to attend and
present their views without formal briefs and to exchange experiences and opinions with the commissioners and with fellow
citizens from their regions, the commission issued a preliminary
report in which it said it had been

> . . . driven to the conclusion that Canada, without being fully
> conscious of the fact, is passing through the greatest crisis in its
> history.

The report continued:

> The source of the crisis lies in the province of Quebec; that fact
> could be established without an extensive inquiry. There are other
> secondary sources in the French-speaking minorities of the other
> provinces and in the ethnic minorities—although a provincial
> crisis at the outset, it has become a Canadian crisis, because of the
> size and strategic importance of Quebec, and because it has in-
> evitably set off a series of chain reactions elsewhere.
>
> What does the crisis spring from? . . . it would appear from
> what is happening that the state of affairs established in 1867,
> and never since seriously challenged, is now for the first time
> being rejected by the French Canadians of Quebec.
>
> Who is right and who is wrong? We do not even ask ourselves
> that question; we simply record the existence of a crisis which we
> believe to be very serious. If it should persist and gather momen-
> tum it could destroy Canada. On the other hand, if it is overcome,
> it will have contributed to the rebirth of a richer and more
> dynamic Canada. But this will be possible only if we face the
> reality of the crisis and grapple with it in time.

That was twelve years ago. Press and public reaction at the time
was either ho-hum or "let's not get hysterical". Later, after hearings at which formal briefs were presented and after weighing
the results of a massive research program that tested the country's patience and pocketbook, the commission presented its final report. Before hardly any dust had settled on it, its recommendations led to Parliament's adoption in 1969 of the Official
Languages Act. The act was supported by all of Parliament's
political parties—though not without some acrimonious debate

and significant individual absenteeism on the day of the vote.

The Act established English and French as Canada's official languages, proclaimed some eminently reasonable rights for Canadians—to be served by their federal government in the language in which it taxed them—and imposed corresponding duties on the government to provide that service. The cornerstone section granted the two official languages the enjoyment of equal status as to their use in all federal institutions.

As a result, language rights flow from the statutory duty of federal institutions to provide intramural opportunity for use of each language and extramural services in the official language of the client's choice, subject to significant demand. Even less-conditional duties are imposed in the National Capital Region, in "bilingual districts", and for the travelling public.

The bilingual districts were to be proclaimed by the government after a report by a bilingual districts advisory board. If service is given anywhere in Canada where sufficient demand exists, such districts seem less and less likely to be needed to protect language rights and promote the desired reform.

A Commissioner of Official Languages was appointed to see to implementation. The Act told him to investigate complaints, to launch investigations on his own initiative, and to make recommendations to the government and to particular departments and agencies to help them fulfil their obligations under the Act.

Meanwhile, the government itself was busy with programs designed to advance reform. As early as 1964, a language-training plan had been established, largely to protect the jobs of unilingual English-speaking public servants. This program has steadily accelerated as an inescapable companion to the Pearson declaration of 1966, the Official Languages Act of 1969, and the parliamentary resolutions of 1973. Also woven into the fabric during this same period were frequent and detailed bulletins from the Public Service Commission as to access to language training, and directives from the Treasury Board as to the nuts and bolts of language service, language of work, and designation of bilingual positions.

THE WAY WE ARE

The best assessment of the way all these programs and rights stand is found in the annual reports of the Commissioner of

Official Languages. Their wit, elegance, and boldness, and their annual language-reform balance sheet and statement of profit and loss have made them a yearly journalistic event. There have been five to date, noting and encouraging slow but steady progress while despairing over our tragic inability to make clear the reform's common sense and simple justice.

Here is a reading of the current balance sheet.

THE RED INK:

- extravagant overkill in language-training programs with a discouraging payoff in on-the-job use of expensively learned language skills;
- overkill in designation of bilingual posts with a further exacerbation of consequent language-training needs;
- bad publicity, outrage over publicized aberrations like civil servants being sent to language school a year prior to retirement, or immersion junkets to learn how to order wine while salaries for them and their replacements are paid by the taxpayer;
- often misplaced concern that the English-speaking unilingual civil servant—for whom all these language-training programs are basically designed—is getting an unfair deal;
- widespread fears that bilingual districts represent another instrument of French-down-the-throat torture.

THE BLACK INK:

- Francophone share of federal jobs getting less unfair (1971 openings for unilingual English speakers ten times more numerous than those for unilingual French speakers—in 1975 ratio falls to six to one);
- actual Francophone share of jobs still short of fair, but rising (from 16 per cent in 1971 to 21 per cent in 1975 in administrative and foreign service categories, 11 per cent to 18 per cent in scientific and professional, 17 per cent to 20 per cent in executive category);
- French gaining as a language of work in federal institutions;
- government's professional development courses given by the Public Service Commission, available in both English and French;
- translation services improving through terminology computer and computerized translation of technical texts;

- federal services to the public slow but impressive when seen in the context of how things stood in 1963 when the B & B Commission started;
- pace of reform encouragingly steady—every day reaching closer to the irreversible;
- extension of French radio and TV (as of November 1976, 92 French television stations and 137 French radio stations in the country);
- the moderates grow more articulate (the usually quiet moderates are gradually becoming aroused and are speaking out from Victoria to Moncton, especially in the field of education);
- a rising interest in studying French (thousands of younger parents in English-speaking Canada are supporting the development of English and French by enrolling some 35,000 children in French immersion classes. Even in smaller centres, experiments are being initiated embracing hundreds of children);
- increased youth-exchange programs and demands for them through monitor plans and summer bursaries.

THE BOTTOM LINE:
- over-all good news 80 per cent;
- over-all bad news 20 per cent.

That balance sheet is essentially a report on the programs or the plumbing. Where do we stand on fundamental attitudes to language reform?

In the last year Canadians have gradually become aware that something in the national bloodstream is not responding to the program. The disease surfaced again with the infamous air-traffic controllers' and pilots' strike of 1975. Suppressed prejudices burst forth under cover of the impeccable cause of air safety and an essentially technical and professional scrap became a call to arms. Here was overwhelming evidence of the failure of the government and of the other political parties to explain the reasonableness of language reform and of the principles all these parties officially support. What erupted was stunning evidence that while programs had been sometimes praised, sometimes damned, attitudes had not changed fundamentally and debate on content of programs suddenly seemed irrelevant. Almost 110 years later, the Plains-of-Abraham virus, with some mutations, was still with us; the English speakers resentful that the French speakers wouldn't give up, and the French speakers resenting the majority's treatment of them as annoying troublemakers rather than partners in nation building.

THE WAY TO GO

How can we develop policies in language rights and programs consistent with the ideals of freedom, responsibility, and inter-dependence; freedom accompanied by individual responsibility? Programs and policies that systematically ask themselves if the moves are really necessary and if there are not other methods and mechanisms capable of accomplishing the same goals but more compatible with private initiative?

First, let's take another look at the balance sheet. If the country's leading full-time expert is right, we can make quick and relatively easy repairs to the plumbing, namely:

- reversing the designation overkill by dropping the number of bilingually designated posts;
- increasing the number of job openings for French-speaking unilinguals;
- offering more opportunities for French speakers to work in their own language;
- streamlining language-training programs with job-related vocabulary training and, where possible, in-house training in the bigger departments;
- hyping up language-training programs for young Canadians for the Throne Speech's "better balance" between the short-term public-service priority and the long-term priority of equipping the next generation with new skills and attitudes.

So much for the structure. What about the concept?

The concept, the ideal, the philosophy behind all the programs and policies starts by accepting the existence of the dominant and distinct cultures or societies that for more than 100 years have shared the northern half of North America as one country. It then holds that the Canadian Confederation should develop in accordance with the principle of equal partnership between these two societies—an ideal overriding the inner heterogeneity of each and their numerical inequality. The English-speaking society is clearly the majority in most, but not all, regions; but linguistic equality, flowing from the ideal and expressed as equality of opportunity, respects the minority and does not reduce the rights of the majority. A majority does not abdicate when it takes a minority into consideration—it remains the majority with all its advantages while at the same time demonstrating its humanity. The reform adds to existing rights, it takes none away.

When such ideals actually function in a modern country, civilization benefits. For a while it looked like Canada might pull it off but now neither we nor the world are so sure we've got what it takes.

If we still think we do, then we must broaden Canadians' —especially English Canadians'—appreciation of the reform's reasonableness and importance. At the same time Francophones must be convinced that the reform is serious and not just another federal snow job.

Given the needed repairs to the present plumbing and the maintenance of a vigilant watch for future errors, can we say we have ever tested the value of a carefully evolved, vast, sustained, and relentlessly truthful information program? If we don't believe in the reform, let's scrap it. But if we do believe in it, nothing should Mau-Mau us into fear of preaching the gospel. In the present crisis, streamlined and solidly supported language reform can earn the support of the people and of provincial governments. And it will surely find an attentive audience. We are seriously accepting for the first time that the nation might not survive and are eager for prescriptions and programs we can support and participate in ourselves.

Any programs that Liberals put forward should be rigorously tested against the principles already stated. Are they really necessary and, if they are not, are there other methods and mechanisms capable of accomplishing the same goals compatible with private initiative, freedom, responsibility, and interdependence?

But even that will not be enough unless we brutally retest our belief in and understanding of this historic reform. Only then can we commit and rededicate ourselves to its implementation. If we believe it is right, we can convince others.

CHAPTER NINE

MAJORITY MUST BEND TO QUÉBEC

MANY PEOPLE THESE DAYS seem to think that the chief call of the B & B Commission was for bilingualism—for nearly everybody in Canada to be able to use two languages; for bilingual services and signs everywhere; for French classes to be forced on hordes of English-speaking federal public servants.

That view of the commission is very, very erroneous. We assumed that the great majority of Canadians would continue to be essentially unilingual in one or other of the official languages. Incidentally, we did not recommend that cereal boxes should have to carry texts in two languages, nor that there be an enormous expansion in public-service language training.

What did the commission find and what did it say?

First of all, we found that there was a crisis in Canada. Our preliminary report, issued in February 1965, makes interesting reading these days. We said then that " . . . Canada, without being fully conscious of the fact, is passing through the greatest crisis in its history."

We did not know whether the crisis would be short or long; we thought the signs of danger were many and serious. We found that French Canadians of Québec were tending to reject the Confederation of 1867 as it had evolved. We thought that unless there were major changes the situation would worsen with time. We emphasized the frustrations of Québécois, and the strong potential appeal of the separatists, then rather small in number.

In the volumes of its main report the commission dealt with changes it thought necessary to make possible a sense of equal partnership.

In the area of language rights the federal government

* Lecture, originally titled "Equal Partnership", delivered on April 19, 1977 at McGill University. Published here in modified form by kind permission of the author.

DAVIDSON DUNTON

would fully recognize French as an official language. It would provide services in French in any areas of the country where there was a reasonable number of Francophones. (We suggested 10 per cent.) Ontario and New Brunswick would declare themselves officially bilingual, in addition to Québec, and also provide services in French in "bilingual districts". Other provinces would make special arrangements for services in French in their few bilingual districts.

The same general approach was adopted for education. Wherever there were sufficient population groups of either official language they should have facilities for full schooling in their language. Parents should have the right to choose between schools with different media of instruction. We thought this a cardinal principle.

The main thrust of our recommendations in language rights and education was to put Francophones living in other provinces on somewhat the same footing as Anglophones in Québec, taking into account relevant circumstances.

In the economic sphere the commission published dramatic findings showing how far Francophones were below Anglophones in average income, in occupations, in ownership of businesses, and in middle and upper industrial management.

Language of work in the province of Québec struck us as very important. We urged that steps be taken to make French the main language of work in Québec, except for head offices and smaller concerns serving English-speaking clienteles.

The commission did not think it had produced a full response to the Canadian crisis. We did think we had written a prescription for a minimum series of changes without which, or something like them, there could be little hope for the future of Canada as one country. And we felt that the spirit in which English-speaking Canadians approached the changes would be almost as important as the concrete measures themselves.

A great deal has happened since the commission reported. The federal Parliament passed the Official Languages Act with all-party support. The federal government has made substantial progress in providing services in French in Ottawa and to significant Francophone population groups across the country. Recruitment of French Canadians to all ranks of the public service has improved.

There has been less progress in the development of French as a language of work in the service.

In the provincial sphere, developments have been mixed. As the commission recommended, New Brunswick declared itself to be an officially bilingual province. Government services are now available in French much more widely than before.

Ontario did not follow our recommendation that it declare French an official language of the province. It did take steps in education that broke with long-standing traditions. A major one was a provision making possible full secondary education in French in publicly supported schools, something previously banned. In fact a number of such schools were soon established in Ottawa and in other areas of the province.

Progress, however, has been uneven . . . . It seems unfortunate, for example, that in 1977 local opposition continued to block a French secondary school in Essex County, where there has been a substantial French-speaking group for two centuries.

French is still not an official language in the courts of Ontario, nor in the legal system, nor in provincial services. In the capital of his country a French-speaking Canadian will still get a traffic summons in the other language, and will have to plead his case in court in English or through an interpreter.

While there has been some unofficial improvement, a member of the large Francophone minority in the Ottawa area —about the same proportion as the Anglophone minority in Québec—still can obtain few provincial services in French.

In other provinces, particularly Manitoba, there has been some improvement in educational possibilities for Francophones. On the whole, however, development of facilities for French-language minorities has been substantially less than as recommended by the commission.

In the field of the teaching of French as a second language the saddest thing is that the actual studying of French in the high schools of most provinces has actually diminished in recent years.

In the very important matter of working languages in the private sector, chiefly in the province of Québec, the commission thought that major changes should come about through actions of business concerns themselves, spurred by government leadership and influence. Some large corporations in Québec did move early to increase the use of French and the participation of Francophones in different levels of management, but, in general, change was rather slow.

It is not just a question of formal changes in language

rights and usages, in education, and in participation of Franco-phones in various institutions, public and private. It is also the spirit in which the changes are discussed by English-speaking Canadians.

Quite a lot of good will has been expressed by members of the English-speaking public across the country. But a lot of ill will also came out; examples of it seemed to be increasing in 1975 and 1976.

The cry, "They're shoving French down our throats", came from individuals living in areas where the only possible evidence could be some arrangements for French-Canadian children to have the chance of being educated in French; or a few French signs on federal property; or a television station broadcasting in French; or an airline stewardess making announcements in French.

Actually the chief irritation in many cases has probably been French on marmalade jars or cereal boxes. Incidentally, I thought the federal insistence on bilingual labelling of products was not very bright, or necessary, in a country in which it is assumed that there will continue to be huge essentially unilingual areas. But why can people be so upset about little things that take nothing away from anybody—if there really is good will?

Then there are the endless stories, all across the country, about able, middle-aged public servants with language-learning disabilities being dragged into French courses to help their jobs.

It is my view that unnecessarily large numbers of bilingual posts have been created. But according to one view, free French courses and the time to do them are a rather nice perquisite for some Anglophone public servants.

For generations any French Canadian wishing to get anywhere in the federal administration had to make sure that he became really proficient in English, on his own account. And even today the prospects of a unilingual Francophone in the public service are far less good than those of a unilingual Anglophone.

Backlash also snapped in the dispute over air-control language. It would be nice to think that deep in the hearts of all those opposed to the use of French at Québec airports was only concern for safety.

How much better would it have appeared to millions of Québécois if those same people had said: "We understand the intense desire of Québec pilots to be able to use French talking to airports in their own province. Let's try to work out the safest way of providing for the use of two languages, as in so many international airports of the world." The air-control row was probably worth scores of thousands of votes to the Péquistes in the November election.

In the field of language and education an essential part of the design was to put Francophone minorities in other provinces onto about the same footing as the Anglophone minority in Québec.

While there has been a good deal of progress in this direction, movement has been in general slow, grudging, incomplete.

As of today the position of the English-speaking community in Québec is still well ahead of that of French-speaking groups outside it.

Discussion about the Québec White Paper on language would have been clearer and the views of many Anglophones better supported if the situation of Francophones outside Québec had evolved as the commission recommended.

The arguments of English-speaking Quebeckers would have much more moral force today if a member of a sizeable French-speaking group in Ontario could plead his case in court in his own language, or get even a copy of the judgment in French, or get a provincial statute in French.

It can be said that, in one sense, the White Paper constituted an attempt to redress an imbalance—to give French the position in Québec that English has in other provinces. In some fields it proposed to do by law and regulation what is brought about elsewhere by the general weight and pressure of the English-language fact.

I do agree that there is a major problem about the future relative size of the French-speaking population if present trends continue. My view, as was that of the commission, is that it is best to rely on the vigorous promotion of French as a language of work. When newcomers see that a high proportion of business of all kinds and at all levels is carried on in French, they will be drawn to opt for French schools.

Actually much of the body of the White Paper, apart from its specific proposals and some of the rhetorical statements, was close to the majority thinking of the commission about the situation in Québec. The commission thought that French should become the principal language of work in the province, and that there should be much higher participation of Francophones, with the opportunity to work in their own language, in the higher levels of business; and that French should become more apparently the prime language of the province. And that was a main thrust of the White Paper.

Incidentally, the resounding declaration in the White Paper that "there will no longer be any question of a bilingual Québec" is an example of the different meanings that can be given to that awkward term "bilingualism".

Some other provinces might well say that they had attained a high degree of bilingualism if they allowed French speeches in their legislatures, quickly published French versions of statutes, provided service in French to individual members of the public, and had a solid French school system in the province for most Francophones, and for their descendants, and in places where French was obviously going to be one of the main languages of business.

Even in spite of such far-reaching language legislation, the position of the minority in Québec will still be better than that of Francophone minorities in the past, and better than in the present under slow changes of policies.

In this age, however, reduction in the privileges of any minority seems out of kilter with the times. The authors of the White Paper claimed they were simply trying to assert and assure the due position rights of a provincial majority, which is a minority in a country and a continent. I think they can do that without some of the disrupting changes they proposed.

While it is probably too easy for someone living on the other side of the Ottawa River to say, I believe that Québec Anglophones would be wise to accept, and say that they accept, the general lines of the legislation, while pressing for modifications in some of its draconian measures.

Some of the cries of alarm and hostility have hardly been helpful. Even with such sweeping changes, one can be confident that the English language and an English-speaking community will continue to have a substantial place in Québec.

I do not find comfort, either, in the fierce cries of some of those who would challenge such measures on constitutional grounds. The main questions do not lie in fine interpretations of sections of the BNA Act; the real issue is whether or not in the future there is going to be one constitution at all for Canada as we know it.

Often the question is asked: "What is a nation?" The best

answer I have found is, in simple terms, that a nation is a collection of people who feel they are a nation. And that kind of collective feeling has been working strongly among Québécois.

That is why I have thought for about ten years that there is perhaps a 50 per cent chance of Canada staying together as one country. I do not predict separation *will* occur. I do think it *may*, because of the proven power of nationalistic calls for self-government, because of the long-tempered sense of identity among Québécois, and also because of a weak response by English-speaking Canadians in the past.

Many chances have been missed. Too often changes have been made too late to appease Québécois feelings.

I believe that if separation is not to occur there will have to be important developments in several different spheres.

For one thing, there will have to be major changes in the roles of Francophones in the economic sphere. Presumably this will occur in large part through policies concerning the language of work in existing Québec business.

Another sphere—the political—is, of course, supremely important. The question of separation is going to be decided by the people of Québec, although this seems to be forgotten sometimes by some people in English-speaking Canada. Unfortunately a strong provincial opposition to the PQ is lacking at this stage.

The best prospect and hope is probably for the development of an alternative political approach built around the thinking of men such as Claude Ryan, Claude Castonguay, Léon Dion, Paul Lacoste, Rector of the Université de Montréal, some of the ministers of the late Liberal government, and many others.

This approach would reject separation but would envisage changes in the constitution and in federal-provincial arrangements to give Québec more freedom of action in some fields.

It has become quite fashionable lately in English-speaking Canada to talk about devolution of powers to provinces as a means of mollifying Québec and solving the problems of Confederation. A difficulty is that the present government leaders in Québec have said insistently—and I for one believe them—that they are not interested in any fiddling around with the constitution; they want sovereignty for Québec and then a freely negotiated association with Canada—and nothing in between.

While waiting and working to win a referendum they may be ready to take any concession going. But there seem to be no realistic prospects of negotiations with a PQ government leading to a restyled model of Confederation.

A main hope, and a prerequisite for the continuation of Canada as one country, therefore, appears to be the rise of a strong provincial party or movement dedicated to remaining in Canada under revised constitutional arrangements.

Some observers are talking about throwing the constitution out and starting to fashion a new one on a *tabula rasa*. Usually they envisage some kind of broadly based constitutional convention, bypassing the "politicians in power". This seems to me a dream that ignores the history and realities of Canada. The provisions of the BNA Act were negotiated by elected leaders of political entities, and I am convinced that any revisions in the future can be accomplished only through a similar process.

For the same reason I am not very confident about the value of a commission or task force of experts on constitutional changes. Such a body might have educational value, and might come up with useful studies and suggestions to put before federal and provincial leaders. But it is these leaders who would still have to hammer out revisions.

Psychological elements are going to have much to say about the question of separation or not. Québec nationalism in its different forms is an expression of strong collective feelings. Many English-speaking Canadians and some French-speaking ones have a strong emotional attachment to the idea of a Canada stretching from sea to sea.

Avoidance of separation is going to require keen psychological sensitivity on both sides.

The keenest sensitivity will have to be shown by the stronger party, the Anglophone majority in Canada. When the commission looked around the world we noted that bilingual and multilingual states had tended to be successful in the measure that the large group was generous to the smaller. By definition a majority is not threatened; it can afford to lean over backwards in agreeing to provisions for the smaller.

Mr. Lévesque and his associates are not going to be deterred by even full and immediate recognition of Francophone aspirations in other provinces. But dramatic moves in this direction could still have an effect on the feelings of other Québécois about Canada. A dampening of the cries "they're trying to shove French down our throats" could greatly help the psychological climate.

What is needed on the Anglophone majority side is not just vague appeals about keeping Canada together, but a manifest recognition of the intense feeling of Québécois for the integrity of their society, and a real acceptance of equality for French-speaking Canadians.

René Lévesque would probably say that the only possible kind of equal partnership lies in his formula of sovereignty-association. There is an alternative that would be much better for all the inhabitants of Canada; an equal partnership, within a continuing Confederation, based on a true mutual sense of equality and partnership.

For that kind of Canada to be in the future I believe a number of developments have to occur:

- French must take its place as the prime working language in Québec, without the excesses of the White Paper;
- Francophones must come to participate much more fully in the upper reaches of the Québec economic system;
- French and French-speaking Canadians must have the same rights, privileges, and opportunities in other provinces, and at Ottawa, that Anglophones want to hold in Québec;
- an active dialogue has to develop among Québécois on the provincial plane with the alternative to independence being put forward by a vigorous political movement powered by a clear perspective for the future. This movement will have to convince Québécois of the economic dangers that lie in separation, and of the prospects of fruitful constitutional negotiations with the federal government and other provinces.

At a later stage there will need to be productive discussions between Québec and Ottawa, and with other provinces, on constitutional adjustments.

If all this happens—and it is going to take an enormous amount of good will and sensitivity, and some unselfishness on all sides—we shall all be able to see a great destiny for Canada and all its people.

CHAPTER TEN

A NEW CONSTITUTION FOR THE CANADIAN DUALITY

IN 1967, the centennial year, the Protestant and Anglican churches issued statements thanking God for the first hundred years of Confederation. The Catholic church was unable to make such a statement: the French-Canadian bishops feared that thanking God for Confederation would be read by their people as interference in party politics. Instead, the Canadian bishops had to compose a thoughtful statement on Canada, its problems, and its possibilities. They concluded that the duality of Canada—the relationship between the two majorities, the two civilizations—is the axis that defines Canadian existence and, at the same time, the locus of its gravest malady.

The bishops' 1967 statement reminds Canadians that the French in Canada are not a minority, not a subculture—not simply an ethnic group attached to its past. Rather, French Canadians constitute a people attached to the land, its language, its culture, and its political, legal, and educational institutions—and this for over three centuries. French Canada easily sees itself as a nation.

In 1967, the bishops spoke of "the deep discontent felt by a growing number of French Canadians at the difficulties which their community must face in its attempts at growth, and the uneasiness which the claims of the French-speaking group arouse in other parts of Canada". This episcopal statement concludes that there can be no justice—and hence no peace in

* Prepared for this volume.

GREGORY BAUM

Canada—until French-Canadian peoplehood is fully recognized.

The bishops defend this position as a demand for social justice. They define social justice in terms of equal opportunity, but instead of applying this principle only to individual citizens —as is usually done in the liberal tradition—they also apply it to communities, to peoples, to nations. Hence the two founding nations, the two majorities that define the Canadian duality, must have an equal opportunity—assured by law—to grow and find their appropriate self-expression.

The 1967 episcopal statement is also concerned with justice for minorities in Canada, beginning with the native peoples; it demands that the government protect minorities' rights and promote their cultures. Because of the drastic way in which the school questions were resolved in Manitoba, Saskatchewan, and Ontario in the decades before and after the turn of the century, French Canadians in these provinces have become minorities. As a people, they exist today only in Québec.

I whole-heartedly agree with the conclusion that the French – English duality is the axis of Canada's self-definition and the place where its existence is most gravely menaced. It seems to me, however, that this duality, so visible to the Canadian Catholic bishops, is not as visible to the great majority of English-speaking Canadians. Since the Canadian Catholic episcopate is half French- and half English-speaking, the Catholic church in this country operates, on its highest level, out of the Canadian duality at all times. What are some of the reasons why this duality is disguised from so many English Canadians?

There is, first of all, the obvious link of English Canada with the United States. Through radio and television, through newspapers and magazines, we are culturally attached to the United States. We may have doubts about who we are as Canadians, but we have no doubts whatever what it means to be North American—and speaking English is part and parcel of this. From this perspective, French Canada is a minority—even an anachronistic minority, a people unduly attached to their ways. Why can't they be like the rest of the continent? Nothing is further from the mind of most English-speaking Canadians than to define Canada in terms of a duality.

The second reason is our new multiculturalism. Until the Second World War, English Canada—certainly in Ontario and the Atlantic provinces—constituted a homogeneous British

North American culture, almost as cohesive in its social make-up as Québec and untroubled about its identity.

Since then, many ethnic minorities have, with much confidence, come to call Canada their home. Some of these remain strongly attached to their own cultural heritage and, quite rightly, demand that Canada should support them in preserving this heritage as a precious subculture. But these minorities are quite willing to fit themselves into the English-speaking public society. In this sense, English Canada today is pluralistic. It differs, now, from Québec not only in language but also in the style of its social make-up. English-speaking Canada is a society defined by legal or contractual bonds between people, while Québec is a society defined by profound social bonds including a common history, a common style, common values, a common dream.

In this social context, then, English Canadians tend to hear the claims of French Canadians as the voice of yet another ethnic minority, and can't understand why French Canadians are not satisfied with what they have—which is, after all, so much more than the Ukrainians and the Poles. The duality has become invisible.

Still, the voice of French Canada will not weaken. The election of November 15, 1976 has proven this. The conclusion of the bishops' statement of 1967 seems ineluctable to me, even though it may be hard to follow for many English-speaking Canadians. Unless this duality can be given an equitable constitutional expression, Canada cannot survive.

But should Canada survive? Why should a country made up of two solitudes continue to exist? Would it not be more reasonable to divide Canada into two independent nations? There are many reasons why the Canadian duality should perdure as a political unity. One has to do with the overwhelming presence of the United States. Another has to do with social justice—for, more important than Canadian nationalism or Québec nationalism, is the pursuit of social justice. More important, also, is the political struggle for a just distribution of wealth and power. More important is breaking the power of the corporate elite that controls access to the world's resources. Within an international capitalism increasingly ruled by a limited number of giant corporations, the smaller the state, the weaker the national government, and the more dependent and vulnerable the national economy. The only way to control the transnational corporations is through united political action by many governments. Canada can defend itself better together than apart. A more united political effort to plan our economy and survive as free people even demands that we transcend the nation-state or the binational state and reach out for wider coalitions. In this sense, nationalism is passé!

How then, can political unity be brought about? Only by giving the Canadian duality a constitutional expression that satisfies both partners. One strategy, recommended by Prime Minister Trudeau, is bilingualism. By this, one means that Canadian citizens, whether English- or French-speaking, can address themselves to public institutions in any part of the country in their own language.

I regard this strategy as theoretically inadequate and practically unworkable! It is theoretically inadequate because it defines linguistic rights only in terms of individuals and not of communities. And it is unworkable because Canada is basically a unilingual country: people learn a second language only if there is economic pressure on them. For most people good will is not enough; there has to be a "need". And this need does not exist in English Canada. Toronto and Vancouver are as unilingual as San Francisco: while there are many languages spoken in the homes of the ethnic minorities and in their subcultural institutions (and the San Francisco school system supports these languages more than Canadian cities do!), there is only one public language, English—the one language spoken by the educated and successful classes. The model of bilingualism promoted by the government is derived from the local Ottawa experience, but it reflects complete ignorance of English-Canadian culture.

The other way to find constitutional expression for the Canadian duality has sometimes been referred to as "special status" for Québec. If Québec received the powers to promote its culture and develop the aspirations of its people, then the Canadian duality would be protected by law. Canada would then be a truly binational state.

Many Quebeckers are not satisfied with this solution. But there is no reason why we cannot change the British North America Act—written for conditions of a hundred years ago—and constitute ourselves as a Canadian Commonwealth in which the two founding nations are associated. I belong to a Toronto-based group, the Committee for a New Constitution, which pleads that both Québec and English Canada pursue their own self-definition in freedom and express their association in something like a Commonwealth, made up of partners equal in principle. In such a constitution, it will be much easier to protect the rights of minorities. In such a Commonwealth, even the English minority in Québec, sociologically so singular, can be promoted by the Québec government without fearing that their superior financial resources, their link to the industrial, commercial, and intellectual world of English Canada and the United States, will undermine the cultural cohesion of the French population. Only after Canada has solved its constitutional problem can it turn to the more urgent problem which it shares with the rest of the western world: the growing crisis of capitalism.

CHAPTER ELEVEN

"LEAVE 'EM ALONE AND THEY'LL COME HOME": CAN THE BOTTOM LINE HOLD QUÉBEC?

SOME PEOPLE hold the Little Bo-Peep view of Québec separatism. When Little Bo-Peep lost her sheep and didn't know where to find them, she was told: "Leave 'em alone and they'll come home, wagging their tails behind them." Canada's commercial community holds out the bottom line of profit and loss to hold Québec to us, displaying indifference to the Québécois' rich cultural history, and to their passionate need for the respect and justice they feel was their right, as Roger Lemelin insists, "since the first moment this country was founded".[1] He notes that cold, commercial logic was not the reason for the sudden acclaim of Trudeau following his Washington speech. Québec responded to "his heartfelt appeal to the generous, abstract values of mankind, the higher of these being liberty and tolerance, values without which any political society is in danger of running into social disorder and crypto-fascism."

The British have made the same mistake with Ireland that we have made with Québec, denying their right to imaginative recognition and questing, and even the indomitable Irish have

*Appeared first in *Perception*, Vol. 1, no. 2 (November-December 1977), pp. 66-71. Copyright: McLuhan Associates Limited and Barrington Nevitt, 1977. Published here by kind permission of the authors.

MARSHALL McLUHAN & BARRINGTON NEVITT

been "hurt" into poetry and song. Perhaps it is characteristic that the most memorable date in British history is 1066, the date of a big defeat, and the birth of a nation. It is a basic human trait that the victors never remember and the losers never forget, which is one of the noteworthy clues to the character of our own time, namely, the great waves of nostalgia for things of the past, pointing to a craving for both personal and group meaning and identity, such as appears in the current success of *Roots*. It could be argued that the international motley of jeans and beards of the young TV generation shows subliminal nostalgia for the work costume of our grandfathers of the frontier time. Nostalgic sentiment extends even to the craving to restore old furniture to its earlier state, and antique shops are a large industry that keeps the shops well stocked with "genuine fakes".

In a larger perspective it would appear that the old centralized forms of social and political organization have become unacceptable in the new environment of electric information. The older arrangements in home and society had a kind of legalistic hierarchical quality of central and personal authority from which the TV generation, at least, feels quite alienated. There has been a kind of split in the consciousness of the young which is involved in their recognition of the "peer group". As the phrase indicates, it is a group and not a private individuality that has come into play as a pattern and guide for behaviour.

Nineteenth-century individualism is quite out of vogue at home and at work alike. Wherever we look, we shall find today that the conduct of the individual *figures* of our world, whether they are people or corporations or nations, seem prompted to adopt fragmented attitudes and positions, as if impelled by some hidden force. The French Canadians are inclined to suppose that their passions merely concern themselves, just as France imagines that its separatist problems are peculiar to itself:

> The trend, however, is not confined to France: what one theorist calls the "regionalist revolution" is a general European phenomenon. Four revolutionary minorities already have clandestine radio stations: there is Radio Scotland, Radio Euzkadi (Basque), Radio Free Tyrol, and the Voice of Serbia. Every sizable nation in Western Europe has its ethnic minorities, and within these minorities agitation for more self-government and cultural expression has been growing in recent years—accompanied in some cases by revolutionary violence.[2]

Thus, dislocation of the family, its separation from older people, the universality of divorce as a kind of "dropout-ism", is matched in the commercial sector by obsolescence of the organization chart with its old classifications of jobs and activities. Likewise, in the school there is a prevalent separation of students and curriculum as well as a gap between students and teachers. Everywhere there is a craving for autonomy and separation from previous patterns of work, for which Women's Lib stands as the most obvious instance.

Going along with this pervasive alienation from the self and society, there are equivalent waves of violence, both inner and outer. The world of entertainment and pornography stands for the world of inner violence, while political upsets and revolutionary programs of social action point to the external manifestations of the same inner unrest. It helps to know that violence is most frequently the accompaniment of individuals and groups who have lost their image and their personal, or corporate, identity:

> . . . Southerners of the generation before the Civil War suffered the most painful loss of social morale and identity that any large group of Americans has ever experienced. . . . [3]

On the private side, an individual who goes to the frontier, or to an area where he has no friends or acquaintances, tends to go "activist" and tough as a normal way of finding out what kind of situation he is meeting and whether he "has what it takes". The same response to the challenge of loss of group identity occurs when a group becomes aware of the degradation of its image. The Wild West and the cult of the Western movie occupies an important place in the minds and hearts of young and old alike, in our time. In the Western everybody is on trial and is tested daily for his adequacy in being able to "take it" or to "dish it out". The Western puts a top priority on the constant assessing of inner resources and the command of primal outer skills, whether camping or shooting. In so doing, the Western has created a type of situation which also finds universal approval in Japan, or Italy, or Spain, or Britain, or wherever movies are available, or where identities are in jeopardy. The hijacker and the political activist alike are seekers of attention and identity by seizing the media.

The *figure* of violence in the Western invariably is sustained by the hidden *ground* of loss of identity. Our pioneers confronted a wilderness that had to be subdued and tamed by the most extreme exertions. We have since transferred many of those habits of lonely exertion to the commercial sphere, which has given us the bizarre and obsolete image of the tycoon, whether Citizen Kane or Howard Hughes. The exertions achieved by these *figures* are always irrelevant to current social needs or patterns, and represent a frantic assertion of a nonentity determined to prove itself in terms of some forgotten nostalgic pattern. Today, national groups in every part of the globe are behaving in this extreme way, without any awareness of the hidden *ground* that feeds and impels their passions. Such a revolutionary *ground* which can inspire or motivate people everywhere must needs be both new and of colossal scale. There have been past times of private and social unrest, also prompted by new *grounds* and new kinds of social service and action.

Today, however, the unrest, inner and outer, is universal and always takes the form of crisis:

> The declining prestige of the nation-state has been accompanied by a decline of the political, business, and bureaucratic elites most closely identified with it—usually members of the dominant ethnic element in the nation (one example being the WASPs in America). The former phenomenon tends to release or reactivate earlier, more parochial loyalties that were previously submerged in the general cult of the nation; the latter encourages members of ethnic minorities to assert with pride, sometimes even arrogance, a cultural personality their fathers were secretly ashamed of and deliberately tried to suppress in the attempt to "pass".[4]

There is only one environmental innovation which reaches everybody on the planet. The railway and the industrial plant reached many people in the nineteenth century, but there were many areas of the world untouched by them. Today there is, in fact, a new and unprecedented force which reaches everybody on the planet, in China, or India, or Africa. This new force does not have the form of *hardware* of the age of steam and steel, but it is *software* in the form of electric information. The Arab and the Black, as much as the Hindu or the Chinese, listen incessantly to the transistor radio which never ceases to alarm or to enrage with political data, and to soothe or to tranquilize with Muzak. In both cases, the decrease of private identity on one hand, and group identity on the other, is always in progress, creating deep insecurity and anxiety with the ensuing response of violence. Radio enhances tribal identity and extreme group passion, just as print releases private individualism and nationalist competition.

The effect of electric information has a special quality that relates to its instant speed. Living at the speed of light deprives us of the stability and endurance that goes with our physical being, for at the speed of light, whether "on the telephone" or "on the air", or on x-ray, both individuals and populations are disembodied. "On the phone" or "on the air" our images are everywhere, but minus our physical being. In political terms, discarnate or disembodied man has no goals and no objectives. Yet he finds that such nostalgic patterns form scars which remain deeply ingrained, even at the speed of light; however, at the speed of electric information they have another meaning, or no meaning at all. The figure of Howard Hughes, as much as that of nationalism, stands out as a stark archetype of the imperialist drive of the go-getter of yore transferred, incongruously, to the electronic age, illustrating how, at instant speed there is nothing to relate to that is in accordance with any previous experiential *ground*. When our forefathers had devised the electric cable and telegraph, the pundits wagged their heads and said: "What hath God wrought?", and "What have we got to say to India?" However, when one is "connected" to India by wire services, the new merger of identities and images breeds a non-stop flood of jabberwocky comment without any need for sense or inspiration.

Turning to the situation of Québec, immersed in this new electric environment, we note how electrically immersed Québec has become intensely aware of its older traditions and aspirations. These have surfaced, so to speak, surrounding the Québécois with resonating rhythms and haunting memories. When they look at their bureaucratic fetters they say, as it were, "We have been freed from our bodies in this electronic age, and yet everywhere we are meshed in the old hardware chains and legalism of the WASP, and gripped by the centralized bureaucracy of the business world." The electronic age is one of auditory imagination which makes for simultaneous awareness of past and present. The simultaneous structure of sound permits all kinds of information to be present at once, the most ancient and the most recent tending to encounter each other.

On coming to Québec, Alexis de Tocqueville recorded in

his notebook on August 29, 1831: "We have arrived in this country precisely at the moment of crisis." The crisis which he confronted then was rather similar to the Québec crisis of 1977, a problem of identity, with a conflict over the rearrangement and redistribution of political power. The same problem confronted Québec Premier Daniel Johnson in 1967:

> In sociological terms, Quebeckers have witnessed the disintegration of the way of life which traditionally protected them. They had survived in good part because they lived in isolation, locked in upon themselves, clinging to the past in a typically rural environment where the state's presence would be marginal. Almost overnight they found themselves in an industrial society requiring massive intervention by the state, open to the whole of North America, and exposed to the influence of foreign, especially American, culture backed by such powerful means of communication as speedy transport, highways, cinema, radio, and television.[5]

Today, as Roger Lemelin puts it: "The question now is not What does Quebec want? It is How does Quebec feel?"[6] It is not a question of goals, but of inner identity and dignity.

Sensing that there might well be some parallel between the current feelings about the separation of Québec and the feelings that led to secession of the southern states from the American Union, we looked for information on this subject and found a book entitled *The Causes of the Civil War* edited by Kenneth M. Stampp. On the first page we read:

> And yet, in spite of all the attention given to the Civil War, historians seem nearly as far from agreement about its causes as were the partisans who tried to explain it a century ago. In recent years the social science methodologists have also attempted to solve this problem with their analytical tools, but the results thus far have not been encouraging.[7]

Even now there is confusion and uncertainty about the reasons for the Québec needs in withdrawing from Confederation, yet nobody doubts the reality of the impulse. There may seem to be an insufficiency of any *particular* cause to justify the move. When political entities experience unrest and discontent, there has usually been some new kind of ground-swell, some abrasive

environmental alteration that causes the political groups to seek
new relationships. There is indeed a major parallel between
Québec and English Canada, on the one hand, and the southern
and northern states, on the other. The parallel in question is that
Québec, like the American South, is dominated by an oral tradition, whereas English Canada, like the American North, is predominantly an area of the written word and of analytic goals
and procedures. Since the industrial revolution at least, written
cultures are heavily industrial in their concern with trade and
commerce as a way of life. Such concern is by no means
paramount in an oral tradition. Stampp explains:

> When Charles A. and Mary R. Beard examined the background
> of the Civil War, they came to the conclusion that there had
> existed an "irrepressible conflict" between the static, agrarian,
> staple-producing South and the expanding, commercialized, in-
> dustrializing North. The ultimate triumph of industry over ag-
> riculture—of North over South—they described as a "Second
> American Revolution."[8]

Today the abrasive encounter between Québec and English
Canada has, in many ways, been softened by the new electric
services, for these have dissolved many of the dominant industrial patterns of the old hardware world. But, more important,
the electronic situation drives people inward and does not encourage them to look outward and forward. This is the new
Quiet Revolution that leads to the quest for Québec secession.
Québec finds its inward look is enormously more satisfying than
anything it can see outside in the WASP world. As pointed out by
Stampp, the South won a software victory over the industrial
North:

> Literature in the end came to terms with these sentiments by
> yielding to the South in fantasy the victory it has been denied in
> fact. . . . [9]

Gone With the Wind is a victory of the spirit which grows ever
stronger in the decentralist electronic age. Such is also the experience of Québec as it turns inward, today. It is rediscovering a
world of values far richer than anything available in the industrial world. Québec art and literature have roots inaccessible to
English Canada, and they are in strong contrast to the victor's
style of merely quantitative achievement. The world of an oral

tradition reverberates with a romantic appeal which is absent from the world of purely literate culture. One has to look no further than the difference between Southern and Northern Ireland to find the contrast between a Romantic culture and the attitudes of the Yankee North.

In the nineteenth century the new technological environment of industry and commerce released nationalist patterns which are quite alien to an oral culture. Nationalism goes with the rise of print culture with its power to give high definition to specific features of human identity and aspiration. Stampp quotes a letter from the *New York Times* (December 13, 1860):

> . . . Nine-tenths of our people in the Northern and Northwestern States would wage a war longer than the war of Independence before they will assent to any such surrender of their aspirations and their hopes. There is no nation in the world so ambitious of growth and power,—so thoroughly pervaded with the spirit of conquest,—so filled with dreams of enlarged dominions, as ours. In New England these impulses have lost something of their natural force under the influences of culture and the peaceful arts. But in the Center and the West, this thirst for national power still rages unrestrained. [10]

Fortunately for the present Québec crisis, driving ideals of Canadian industry and nationalism lie behind us, while the present is pervaded by an environment of electric services of a strong decentralist character. The Québec wish for independence in these electric circumstances cannot arouse the rancour or frustration in our commerce quarter which would have been felt even sixty years ago. The paradox is that the closer we are by communication, the less we feel the need for each other's society. If historians still fail to perceive the causes of the Civil War, it is because those causes were not specialist but of environmental abrasiveness. It is typical of the mosaic of Stampp's historical reports that anthropologist Eckenrode observes:

> If there had been no negro slaves, the development of the South would have been much what it was. A tropicized Anglo-Saxon population in the Gulf region would have preferred planting to mill-owning, would have attempted to extend farther southward, and would have defied the industrial North. Slavery has been too much glorified. It was but an incident in the conflict. . . . [11]

The gist of the book is in the following statement:

> It is this tragic bad bargain with fate, this payment of so much for
> so little, that nationalism cherishes as our tradition of triumph![12]

What had been merely hidden *ground* often surfaces unexpectedly as a *figure* in a dream. The French once had a great dream for Québec, and, indeed, for North America; and the retrieval of that dream in a great resonating image is a natural side effect of our electric simultaneity. The French encountered North America during their own Age of Enlightenment when the dream of new territories, both for the mind of man and for his empirical aspirations, seemed possible. Paradoxically, the Age of Enlightenment also bred the tycoon Napoleon with his dream of a Continental System which would command the world. By contrast, the English had no dream and no plan beyond the acquisition of territory, markets, and resources. George M. Wrong indicated that "it was the weakness of the English colonies that they could not unite to work out a great plan."[13] The French had an ideal, while the English were empirical. Today the dream gets more intense, while the new electric surround renders the old empiricism irrelevant.

In 1867, following the purchase of Alaska from Russia, Senator Sumner openly announced: "The present Treaty is a visible step in the occupation of the whole American continent." The ties of Confederation were initially vaporous, the very word reverberating with the desire for an informal union. The word had the sympathy of the British element for whom the Southern Confederacy evoked congenial sentiments. The hardening of the Confederate bonds followed the completion of Canada's transcontinental railway which led to a more centralized federation of a monetary and financial character. Lévesque has freely compared the Québec dropout-ism with the defection of the American colonies from British control; but Canadians might well consider the defection of the American South which culturally and economically has much in common with the current attitudes of Québec. It was very much the commercial estimate of the "bottom line" variety that triggered the clash between the North and the South. Mere calculation cannot save the holistic reality of Canada.

In summary, Canada has three choices: *First Way* — hang on to Québec grimly, at all costs; *Second Way* — just let them go;

or *Third Way* — seek a new unity of heart and mind, using new processes and new media that will assure, in the new software age, new importance and new meaning for Québec and psychological enrichment for all.

NOTES

1   *The Globe and Mail* (Toronto), March 26, 1977, p. 10.
2   Edmond Taylor, "The Fourth World", *Horizon*, Vol. 16, no. 2 (Spring 1974), p. 6.
3   Kenneth M. Stampp (ed.), *The Causes of the Civil War* (New York, 1965), p. 151.
4   Taylor, "The Fourth World", p. 8.
5   Ramsay Cook, *The Maple Leaf Forever* (Toronto, 1971), p. 82.
6   *The Globe and Mail* (Toronto), March 26, 1977, p. 10.
7   Stampp, *Causes of the Civil War*, p. 1.
8   Ibid., p. 60.
9   Ibid., p. 121.
10 Ibid., p. 54.
11 Ibid., p. 177.
12 Ibid., p. 52.
13 George M. Wrong, *The Conquest of New France* (New Haven, Conn., 1918), p. 147.

PART THREE

THREATS TO UNITY: THE PROBLEMS OF REGIONALISM AND THE ECONOMY

THERE HAVE ALWAYS BEEN serious flaws in Canada's economic structure. According to the classic theories of Canadian development advanced by Harold Innis and his colleagues, the chief source of these flaws lies in our historic reliance on external sources of capital for development and the consequent structuring of our economy around the production of goods for export. Over time, this has meant that the balance of that economy has been weighted towards the extraction of various raw materials—"staples"—and away from the production of semi-finished and manufactured goods.

Thus, while Canada's economy has, since Confederation, continued to grow in terms of the value of the goods and services it produces, this growth has occurred in the context of a larger *dependence* on external capital markets. This is not healthy. Concretely, it has meant that the Canadian economy is unusually sensitive to modest fluctuations in world demand for raw materials; that our own capital markets have been relatively weak and shallow; and that cyclic fluctuations in the size and composition of our labour market have been extreme. The fiscal and income policies adopted by various senior governments in Canada have frequently been directed towards smoothing out these trends and cushioning their effects; but the fundamental structural sources of these fluctuations remain.

Because of this larger dependency, the internal development of the economic forces in this country has always been uneven. The most obvious effect of this, in turn, has been the creation of a strong regionalism which pervades every aspect of our national life. Throughout Canadian history, it has been a barrier to the global integration of our economy. It has also been the axis around which much of our political conflict has turned. In the past, where regional disparities have combined with ethnic or cultural differences, political conflicts have manifested themselves in inter-group rivalries and social confrontations. This is precisely what has occurred in regard to Québec today. This phenomenon is not new: it has gone on throughout our history. Where cultural and ethnic minorities have existed within regions which are dominated by other groups—e.g., English Canadians in Montreal or Francophones in Manitoba—much of the animus arising out of regional conflicts has been directed towards them. But the genesis of these conflicts has been in regional inequality.

Regional differences have also manifested themselves in class conflict. While some form of confrontation would probably have occurred between the English-speaking minority and the French majority in Québec in any event, the fact that Anglophone Quebeckers were, and are, a privileged minority lent fuel to the encounter. And while class conflict cannot be entirely explained in regional terms, the fact that the prosperity and power of Québec's English minority has ultimately rested on its ties to commercial and financial powers in Ontario was and is the source of much of the resentment directed towards it.

One could argue, then, that the "cultural" or "language" conflict in Québec, and between Québec and English Canada, is not qualitatively different from the resentment directed against business classes with ties to "the East"—or from the perceived conflict between the "West" and "East", generally—in, say, Saskatchewan. Class and cultural confrontations in Canada have always been closely associated with and exacerbated by regional rivalries and power struggles.

In short, we could almost reduce all of the various questions confronting us at the moment—the Québec question, the question of regional disparity, the question of national *versus* provincial power, and so on—to a single issue: the Ontario question. Since Confederation, central Canada has played a dominant role in Canadian affairs, and Ontario has become increasingly hegemonic within it. So when we talk now about "regional inequality" or "economic disparities" or "cultural concentration" what we really mean is inequality relative to Ontario, economic disparities measured against Ontario, and cultural concentration in Ontario.

But why is this the case? Why has Ontario come to play such a key role in Canada's industrial, financial, political, and cultural life? Why has Ontario become the object of so much resentment by Francophone Québec—and by other regions as well? The answer to these questions is simple: foreign investment. Since Confederation, Ontario has increasingly become the most conspicuous focus for foreign penetration of our economy. In the 1870s and '80s, domestic capital began moving out of places like the Atlantic provinces and into Montreal. But while this trend continued up until the First World War, it was soon dwarfed by a second and more powerful movement of foreign industrial capital into southern Ontario. As a result, Ontario—not Québec—became the commercial and financial centre of the country. Today, Ontario continues to dominate Canada's economy because of foreign capital. Ontario also predominates in federal economic thinking because it contains so much of our industrial base. And Ontario dominates commerce because of its role as a financial and industrial centre serving foreign interests.

The Ontario question, then, arises from the fact that while Ontario has been relatively prosperous until quite recently, this prosperity appears to rest on the lack of development in other regions. Atlantic Canada has been in a kind of Quiet Depression for over a decade. Major industries in Québec have been dying. The Prairies have, until recently, been chronically short of capital investment. And B.C. has had only sporadic periods of economic well-being.

In this economic contest, then, Ontario appears to be the conspicuous "winner". But this perception can be, and is, quite misleading. Ontario's so-called prosperity has not, after all, been a product of the systematic and even growth of its own human and material resources. With rare exceptions, Ontario's industrial base has been built on foreign capital and externally produced industrial technology. Thus, although the lion's share of Canada's manufacturing takes place within Ontario, some 60 per cent of its industrial capacity is owned abroad. As a result, while Ontario has benefited from Canada's uneven development, it has not caused it.

In this Part, a number of contributors propose ways of correcting, or at least offsetting, the effects of this pattern of dependency. Berkowitz and Corman suggest that Canada can and should change her industrial structure through the extensive use of state-owned enterprises. Felt warns that developments of this kind should be undertaken only where they can quickly become self-sustaining—and that governments should avoid costly and unrealistic "showpiece" projects. In the short term, he argues, extensive and rational use can be made of transfer payments in order to sustain minimum standards of living in disadvantaged regions. Dukszta and Berkowitz propose a structure through which rational and equitable development of our health-care system can occur across provinces. And Waverman and Kinzel suggest different but complementary ways in which public policy can be used to foster exploitation of our natural resources in the public interest.

While the means they propose and the problem areas they focus on are quite different, then, the authors of the articles which appear in this Part are united in the common belief that regionalism and regional inequality—and their structural sources within our economy—underlie many of the other societal problems which we face today.

CHAPTER TWELVE

FORMS OF STATE ECONOMY: ALTERNATIVE FUTURES FOR CANADA

BACKGROUND

WHEN IT WAS REVEALED, recently, that a federally owned Crown corporation, Atomic Energy of Canada Limited (AECL), had paid considerable amounts of money to foreign go-betweens in order to further sales of Canada's CANDU nuclear reactor, many Canadians were forced to examine a series of questions which most politicians, many economists, almost all sociologists, and all but a handful of government planners choose to ignore: What are Crown corporations? Why do we have them? In whose interests should they be operated? And what role do they, or *should* they, play in our economy?

These issues surfaced because AECL's management on the one hand, and some opposition MPs on the other, held conflicting views about the nature of, and fundamental rationale for, state-operated enterprises. AECL held that they are simply normal businesses with one stockholder—the government—and that payments to agents in order to make sales were part of "normal business practices". The MPs retorted that Crown corpora-

* Prepared for this volume.

S. D. BERKOWITZ & JUNE CORMAN

tions are not normal businesses: they are instruments for carrying out the policies of governments. Leaving apart the question
of what constitutes "normal business practices", they argued
that, as instruments of governments, Crown corporations can
and should abide by a higher set of moral standards. The Liberal
government in Ottawa waffled on the issue. Sometimes it argued
as though the government were simply an interested stockholder; sometimes it acted as though that convenient and omnipres-
ent parliamentary phrase "the Minister responsible" really
meant what it said.

In fairness, we should not think too harshly of the Prime
Minister and Cabinet for getting the whole thing confused:
Canadians, as a rule, have not thought systematically about
Crown corporations, their purposes, and how they should be
run. There has been almost no public discussion of the broader
issues surrounding state-operated enterprises in this country.
Journalists ignore them—except when some scandal is un-
earthed. Politicians in places like Ontario and British Columbia
grow hoarse lauding the virtues of "free enterprise" while
operating massive public corporations. And social scientists,
generally, labour tirelessly to increase our ignorance of the subject. Writers for financial and trade journals and the financial
pages of daily newspapers chortle with glee at the merest mention of some difficulty or disaster which has befallen one of them
—thus pandering to the supposed biases of their businessmen
readers. Where are our careful, reflective, feature stories on, say,
Sasktel? Ontario's William Davis—perhaps the country's
champion harumpher on the subject of state-owned enterprises
—heads a government which has acquired or built up state
enterprises exceeding $8 billion in assets. Why hasn't he been
forced publicly to explain how he manages to do this? And the
Alberta government, loyal Tories all, may, in time, own and
operate half the country—in the name of "free enterprise" and
"minimum government intervention", of course.

As a rule, our record in forcing politicians to discuss state
ownership openly is not good. We are far more comfortable with
nineteenth-century clichés than with realistic and practical
present-day discussion. Socialists—ranging from the suet-soft
social democracy of the Ontario NDP to the strident and dog-
matic socialism of the micro-psychotic left—speak glowingly of
the virtues of state ownership without the slightest practical
knowledge of how it actually operates in Canada. Can you imag-

ine, for instance, a member of the Canadian Communist Party (Marxist-Leninist) running Ontario Hydro? The ludicrousness of this image is only exceeded by the consternation which would follow the introduction of genuine, Adam-Smithian free enterprise in the boardroom of Bell Canada. What would happen, for instance, if we really made Ma Bell a common carrier and allowed patrons to buy their telephones—carefully tested electronically—from, say, Canadian Tire rather than Northern Electric? Anyone who suggested such a thing would immediately be labelled as a foe of "free enterprise".

Public ownership in Canada is like crazy old Aunt Nellie whom the family keeps locked in the attic: everybody knows she is there—some are even fond of her in their own way—but it is unseemly to talk about her in public.

It is time we let her out: state ownership is an increasingly important part of Canada's economy; as indeed it is in most Western countries. Moreover, public management of the economy is one of the key underlying issues in the current debates about constitutional forms and federal-provincial relations in this country. In another article in this book, John Kinzel argues convincingly that regulation and management of provincially owned natural resources is one of the central bones of contention between Ottawa and the provinces. After he wrote his article, a slightly different version of the same issue surfaced in a confrontation between the federal government and Alberta over the latter's plans to take over and operate Pacific Western Airlines. Both Québec and Saskatchewan—in each instance, for largely cultural reasons—are at loggerheads with the federal government over their respective roles in the operation and regulation of cable TV. The present confrontation between Ottawa and Québec City is, in this sense, not unique: it is going on, and has been for some time, in areas of federal-provincial relations all across this country.

It is important to bear this in mind as we approach our national debates over the future of Confederation. All too often the press portrays Québec as the odd man out in all sorts of federal-provincial schemes. This is not true, or, at least, not the whole truth: when Ottawa and Québec disagree, it becomes the leading story in all our national media. When Ottawa and Saskatchewan are at loggerheads, it becomes a matter for the third page of the *Globe*'s business section, at best.

To the extent that these confrontations have centred on

economic issues, the reasons for this are clear enough. In all the provinces except Ontario and, possibly, those in Atlantic Canada there has been a gradual—at times, almost imperceptible—movement towards a greater role for the state in organizing, managing, and operating the economy. In some cases, the method-of-choice of provincial governments for doing this has been (as in Saskatchewan) proprietary Crown corporations. In some, as, for instance, in Québec, joint ventures with private capital groups have predominated. In all provinces, there has been some mixture of both.

The federal government, by contrast, has not viewed either Crown corporations or joint ventures as a means of shaping the economy, but as a way of supplementing or extending the private sector. As a result, federal economic policy (which, under the BNA Act, includes such things as banking, monetary policy, tariffs and trade, etc.) pulls in one direction, while provincial policies—in some cases in spite of ideological proscriptions, as in Alberta—pull in the opposite direction.

The confrontations which arise from this state of affairs will continue and intensify as long as Ottawa continues to behave as if Canadian economic policy was a matter solely for private discussion with Toronto. Many Torontonians, as a result of the Canadian unity debate, are beginning to realize that the country does not stop at the Québec and Manitoba borders (and with "those unpleasant people out in Alberta who are always trying to turn off the lights"). It is high time Ottawa did the same.

In the rest of this article we will: (a) try to establish a framework within which discussions of the role of the state in our economy and of the related issues of federal-provincial relations can go on; (b) lay out a series of models of state economy which bear directly and realistically on the directions in which the Canadian economy can go for the next several decades; (c) draw out the implications of each of these for various provincial economies; and (d) outline the directions in which national policy might best move if Canada is to survive and prosper over the long term.

MODELS OF STATE ECONOMY

In earlier work, Berkowitz, Kotowitz, Waverman et al., have argued that the Canadian economy is highly concentrated. This is largely the result of a series of normal forces at work within the world economic system, and of the close links between the Canadian and U.S. economies.

These factors have operated here from the beginning. In reaction to them, Canada has always had a high degree of state participation in the management of her economy. Initially, this participation took the form of the granting of monopolies by the Imperial government for the exploitation of her resources. (One of the recipients of these grants—the Hudson's Bay Company—continues to play an important role in a number of areas to this day.)* Britain was concerned that, given its closeness to the United States, Canada would simply be gobbled up in the course of American westward expansion. To guard against this, it granted "loyal" firms the exclusive right to develop large parts of Canada's western frontier.

By the 1870s and '80s, when western settlement in this country began in earnest, the period of rootin' tootin' free competition in world capitalism was over. In the United States, through a process called "Morganization" many separate capital pools were knitted together into larger ones. The "syndicate" was the order of the day and, in this context, the Canadian Pacific Railway Company was just one among many. Syndicates, then, presided over the later development of our western frontier. The history of settlement in the Canadian West is a history of syndicates.

In fact, competitive capitalism never reigned supreme in Canada. We passed from a period of domination by Imperial monopolies into one of subservience to large international syndicates. In our industrial sector, which has always been weak, we have witnessed the latest phase in this pattern; the branch-plant syndrome. As of 1972, according to Statistics Canada, almost 60 per cent of our manufacturing was controlled outside the country.

Successive federal governments have played a usually bumbling and ineffective role in trying to alleviate the most serious effects of these processes. Tariff barriers—originally introduced to protect domestic industry—became an incentive to

* One which most Canadians are not aware of is Hudson's Bay's role as the owner or proprietor of sub-surface mineral rights. In Saskatchewan and Alberta almost all rights of this kind are held by the Crown, with the exception of those granted to the CPR in exchange for building the railroad, and those residual rights retained by HBC from the period when it owned much of these two provinces.

Americans to jump the tariff wall and set up branch plants. Incentives for domestic investors have been coupled with inconsistent and contradictory tax policies. Branch banking has produced a secure system for domestic savings and investment—but much of our bank capital has either been channelled abroad or given over to the multinationals. Regional inequality, which has been perpetuated, in part, by the chartered banks, has been met (as Felt documents later) by half-hearted and ineffective grants programs. And so on.

This lamentable record results partly from the fact that our national government has never had a realistic set of models for our economy. Is the Canadian economy—as the Bank of Canada would have us believe—simply a smaller version of the American one? That is to say, can we really effectively regulate our economy largely through monetary and fiscal policy? Can this realistically be done when capital flows more or less freely across our border with the United States?

The federal government continues to behave as if it can. Its two most recent white papers on the subject—one on the new bank act and one ("The Way Ahead") which was designed to allay jittery businessmen's fears about creeping socialism—promise more of the same. The first, if its recommendations were put into practice, would *increase* the chartered banks' monopoly over commercial lending by limiting foreign competition. The second would make the government's regulatory policies even weaker than they are at present.

We submit, by contrast, that any set of consistent and productive economic policies in Canada must reflect three essential facts of life: First, that a modern Western government cannot avoid playing a significant role in its economy—that, in other words, *all* such economies are really one form or another of "state economy". The trumpeting about "free enterprise" in "The Way Ahead" is, in our view, so much blather—possibly harmless, probably not. Second, that Canada has always been developed by large aggregations of government-sanctioned capital. This historical fact is probably the product of the structural position it has found itself in over time. It is also not unlikely that this pattern will continue in the future. The only serious question which remains, then, is: who shall control these capital pools? And third, that no country can long live off the avails of foreign investment without losing its economic, political, and cultural sovereignty. If Canada is to avoid doing this, it must find ways and means of retaining and reinvesting capital within its borders, promoting innovation, and increasing its share of the wealth generated by its natural resources.

Most of the provincial governments—by virtue of their responsibilities as laid out in the BNA Act—have been forced to confront these facts already. The federal government has not been forced to examine these issues and, consequently, has not done so.

In the table appended to the end of this article we present some of the alternative forms of state economy present in the world today and indicate what we think some of their principal strengths and weaknesses are.

It should be noted that, in terms of our model, Canadian provincial economies spread out over the entire less-interventionist half of the spectrum. This is probably one of the reasons the federal government has palpitations every time it tries to get the provinces to agree on some sort of common economic policy. (British Columbia and Newfoundland do not appear on the chart because it is difficult, for various reasons, to evaluate the accuracy of the assets they report for their proprietary Crown corporations.)*

The data on which these categorizations are based, however, are for 1972—and some changes have been going on. Alberta, for instance, appears to be rapidly moving from a mildly interventionist "state-directed" category towards a "state-centred" or even "state-based" pattern. If these trends continue—and the present government in Québec seems committed to a "state-centred" model as well—Ottawa may soon find itself faced with a united opposition—composed of Québec, Manitoba, Saskatchewan, Alberta, and British Columbia—on economic matters. By coincidence, these provinces contain almost all of our known sources of exploitable energy reserves.

The long-term implications of this model, if it is correct, are crystal clear: since the principal historical difficulties in the Canadian economy have been, (a) a shortage of domestic venture capital, and (b) a boom-and-bust cycle in employment, there will be considerable pressure on provincial governments in the future to move towards either the "state-directed" or the "state-centred" model since, in these, governments take a direct

---

* Canadian Crown corporations are typically divided into three types: "departmental", "agency", and "proprietary". The latter type, which functions in much the same way as a business firm, is the only one we are concerned with here.

role in solving problems. Provinces can only do this, however, within the limitations of their resources and their degree of understanding of the processes in which they are involved. The various enterprises of the Newfoundland government—the Come-By-Chance oil refinery most conspicuously—would have moved that province in the direction of one of these models. These attempts were scuttled by poor conceptualization of the role the government ought to play in these ventures and, as a result, by poor management. In addition, without a clear partnership with either the federal government or some other provincial government, the poorer provinces cannot invest on a sufficient scale to turn their economies around.

The Québec case has an added meaning because of the current debate over Canadian unity. Québec was well on the way towards a "state-centred" economy under the Bourassa Liberals. The James Bay hydro development is, perhaps, both in dollar terms and in its potential impact, the most significant project undertaken by a Crown corporation in Canadian history. It has been in trouble from the beginning, however, because of the atavistic notion in Québec that public enterprises are best undertaken with a lot of help from friends in the private sector. Lévesque has inherited this problem, and there is probably very little he can do about it at this point. But a move towards a "state-centred" economy, by consolidating joint ventured capital into fewer provincial Crown corporations, will probably look more and more desirable to him as time goes on.

This would have the added advantage, from a separatist point of view, of giving the Québec government more control over employment: the principal difference between a "state-directed" and a "state-centred" economy is in the degree to which the state, in its role as owner of proprietary enterprises, can actually regulate employment. Continued high rates of unemployment in Québec—combined with the predations of the Olympic and James Bay debts—will almost surely rebound against Lévesque's government. A move towards greater state control over the economy would, therefore, seem to be a precondition for a continuation of it.

PARTNERSHIPS FOR DEVELOPMENT

As provincial economies move along the continuum from "state participation" to "state-directed" economies, their governments tend to take on many of the functions of nation-states. Current trends in many of them could, therefore, be viewed as a potential threat to Confederation. There is some truth in such a view. Sabre rattling about "the East", for instance, has increased in Alberta and Saskatchewan in almost direct proportion to the degree of control each has exercised over its economy. But it is Ottawa's failure to recognize and accommodate these pressures within the context of our national economy that has turned a potential source of strength into an excuse for confrontation. The fact is that Ottawa insists on maintaining economic policies which mollify Ontario—one of the least-structured state economies within Confederation—to the detriment of the others. In this sense, if there had not been a Parti Québécois based on traditional language-group rivalries, it is very likely that one would have sprung up along some other lines. There is, in fact, a social and economic basis for separatism which may go deeper even than language or ethnic issues.

These conflicts are not inevitable, although they are certainly implicit in the way in which things are done at present. There are alternatives, however. First, the various provinces could devise a means—with or without Ottawa's participation—of sharing capital and expertise. Alberta has already taken a step in this direction by lending Newfoundland $50 million out of its Heritage Fund. This capital would be even better used, however, if it were invested in a project which was jointly capitalized and run by both governments. Since past evidence suggests that the efficiency of provincial Crown corporations increases in almost direct proportion to the range of activities in which their parent governments are engaged (Saskatchewan's proprietary Crown corporations have a debt-to-equity ratio of 2:1. Ontario's have one of almost 5:1), Saskatchewan, too, could provide technical assistance if the project resembled one in which it already has experience.

Second, joint federal-provincial Crown corporations could be set up in many fields where a natural monopoly exists. Cable TV would be an ideal place for this: both provincial and federal Crown corporations could supply material to be broadcast over the network. This project would have the added advantage of fostering closer relations between various production staffs. It might even provide regional material which could then be broadcast over the CBC's main network. In the area of resource development, we see no reason, for instance, why joint development of Saskatchewan's uranium deposits could not be undertaken by a consortium of federal and provincial Crown corporations. Tidal power in the Atlantic provinces will probably be developed in this fashion. Joint resource-development ventures of this kind have already begun between some provincial Crown corporations, but without significant participation by Ottawa.

Third, in some areas, such as pharmaceuticals, where governments are by far the largest customer and where no significant production goes on in Canada, joint development of an industry could be undertaken with production facilities in different locales across the country. Although initial capital-investment costs would be quite high in some cases, a ready-made market does exist and the savings to individual provinces would be enormous.

Finally, high-technology industries with few significant locational advantages (computer software, for instance) could be established in areas with high levels of unemployment but natural lifestyle advantages (e.g., Newfoundland). Products from these industries could then be marketed through the federal-provincial Crown corporation network. These ventures could be established out of some kind of rotating capital pool contributed by the provinces and Ottawa, and funds could be channelled into various regions when conditions warranted. In the long run, investment of this kind would be much more likely to reduce levels of unemployment than all the DREE, LIP, LEAP, and UIC money put together.

In every case, since each province would benefit to some degree, confrontations between and among them would be minimized. In addition, a proliferation of arrangements of this kind could knit the various provincial and regional economies in Canada together, reduce competition among them, and also benefit the national economy by reducing dependence on external capital and expertise. In time, devices of this kind might even promote the flow of population between regions, lead to closer working relationships between Canadians in different parts of the country, and generally do a whole series of things Ottawa bureaucrats have been promising to do for a long time. Ottawa itself would benefit from the greatly reduced level of tension in federal-provincial relations and would encounter far fewer problems of co-ordination—since federal-provincial relationships in a number of different areas would be increasingly institutionalized and, hence, routine.

If all of this is to work, however, we must first come to

realize and accept certain things. We must understand, first of all, that Crown corporations must be run efficiently, but that they are principally instruments of government policy. As such, they must be designed to achieve specific and clearly defined goals. They should not be created where there is no larger purpose to be served. Second, we must accept that Canada is most likely to be developed by large agglomerations of capital, and that we have nothing to lose and much to gain from using state mechanisms to mobilize this capital where appropriate. Finally, we must recognize that some mechanisms of this kind must be found if we are—in the national interest—to undercut the strains implicit in divergent provincial economic models. We have nothing to lose in the process except our nineteenth-century consciousness. That's a small price to pay for a country.

Table 12:1   Forms of State Economies and Their Principal Effects

Forms of state economies	State Participation	State Directed	State Centred	State Based	State Dominated	State Controlled
Definition scope	• state participates in various sectors of the economy on a hit-or-miss basis • over-all state investment is a small part of the total • not rationalized	• state participation in natural monopoly areas • over-all state investment is an appreciable part of total • decision made to enter high-risk areas through joint ventures	• state role in some principal sectors • over-all state investment is an important part of total • decision made to dominate some key areas of the economy	• state role in all principal sectors • over-all state investment in the majority of economic activities • clear development plan with definite allocations between state, private, and co-operatives	• state dominates all areas and markets • over-all state investment is more than 80 per cent • over-all planning of capital allocation, with local planning of specific economic activities and work process	• state controls all areas of economy • all investment through the state • centralized planning of capital allocation, development, and work process
Goal of intervention	• supplement and support private economy • protect existing employment	• supplement and support private economy • increase supply of venture capital • increase employment opportunities	• direct the economy towards socially desirable goals, e.g., redistributing income • increase and organize supply of venture capital • increase employment opportunities	• direct and regulate the economy to minimize income inequality • dominate and regulate capital allocations • create new mechanisms for capital allocations • shape and co-ordinate labour supply, education	• dominate and control all aspects of economic life, e.g., standardize wage rates by occupation • make all fundamental capital allocations between sectors • manpower decisions tied to development plan	• complete control of the system of production • makes virtually all capital allocation decisions • all manpower-training allocation decisions made through state agencies
Management and control (locus of control)	• largely in private hands • government offices have little power to intervene only in most enterprises	• largely in private hands • state officers can intervene only in certain sectors	• competition between private and gov't officials over control of key sectors • possibility of	• largely in gov't hands • possibilities for worker participation in some sectors	• all key decision areas in hands of state officials • private and worker participation confined to less cen-	• centralized control by government officials of all areas of the economy • workers' control is nominal

Forms of state economies	State Participation	State Directed	State Centred	State Based	State Dominated	State Controlled
Principal difficulties	• constant necessity for government intervention to shore up, restrain, and regulate economy	• difficulty in protecting public monies • process inequalities in capital allocations and income distributions • structural opportunities for theft	• often difficult for government to carry out socially desirable plan in face of private enterprise opposition • getting competent management staff • political interference with Crown corporations	• adjusting to sectoral demands in time • interfacing between private and public economy	• more difficult to ensure co-ordination of production as economy becomes more industrialized • tendency towards over-reliance on expertise	• establishing parameters and goals over time • over-reliance on expertise
Cases in which this form predominates	United States Ontario Nova Scotia Prince Edward Island New Brunswick	Québec Italy Alberta India United Kingdom Brazil Australia West Germany	Saskatchewan Manitoba Sweden Finland Algeria	Yugoslavia Tanzania Norway Guyana	China Romania Bulgaria	Cuba U.S.S.R. East Germany Albania

Table 12:1 Forms of State Economies and Their Principal Effects (cont'd)

Forms of state economies	State Participation	State Directed	State Centred	State Based	State Dominated	State Controlled
Positive consequences	• minimal response time in allocation of resources • administration costs largely confined to regulation of economy instead of operating costs • many alternative career paths (mostly in private sector) • less obvious constraints on individual choice	• some more rationalization of capital and manpower allocation • increased visibility and accountability of administrative costs for infrastructure, health, and welfare • opens up opportunity structure in certain areas, through government employment	• rationalizes capital and manpower allocation and allows government to look at alternative ways to allocate the above • greater control over, and knowledge of, the effects of taxation, hence simplified taxation • increased visibility and accountability of administrative costs for infrastructure, health, etc. • positive effect on income structure • earlier identification of manpower needs • opens up career opportunities in the public sector • low unemployment	• optimal allocation of resources across sectors • optimal control without having to make all detailed decisions • simplified system of taxation (reduction of number of taxes) • virtually eliminates regulatory procedures • eliminates recessions and inflations • gov't can estimate rationally demand for labour and co-ordinate demand with educational decisions • balanced opportunity structure • virtually no unemployment	• enables government to allocate capital most efficiently for over-all development • market decisions virtually automatic • eliminates necessity for many forms of administration of non-state economy • perfect control over costing • eliminates major forms of crime, by eliminating all opportunities for criminal activity • no employment, no unemployment	• allows for full social costing of social effects • enormously simplified tax system • eliminates opportunity for major forms of crime • opportunities for new labour specialities • no unemployment, no employment

Forms of state economies	State Participation	State Directed	State Centred	State Based	State Dominated	State Controlled
Negative consequences	• no method of determining efficient allocation in most cases before the fact • high administration costs as the government tries to control the economy through complicated tax structure, legal regulations, and incoherently planned state ownership • over- and under-production • large-scale direct and indirect subsidies to private economy • full accounting of infrastructure is impossible • minimal impact on income structure • relatively high unemployment • intergenerational occupational mobility is relatively low	• difficult to separate allocations to private and public sector • very complicated tax structure and legal regulations as government introduces more controls • typical high rates of inflation • minimal and possibly negative impact on income structure • Crown corporations tend to develop autonomous goals and power	• tends towards uneven growth in different sectors of the economy • time lag in allocating resources due to complexity of planning • rates of individual taxation tend to be variable but high • imperfect mechanism for accounting for private-sector costs • sectoral income differential is high • labour structure in less capital-intensive areas of economy tends to lag behind	• eliminates many small, inefficient units with negative consequences for those directly affected • capital shortages in some areas • high rates of taxation for private enterprise • increased operating costs borne by government • highly structured job opportunities	• inflexible allocation in some sectors • long lead time in planning • necessity for large centralized planning departments • entrenched bureaucracy • requires a regimentation of labour force and highly restrictive choice	• moderate to high administration and operating costs • entrenched and unresponsive bureaucracy • capital allocation tends to become arbitrary and unbalanced • very long response time for planning • difficulty in shifting capital from sector to sector when needed • pricing of goods tends to become arbitrary • over- and under-production • strong formal mechanism of social control in workplace • high rates of underemployment • requires regimentation of the labour force and virtually no choice by the individual • tendency to lock up manpower

CHAPTER THIRTEEN

CANADA'S SOCIAL-WELFARE CRISIS

CONSTITUTIONAL CRISES do not arise on their own. They are not causes of social change—although they may result in profound alterations in a society. They are symptoms of structural problems which underlie and shape public issues, sentiments, and reactions. A constitutional crisis is a signal that something is wrong, not a cause in itself.

As several of the essayists in this book recognize, Canada's difficulties today stem from a number of such structural faults. Probably the most important of these is regional inequality. This pervasive fact of Canadian life divides Québec from English Canada, the Atlantic provinces from central Canada, the Prairies from the rest of the country, B.C. and Alberta from the East, the "North" from the "South", and so on. It is not confined to antagonisms between provinces, but goes on within provinces as well. In this regard, northern Québec and northern Ontario are more similar to one another than either of them is to Toronto or Montreal. The reasons for this inequality—this structured inequality—vary somewhat from region to region but, in each case, are a legacy of our history as an economic appendage and political vassal of foreign powers.

A second important cause of our present dilemma is a particularly and peculiarly timid and self-serving local and national elite which has perpetuated foreign domination to the detriment of the national interest. The economic policies and social goals formulated by this elite have, not surprisingly, been characterized by a certain caution and lack of imagination.

Third, partly as a result of the first two factors, we lack a truly *national* culture. As a result, to the extent that a uniquely Canadian experience is reflected in our culture, it is even now usually expressed in regional rather than national terms. Our

* Prepared for this volume.

LAWRENCE F. FELT

regional cultures, as a result, are as unique and as highly articulated in places like the Atlantic provinces and the West as they are in Québec. But our national media and national cultural institutions, shaped as they are by strong foreign influences, have contributed little to overcoming our endemic regional isolation.

It is in the context of such underlying factors that we should look at any effort to formulate and carry through a policy or set of policies of national scope. In this brief essay, I will focus on one important area—social-welfare policy—where our lack of coherent national goals has been most apparent.

Canadian social-welfare policy—particularly the income-support and employment-opportunity dimensions of it—suffers from duplication, contradiction, and ineffectiveness. I shall attempt three interrelated tasks with respect to overhauling it:

- to provide what I consider to be an adequate definition and rationale for social-welfare policy;
- to review present Canadian attempts at social-welfare policy; and
- to outline some features of what I deem to be a flexible and humane policy.

In regard to point three, I will focus primarily on the issues of income support and the expansion of employment opportunities, including the role of a Guaranteed Annual Income (GAIN) program.

WHAT IS SOCIAL WELFARE?

"Social welfare" refers to the physical, mental, economic, and cultural well-being of a citizenry. "Well-being" can be defined as the opportunity to secure adequate resources (economic and other) to maintain a "reasonable standard of living" in a society at a given time.

The determination of what constitutes a "reasonable standard of living" requires us to consider local needs, preferences, and aspirations as well as any relevant national standards. It is a complex calculus of what the minimum guarantees of citizenship are. All too frequently such a calculus is reduced to a very crude monetary standard (for example, the notorious "poverty line") which divides the population into those below the standard (the "poor") and the rest.

The definition I am proposing here is more difficult to calculate. While adequate economic resources (a job or some other source of income) is necessary for "well-being", there is a wide range of economic adaptations and corresponding lifestyles found within any society. By implication, any social-welfare policy should not only recognize but give concrete support to these differing adaptations (urban *vs.* rural, industrial *vs.* agricultural, western *vs.* eastern, etc.) while simultaneously providing adequate income guarantees. It is clear from a review of present programs, that this is currently not the case.

PRESENT SOCIAL-WELFARE POLICY IN CANADA

The definition of social welfare I have just presented bears little or no resemblance to those embodied in the collection of programs at the federal and provincial levels that pass for social-welfare policy today. While civil service bureaucrats would undoubtedly demur, it is not an exaggeration to say that we simply do not have a comprehensive social-welfare policy. Rather, we find a jungle of provincial efforts—usually cost-shared with Ottawa—combined in no particularly co-ordinated fashion with an even larger and more convoluted maze of federal programs scattered among various ministries. This is even the case if we limit ourselves to those programs which are most relevant to a comprehensive policy—such as health care—but which might reasonably be dealt with separately.

Four of the federal programs directed at income support and employment opportunities are currently most important: those administered by the Department of Regional Economic Expansion (DREE), the Unemployment Insurance Commission (UIC), the Canada Pension Plan (CPP), and the Canada Assistance Plan (CAP).

DREE was created in 1967–69 to consolidate a wide range of federal-provincial programs aimed at redistributing economic opportunities into so-called "underdeveloped" regions of the country. Initially, the program divided the country into various regions based on levels of economic development. Governments and individual entrepreneurs within designated regions were given incentives and expert advice to undertake job-creation projects in the agricultural, manufacturing, and resource sectors. In the 1970s, an "infrastructure" funding program was added which provided federal funds for school construction, road building, community water and sewage facilities, and other projects which generated short-term construction employment and were thought to be a useful foundation upon which later, more permanent, industrial development could be built.

Except in a few scattered cases, DREE has not worked to redistribute economic opportunities. Indeed, by 1977 DREE has come to look more and more like yet another public-welfare institution providing short-term, make-work funding and having little lasting effect. Partisan politics has also interfered with DREE's original mandate to the extent that virtually the entire country (except for parts of Alberta and the Toronto area) have now become eligible for funding. Moreover, according to one study by Keith Storey,[1] regions with a long history of support for the Liberal party are overrepresented in the awarding of grants.

Inflation, federal anti-inflation policies, and poor planning have placed the Canada Pension Plan and the Unemployment Insurance Commission in jeopardy. In 1977, eligibility for unemployment insurance was made more stringent. This change was necessitated by the heavy subsidization from general revenue required to keep the fund solvent. Pension levels for Canadian senior citizens are lower than those in many European countries with lower material standards of living than ours. Moreover, analysts predict a considerable short-fall in pension funds in the near future, given anticipated retirements, present levels of funding, and the investment strategies currently pursued by those administering these funds. While the program is partially indexed to inflation, this has still resulted in a decline in the real purchasing power of pensioners over the last two years. This, in turn, has had, and will continue to have, a marked impact on provinces such as Québec and Newfoundland, where the population is aging more rapidly than it is in others: less purchasing power for an increasingly large part of the population means weaker demand for goods and services and, indirectly, higher rates of unemployment.

The Canada Assistance Plan is a series of programs cost-shared between the two senior levels of government (welfare assistance is largely a provincial responsibility). As revised in 1976, CAP provides funds for a wide range of income support, counselling, and rehabilitative services. It suffers from excessive bureaucratization, however, and levels of assistance are considerably below adequate levels for maintaining households.[2]

A host of other federal programs are involved in income support and employment creation. The Canada Manpower Department provides job training, career counselling, and some occupational placement. Several studies have indicated, however, that the program is unable to anticipate future labour-force needs, has failed to experiment with new training schemes, and does not aggressively pursue job placement. This is in stark contrast to manpower programs in Europe where, for example, more thorough research is done on future occupational needs, imaginative efforts are made to develop retraining schemes which bypass many barriers in access to programs (minimum educational requirements, for example), and much more aggressive attempts are made to create new jobs and convince firms that these jobs can improve economic performance.[3]

In Canada, the counterparts of many of these projects are mired in bureaucracy. Typically, there is currently a batch of programs at the federal level which might be referred to as "alphabet soup": Opportunities for Youth (OFY), Local Initiatives Program (LIP), Young Canada Works (YCW), Canada Works, Horizons, LEAP—I confess I have not been able to find out what it stands for—and a host of lesser-known ones. All are short-term make-work projects directed at those regions and/or subpopulations in Canada most hurt by the present recession. While some good individual projects have resulted from these efforts, they are viewed cynically by both provincial governments and recipients as sops in lieu of long-term economic opportunities. To further complicate and confuse issues, it should be noted that most of the above programs have provincial counterparts. Indeed, many federal programs *require* that parallel provincial bureaucracies be created to provide a liaison with the corresponding federal organization. A local component to these programs, thus, does not bring them closer to people: it simply makes them more complicated.

The end result of this maze of programs has been noted by the Senate Committee on Poverty chaired by David Croll.[4] It characterized these income-support and job-creation programs as: excessively bureaucratic and involving a great deal of duplication, inadequate in their amount of income support, and ambiguous—and sometimes contradictory—in their goal(s). Depending upon what measure of adequacy is taken, estimates of the number of Canadians living at inadequate levels varies between 20 per cent and 40 per cent.[5] Little evidence can be adduced to demonstrate any great impact of these programs on the number of Canadians living in such a state. Moreover, as stagflation continues and the federal government continues to place a higher priority on fighting inflation than combating unemployment and poverty, the performance of these programs can only deteriorate further. Unemployment is presently the highest Canada has had since 1951; and indications are that it will go higher. The national average percentages for unemployment should be doubled and even tripled in the poorer regions such as Atlantic Canada, eastern Québec, and the Northern Territories. Under our present arrangements, only provincial governments with strong, relatively independent financial bases (Alberta, for one) can offset these effects on their own.

THE BEGINNINGS OF A PROGRAM

In a country as wealthy as Canada, there is no excuse for the large number of people living at these inadequate levels. The first and foremost task for us, then, is to provide some means of raising the income levels of those in need. The most efficient mechanism for doing this is a Guaranteed Annual Income scheme (GAIN).

GAIN would considerably simplify the myriad of programs which are now either directly or indirectly playing income-support functions. The basic function of such a plan is conveyed in its name: to provide a guaranteed annual income level for every member of society. The amount of such a guarantee will vary depending upon the resources of a society: it should be large enough to provide an adequate level of existence relative to the general living standards prevailing at that time within the society, but the actual amount will vary depending upon the size of a given living unit. I would propose that the level for such a plan, in Canada, be pegged at approximately six thousand dollars for a single individual, with increments dependent on family size. A family of four, for instance, might require eight or eight-and-a-half thousand dollars.

A comprehensive program such as this would replace the hodge-podge of income-support schemes we have at present— from LIP to the Canada Pension Plan and would reduce bureaucratization. Operationally, this plan might take a number of forms. While Green[6] and Lekachman[7] have systematically reviewed and commented upon various schemes, a few general comments may help us to understand the operation of GAIN.

In addition to determining the income level to be guaranteed, any particular type of GAIN must also decide (1) what the appropriate units are to which payments are to be made, and (2) whether the program employs a "means test" for eligibility, or if it is a universal, demogrant type—such as family allowances—which makes payments to everyone but then taxes back these groups at levels approaching 100 per cent for those not needing support.

It is normally argued that the census categories of "families" and "self-resident adults" are the most workable. Most children and adults can be conveniently classified in one of these categories.*

Advocates of both the "means test" and the demogrant patterns can be found: demogrants have the advantage of reducing the social stigma associated with many current types of income support such as public assistance. They are, however, more complicated to administer than "means test" methods.[8] At the moment, there is no general agreement among experts on which type of mechanism is preferable.

Two objections are typically raised against the implementation of Guaranteed Annual Income schemes, generally: their alleged excessive cost; and that they will destroy the work ethic by providing a disincentive to working. Politicians—particularly though not exclusively those from the poorer regions of Canada —rhetorically declare themselves in favour of GAIN, in principle, but find themselves unable to undertake such a program because of insufficient funds. Despite this, these same politicians are willing to throw away hundreds of millions of dollars on industrial projects designed to turn their regions into an industrial heartland, only to have their efforts end in failure. The worst examples of this have occurred in Newfoundland. It is estimated that the now bankrupt oil refinery at Come-By-Chance cost various levels of government upwards of one million dollars for every job created there.

Estimates from the Croll committee place the cost of an income-guarantee program at between two and eight billion dol-

---

* "Self-resident adult" refers to an individual who lives alone and is self-supporting. Individuals resident in caretaking institutions such as nursing homes can be classified as self-resident adults with a certain percentage of their income allocated to cover the cost of residence in the institution.

lars, depending upon the income level chosen. Of particular importance in determining whether or not Canada can afford such a program is providing an answer to the question "Who will pay?" Politicians appear to believe that the already hard-pressed middle-income earner must bear the brunt of any tax increases for the program. This is far from clear: restructuring of corporate tax policies, savings gained from reducing much of the inefficiency in the current conglomeration of programs, and a saner strategy towards creating greater economic opportunities— which I shall discuss shortly—could allow GAIN without large increases in taxation for the middle-income earner. It certainly *does not* follow that there is no money, and no place to expand government revenues, without forcing ordinary wage earners to contribute more to the taxes needed for GAIN.

But if we pay people a guaranteed annual income, who will work? This work-disincentive argument does not appear to be a serious one when examined carefully. In both the United States and Canada, a large number of studies have been done of the potential effects of GAIN. *All* of these studies have clearly demonstrated that *work-incentive features can be built into a guaranteed income plan while leaving the funding at adequate levels*. Tobin has demonstrated this for the United States.[9]

One possible work-incentive effort is contained in *The Real Poverty Report*.[10] The desire to work is still a deeply ingrained cultural value in Canadian society—so deeply ingrained that even with today's inadequate levels of welfare assistance, thousands of individuals prefer to work at low-paying, dirty, dead-end jobs than to receive the same or even slightly higher incomes from public welfare.

If a guaranteed annual income plan were pegged at an adequate level, it could, at least, eliminate poverty in Canada. By itself, however, it would not increase employment opportunities for the millions of Canadians either unemployed (914,000 in April 1977) or working at low-paying jobs commanding no respect and leading nowhere. Substantial regional inequities in employment opportunities would still exist.

Given a commitment to the work ethic, then, a sound social-welfare policy must also promote greater opportunities for employment. For this to occur, our manpower and job-creation efforts must be overhauled. I suggested earlier some of the changes that are needed in manpower policy. Our basic approach to job creation must be altered as well.

Past policy in job creation might be characterized as the "big bang" strategy. That is, millions of dollars are invested in gigantic showpiece projects (often with associated costs of hundreds of thousands of dollars per permanent job) with the hope that such projects—be they pulp complexes, oil refineries, or heavy water plants—will generate further industrial growth. As one after another of these projects have failed, the poorer regions have experienced an exodus of thousands of workers to the "Golden Horseshoe" of Ontario or the boom towns of Alberta. This has historically been the pattern in places like Atlantic Canada. With a guaranteed annual income program as a support, a more creative and flexible attitude towards job creation could be used. Not every part of Canada can—or should—become another Hamilton or Calgary. This does not mean that *no* industrial development is appropriate for such regions. Rather, such development should be more geared to their economic and human resources. A considerable amount of the natural resources extracted from our poorer regions (be they fish or iron ore) could be processed locally. Most types of large-scale manufacturing are not likely to be competitive, in any case, with similar plants in central Canada or the United States.

It follows from this that greater emphasis should be placed on developing decentralized, relatively low- or intermediate-technology industries. Although I only note it in passing, Scandinavian societies have been highly successful in promoting relatively high-paying, efficient industries—without high degrees of subsidization—in their marginal regions. This has stabilized population migrations, thereby cutting down on problems of urban growth in the heavily urbanized industrial areas and, simultaneously, allowed such regions to retain their own economic and cultural distinctiveness.

It would be excessively romantic to argue that such employment strategies can generate wages equal to those of workers in a large steel complex. Such projects can and do, however, provide more than adequate income levels for many individuals. Such an option is particularly attractive to those people who, for whatever reason, may prefer a trade-off between higher incomes and certain social or cultural preferences—such as remaining near kin, residing in a rural area, or avoiding the bureaucratic nature of industrial work.

Evidence over the last fifty years suggests that we *cannot* employ all Canadians who wish to work in industrial settings.

Why then, do we hold this out as the only relevant meaning to the term "economic development"? If an individual or family prefers using the inshore fishery in the Atlantic region as a way of making a living, rather than working in a factory in Brantford, Ontario, why should we not encourage him or her to be a capable fisherman and, if necessary, guarantee him or her an adequate level of income?

Surely in a country as wealthy as Canada, we do not need to convert everyone into service-sector or industrial workers. A goal of any social-welfare policy should be to encourage these diverse adaptations and lifestyle preferences while providing adequate income support. This is the challenge for future policy to meet in this country. If we fail to meet this challenge, we can expect continued high levels of regional inequality with all of the divisive and centrifugal tendencies which these bring in their wake. If we fail to recognize the diverse regional lifestyles which could potentially form part of a national culture, we can expect continued erosion of our national sense of self-worth. We now have an opportunity to reverse these trends which may not occur in so malleable a form again.

NOTES

1   Keith Storey, "The distribution of DREE funded projects in Canada", Department of Geography, Memorial University of Newfoundland, 1976. Mimeographed report.
2   Ian Adams, William Cameron, Brian Hill, and Peter Penz, *The Real Poverty Report* (Edmonton, 1971).
3   Sheila Arnopoulos, "Manpower in Canada", a collection of articles appearing in *The Montreal Star*, 1970.
4   David Croll, Special Senate Committee on Poverty. Printed as *Poverty in Canada* (Ottawa, 1971).
5   Ibid.
6   Christopher Green, *Negative Taxes and the Poverty Problem* (Washington, 1967).
7   Robert Lekachman, "Can more money end poverty?", in Irving Howe and Jeremy Larner (eds.), *Poverty: Views from the Left* (New York, 1969), pp. 58-67.
8   Green, *Negative Taxes and the Poverty Problem*.
9   James Tobin, "The case for an income guarantee", *The Public Interest*, 4 (Summer 1966).
10 Adams *et al.*, *The Real Poverty Report*, Appendix III.

CHAPTER FOURTEEN

THE COMMUNITY-CENTRE ALTERNATIVE: A NEW FOCUS FOR HEALTH

THE HEALTH OF CANADIANS is now an acknowledged government responsibility. The federal government, as well as every provincial government in Canada, now participates to some degree in the provision of health-care services. The kind and extent of this government involvement in health varies from province to province. All, however, have some form of hospital- and medical-care insurance which is cost-shared with the federal government.

In theory, this program was intended to equalize access to health care across the country by subsidizing less populous provinces where economies of scale might make it difficult for them to provide the range of services available in larger ones. In practice, of course, since the larger and wealthier provinces had already invested considerable sums in their hospital and laboratory systems at the time that insured services were introduced, federal payments—even on an adjusted per-capita basis—tended to perpetuate existing inequalities in levels of service. Moreover, given the high levels of outmigration from many of the poorer provinces—such as, for instance, Newfoundland—

* Prepared for this volume.

JAN DUKSZTA & TERESA BERKOWITZ

the per-capita cost of maintaining the same levels of service has tended to increase over time. This has meant, in practical terms, that regional inequalities in levels of service not only persist, but are increasing.

The common element in these schemes is funding: hospitals and other existing institutions are heavily subsidized and the services of medical-care practitioners are insured.

The fiscal basis of these schemes is, however, now in jeopardy at the same time that the division of powers and responsibilities between federal and provincial departments of health—never well-articulated in theory and even more confused in practice—is beginning to crumble. Two developments clearly indicate the magnitude of this crisis: current demographic trends are such that not simply health care, but a whole series of social-welfare programs which Canadians take for granted today, will bankrupt the average taxpayer in 1995 unless they are (a) seriously cost controlled, or (b) eliminated. Between 1980 and 1990, the number of young people entering the labour force will fall radically, and the number of persons over sixty-five will climb. If present trends continue, in other words, fewer active wage earners will be supporting the rest of the population. The federal government realizes this and has chosen to deal with the problem in the way that the BNA Act makes so desirable and possible: it has copped out. It has traded constant dollars today against rising health-care social-welfare costs tomorrow. Under our present system, the provinces have no choice but to go along.

The second development is even more serious: the federal and provincial governments have been playing hot potato with grave threats to the public health. Once again, under the prevailing interpretations of the BNA Act, a germ—say, one being unwittingly transported by an air traveller—is a federal responsibility until it clears customs and leaves the airport grounds. Once it does this, however, it becomes a bona fide provincial germ—say, an Ontario germ. If it then drives to Montreal, it remains an Ontario germ until it crosses into Québec, at which point it is transformed into a Québec germ—and so on. No one, at present, takes full responsibility for it. In recent cases, all the relevant jurisdictions have avoided responsibility successfully.

These two developments exemplify the ways in which the current fiscal and constitutional arrangements between Ottawa and the provinces promote a shirking of responsibility. Fixed tax-sharing today is fine, but how will provincial governments react tomorrow when the real value of these payments declines and they cannot pay for health? And we have not yet had a major epidemic because of government games of hot potato with some disease germ, but what about next time?

The core of these problems lies in a basic unwillingness to rethink the broad general purposes and goals of our health-care system. The provinces, with the partial exception of Saskatchewan, have not established their own publicly controlled, owned, and funded health-care systems serving their own constituents. Rather, they have undertaken to support the existing accumulation of private institutions, hospitals, laboratories, clinics, and practices with public funds. The federal government—which has a clear mandate in public health—has chosen to avoid going beyond rudimentary service.

This government short-sightedness has produced a paradox: although our current health-care system is overwhelmingly publicly funded, its organization and logic are those of a private system. In it, physicians and health institutions behave much as they would in a private-care system. Pre-existing facilities and institutions, located usually in middle-class urban areas, serviced a clientele which could afford the expensive buildings, equipment, and techniques that private Western medical systems favour. This inequitable and disorganized geographic distribution of facilities and personnel, as well as the profit-oriented, wasteful brand of medicine it fostered, remain in operation in most provinces today. Therefore, not only are poor and moderate income earners and their families denied access to adequate facilities, but they are obliged to pay for them through public taxation.

As a result, not only is our larger health-care system disorganized—in part because of constitutional vagueness; and not only is it extremely expensive—because it is a system of private care at public expense; but it is unjust and inequitable as well. We feel that it is high time something was done about these problems. The public foots the bill for medical care in Canada. It is time the public had control of the structure, organization, and distribution of these services. We pay the piper; we should call the tune. This means, in practice, that we should demand: (a) that a comprehensive and co-ordinated health-care system be established in Canada; (b) that this system be under public control to reduce costs; and (c) that it should be geared to the needs of the communities it serves.

The solution to the first of these—the over-all design of a comprehensive and co-ordinated national system—is highly technical and demands careful research before it can be answered thoroughly and thoughtfully in detail. But its broad outlines and theoretical rationale are clear enough. The answer to the second and third issues, however, has already been researched and is almost a truism: it lies in "the Community-Centre alternative".

HEALTH AND ILLNESS

Health is not the simple absence of disease: it involves the social, environmental, and psychological well-being of individuals and communities. There is an intricate relationship between the occupational, familial, and environmental sources of ill-health and the concurrent necessity for dealing with social inequality, poor nutrition and nurturance, and pollution when attacking them.

The inequities, disorganization, inefficiencies, and technical shortcomings of our present system are easily seen. Marc Lalonde has catalogued them very clearly in his *A New Perspective on the Health of Canadians*. What this document lacks, however, is a true change of perspective: a shift away from the present focus on the "cure" of illness to the prevention and elimination of those elements within our society which destroy health. Rather than attempt the complete restructuring and rationalization of the health-care system which such a shift in perspective implies, Lalonde prefers to ascribe the ill-health of Canadians to individual causes. This, of course, eliminates the need for concrete action. It is a cop out. Rhetoric, in which the present federal government excels, replaces it: "Arise, Canadians, repent, abandon your personal, unhealthful practices and be healed."

We maintain that not exhortations, not half-measures, but a new structure and a new orientation are required. A truly public health-care system, under public control, must be instituted. Such a system, acknowledging the interaction of health, work, and education, would shift resources and manpower away from the present "curative" emphasis towards preventive health, primary care, and a broadly based social-service system. This system and these attitudes must be implemented at all levels—federal, provincial, municipal, and community.

In the broadest terms, these developments must be thoughtfully and thoroughly planned with the following objectives in mind:

- quality health care must be accessible to all;
- individuals' participation in those decisions which directly affect their own health must be ensured;
- positive health measures to supplement illness treatment must be instituted;
- the integration and co-ordination of health-related services to promote ease of access, improve service, and eliminate redundancy must be increased.

THE COMMUNITY CENTRE

The basic structural unit around which our proposed new system would be organized is the community-based and run Community Health and Social Service Centre. Each centre would be staffed by teams of professionals with complementary skills. Each would also have an elected Community Board and serve a particular health and social-services district. Each District Board would allocate and rationalize the use of the available resources on a district-wide basis.

A typical centre would provide primary medical diagnosis and treatment facilities, preventive and primary dental care, family services, a basic public-health service, mental-health services, industrial- and occupational-health programs, environmental testing, health education, counselling, day-care services, legal aid, and locally provided social-welfare services as well. Some units would include basic radiological, laboratory, and pharmaceutical services and would handle referrals from other centres as well.

Although the range of services provided in each centre would vary somewhat depending on population, each would contain basic services independent of community size. Each would also maintain a team of health workers reflecting the ethnic and linguistic composition of the district or community it served. Some teams would operate from vans fully equipped with two-way radios, electronic monitoring equipment linked to the service centre by acoustic couples, a basic drug supply for primary treatment, and—in rural areas—a small portable x-ray unit. Mobile teams of this kind would be staffed by nurse-practitioners, paramedics, and social workers.

There are two important principles of organization implicit in the over-all design of our proposed new system. First, that the greatest range of skills and flexibility should be introduced at the point where problem definition occurs. Here, the availability of a single centre which is responsible for providing a broad range of services to a given community member predisposes the system towards the sharing of information and a holistic definition of the situation. Second, to be effectively used, people-centred organizations must present clearly defined paths for access to their services. A "centre" approach would tend to break down barriers to access by introducing a great deal of simplification in allocating services.

Thus, by ensuring that a range of primary services is immediately available many of the more glaring faults of the present system could be avoided. The confusion, delays, and lack of service which result from our present completely random pattern of access would be eliminated. Referrals to hospitals and other specialized services would be made on a systematic basis. The incredible waste of funds and misallocation of facilities, resources, and professional and staff time now commonplace in most provinces would no longer be permitted to occur.

DISTRICT, PROVINCIAL, AND FEDERAL LEVELS

Within this scheme, while communities would be the principal focus for the provision of services, *districts* would act to rationalize and co-ordinate different types of programs and to plan for future needs on a wider basis. Competing claims for funds—for instance, those between nursing homes and home-care programs —would be resolved here. This would allow for both a certain amount of flexibility in terms of meeting local needs and, at the same time, provide a natural experimental laboratory for trying out new alternatives.* Provincial governments would assume primary responsibility for allocating funds for primary, secondary, and tertiary care, compiling over-all statistics, undertaking long-term planning and research, and helping the districts to evaluate the effectiveness of their programs. The federal government would undertake primary responsibility for (a) epidemic and highly infectious disease monitoring, (b) immigration-

* A district something like this exists in Saskatchewan and has been used by the provincial government for this purpose for many years.

related health programs (immunization, testing, intelligence gathering, etc.), (c) high-security isolation and laboratory facilities, (d) standards for bio-medical research, (e) the control of effluents in bodies of water touching upon more than one province or an international boundary, (f) raising the revenue needed for care of those of pensionable age, (g) the training of specialists in rare branches of medicine where it is deemed to be in the national interest to do so, and (h) the provision of critical biologicals or testing agents. Depending on provincial needs and priorities, these services could be provided either directly by the federal government, or by contract with provincial, municipal, or community groups.

CONCLUSION

In this brief space, it is impossible to do much more than provide the barest outlines of how such a system would function in practice. In an article in Part Four, Ernest Chang will take up some of these issues in detail. Suffice it to say, however, that what we need in Canada today is an over-all health system which is sufficiently centralized to allow for co-ordination, planning, and a rational allocation of resources—but one which is, at the same time, sufficiently flexible to allow for (a) local experimentation, (b) the different needs of different regions and provinces, and (c) adaptation to changing circumstances and conditions. The first, we feel, would be provided by focusing on primary contact, testing, and environmental monitoring at the community-centre level. The second objective would be met by placing responsibility for routine funding, planning, and evaluation at the district and provincial levels. And the third could be jointly met by all levels of government—with the federal government enjoying chief responsibility for problems of a peculiarly national or long-term nature. In other words, through a diversity of means and approaches, but with the clear delineation of responsibilities and duties, it should be possible to build a publicly funded, *public* health-care system which will be more relevant to the needs of all Canadians. This is an increasingly urgent national task which we must face right now—or reap the whirlwind in the very near future.

CHAPTER FIFTEEN

CRISIS IN ENERGY: MYTH OR REALITY?

INTRODUCTION

IN 1973, a so-called energy "crisis" gripped the world. OPEC, the Organization of Petroleum Exporting Countries (formed in 1960) saw the posted price of the marker crude — Saudi Arabian light — stay constant, in nominal terms, through 1970, but fall 20 per cent in real terms. In 1971 and 1972 there were substantial increases in the nominal price of crude; 23 per cent in 1971 and 12 per cent in 1972. In the two years following the shock of the Yom Kippur War, posted prices rose 370 per cent.

In the face of these events, a number of Western countries developed policies to cushion their effects. It is widely argued that Canada should follow the lead of the United States in developing similar policies. In this paper I will examine a number of policies — particularly those of Canada and the United States — and show that those pursued in the United States have, if anything, been more inconsistent and unproductive than those pursued here.

It is important at this point to remember the actual events of the early 1970s. There was neither a precipitous fall in world oil reserves nor a great and unusual increase in demand. Between 1969, when most industry experts argued that oil surpluses existed, and 1973 when these same experts announced that the world was running out of oil, the life index of proven world oil reserves *actually rose*.

The "crisis", then, was not due to a world oil shortage but was attributable to two perceptions: first, that of the Western

---

*Lecture delivered on January 19, 1977 at the conference on "Energy: The User's Problem and Response", University of Toronto. Published here in modified form by kind permission of the author.

LEONARD WAVERMAN

industrialized countries—particularly the United States and
Canada—that they were not to remain among the oil-rich areas
of the world; and second, that of the major non-industrialized
oil producers—particularly Saudi Arabia—that the OPEC cartel
could become effective for the first time.

The Western industrialized nations reacted in complete
disorder to the embargo of 1973. Canada announced a set of
policies aimed at increasing self-sufficiency. And the United
States hurriedly initiated Project Independence aimed at making
America self-sufficient in energy. European countries with large
potential oil reserves decided *not* to maximize the flow of oil
from these reserves. Thus, while OPEC appeared to be acting in
unison, Western industrialized nations reacted individually—
each country's policy not necessarily maximizing the interests of
the group. The major group effort undertaken by these nations
was the formation, under American pressure, of the International Energy Agency. Operated jointly by eighteen major Western consumers (excluding France), it aims at bilateral negotiations with OPEC, and the establishment of plans for collective
action.

Just over three years have elapsed since the outbreak of the
"crisis". New energy policies in Canada and other Western industrialized nations can best be characterized as bankrupt. Brave
statements about the ease of a transition away from dependence
on OPEC through the generation of increased internal supplies of
oil, coal, and nuclear power have proven false. The supply trends
of the late 1960s and early 1970s appear unchanged—as, indeed, they must given the long lags involved in bringing new
supplies on stream. In this regard, Canadian policies have been
the best-articulated of those of any Western industrialized
country.

Despite the fact that some cracks have begun to appear in
OPEC, we must assume that OPEC—albeit an increasingly wes-
ternized OPEC—will continue to exist; and we must judge Western policies accordingly. Let us look at these trends in detail.

CHANGES IN WESTERN SUPPLY AND DEMAND

PRODUCTION

Recent trends in crude oil production show sharply divergent
patterns across the world. Because of direct government policy
aimed at reducing exports of oil, domestic Canadian oil produc-

tion has fallen from a peak daily rate of 1.8 MMBD in 1973, to 1.2 MMBD through the first half of 1976. The United States has seen domestic oil production steadily decrease: from a peak daily production rate of 9.4 MMBD in 1970 to 8.1 MMBD for the first six months of 1976.

Production in OPEC member countries differs sharply. Saudi Arabian production averaged 7.6 MMBD in 1973, 8.4 MMBD in 1974, 7 MMBD in 1975, and 8.3 MMBD in the first seven months of 1976. Saudi Arabia appears to have the capacity to move to a production level of 12 MMBD within a short space of time. Over-all OPEC exports fell from 30.8 MMBD in 1973 to 27.5 MMBD in 1975, and approximately 29.5 MMBD through the first six months of 1976.

CONSUMPTION

While most other countries experienced significant cutbacks in oil consumption since 1973, total Canadian oil demand fell only 1.1 per cent through 1975. Through the first nine months of 1976, consumption was slightly up over its 1975 level. By contrast, demand fell by 6 per cent between 1973 and 1975 in the United States. In western Europe, total oil demand fell over 11 per cent since 1973. This decrease has been most pronounced in France, the United Kingdom, and West Germany. Demand in Japan, the other major Western oil consumer, has also fallen by some 11 per cent.

In short, following the large increases in world oil prices since 1973, demand in the Western industrialized nations has fallen. This has been least true, however, in North America and hardly at all in Canada.

ADDITIONS TO RESERVES

In 1975, 8.3 per cent of proven world oil reserves (outside the U.S.S.R., eastern Europe, and China) were in North America and 65 per cent were in the Middle East. The "life index" of North American oil—including Alaska's—is now eleven years.

Additions to U.S. proven reserves of oil (aside from the proving out of the North Slope in 1970) from all sources—revisions, extensions, new field discoveries, and new reservoir discoveries—have fallen short of production in each year since 1968. A similar story may be told for natural gas: except for 1970, additions to proven reserves have not met half the level of production in the last seven years.

Similarly, since 1970 annual changes in proven oil reserves

in Canada have fallen behind annual production. Marketable natural gas reserves (excluding all North Slope and Arctic Island discoveries) declined for two years, in 1972 and 1973, but are now slowly climbing once again.

IMPORTS

In Canada, imports fell by 3.3 per cent through 1975, and fell another 11 per cent in 1976 (to a level of 733 MBD). By 1973, imports into the United States had nearly doubled (to 6.3 MMBD) from their 1970 level. Given the much-vaunted talk of U.S. oil independence, one would have expected imports to be down sharply by 1976—as they are in Europe. Between 1973 and 1975, however, U.S. oil imports fell by only 3 per cent. In the first six months of 1976, U.S. oil imports were *up* 1 MMBD over the similar period in 1975, to 40 per cent of domestic consumption. Given decreases in Canadian shipments to the United States, it is now far *more* dependent on OPEC oil than it was three years ago.

POLICIES

The United States

U.S. energy policy has not developed a significant theme, despite the rhetoric emanating from Washington. In 1973, four major goals were announced: (a) higher finding rates for oil and natural gas combined with (b) rapid development of coal and nuclear capacity in the interim period (5 to 10 years) to reduce dependence on overseas oil. Massive expenditures (c) on non-conventional sources—nuclear fusion, solar, oil shale—would mean that by the end of the century the United States would be (d) independent of all imported oil.

Announcing a goal of less dependence on oil is vacuous without concrete policies aimed at meeting that goal. What *policies* has the U.S. government actually instituted? First, the price at which domestically produced oil and gas could be sold in markets has been held below world levels. While the average price of imported oil landed on the American east coast is now $12.75, the average price of domestic oil is now just over $8.00.*

---

* The elaborate set of U.S. oil price controls distinguish three types of oil —old, new, and stripper. Stripper wells (those producing under twelve barrels per day) can sell oil at the *prevailing* world market price. Old oil (from wells commenced before December 31, 1972) currently sells at approximately $5.15.

The price at which natural gas can be sold in U.S. markets has been controlled since the 1950s. Economists have argued since the mid 1960s that this domestic price ceiling has led to a regulation-induced shortage, estimated to be as high as three trillion cubic feet in 1975.[1] Domestic price ceilings have a two-pronged effect on the oil and gas sector. First, higher prices add incentives to increase reserves through secondary and tertiary recovery as well as stimulating the discovery process to add new reserves. Price ceilings then cut off supply. Moreover, excess demand is encouraged. Consumers do not react to the proper price signals since they are not forced to pay the world price or opportunity cost of these resources. Consequently, any government committed to a goal of less dependence on foreign oil cannot expect that goal to be met when domestic prices are held below the world price. Increasing the price of oil, as the U.S. government is committed to do (up to $13.50 by 1979), will limit oil imports through both increased domestic supply and decreased domestic demand.

Another cornerstone of U.S. policy has been the enhanced role of both nuclear power and coal. It is, however, interesting and frightening to realize that the *future* use of both these energy sources is *now* predicted to be lower than we had forecast in 1972—before the so-called energy crisis. Nuclear power today represents 2.3 per cent of U.S. primary energy consumption. Because of increasing public scrutiny of the real social costs of nuclear power (including environmental and safety aspects), that percentage will be likely to increase to only 13 per cent by 1985. Three new major environmental laws imposed severe costs on coal-using thermal plants in the United States. Moreover, the coal supply faces real bottlenecks in the short term. As a result, the expansion of the coal sector did not meet the rosy forecasts of early 1974.

Other U.S. policies have involved some plans which tend to increase supply. Some policies, such as the change in depletion allowance and the price rollbacks, decrease supply as well. In sum, there is then no clear direction to U.S. policy.

The average price of *all* domestically priced oil is $8.16. After accounting for the production from old and stripper wells, the price of new oil is arrived at as a residual—currently $11.28. (It is interesting to note that the FEA recently underestimated the volume of old and stripper oil shipped and consequently had to roll back the price of "new" oil.) Oil from enhanced recovery can likely sell at market-determined levels.

The IEA

As I said earlier, the U.S.-sponsored International Energy Agency began in 1974 as a potential "front" to negotiate with OPEC. Stated aims included the development of an emergency oil-sharing plan in the event of another embargo. Under such a plan, rather than rely on the oil companies to dole out reduced oil supplies, the member countries would work out their own scheme.

Member countries have, as yet, to fulfil IEA obligations. In fact, Canadian and American price ceilings run counter to IEA conservation programs. The most striking example of dissension within the IEA rests on the notion of the minimum-safeguard price system enthusiastically put forward by the United States: all member countries would agree to a common floor price, guaranteed to safeguard risky investments in conventional energy sources, were the OPEC cartel to break. The United States had everything to gain and nothing to lose by this policy: if all countries—including those with no domestic reserves of high-cost energy—would agree to a floor price, the risks to U.S. energy developments would be minimized. The United States would no longer dream of having consumers in, say, France or Germany, paying $6.00 for OPEC oil while U.S. energy users paid $10.00 for Alaskan oil.

Needless to say, other countries objected to the concept and level of the floor price. All in all, the IEA has not been a notable success—but then few of us thought it would be.

Canada

Canadian policies have, as I suggested earlier, been more definitive than those in the United States. Our goal of increased self-sufficiency *could* be met, since a number of policy tools to accomplish this were available. By reducing oil exports to the United States, for instance, Canadians assured themselves of more domestic oil for domestic consumption—at least in the short term. The marked division between users of domestic oil and imported oil which characterized National Oil Policy since 1961 was broken: not only were tankers immediately dispatched to Québec and the Atlantic provinces in 1973, but the Interprovincial Pipeline was subsequently extended to Montreal. As a result, all domestic consumers partake in the cheap, price-averaged domestic crude.

At the same time that these and other policies (government promotion of northern energy development and tar sands plants) aimed at increasing self-sufficiency were put into effect, a set of policies which tended to *increase* dependence on foreign oil were undertaken. Two stand out: domestic price ceilings combined with an export tax on oil, and changes in tax and royalty provisions.

Like the U.S. government, the Canadian government decided that retail energy prices should not adjust instantaneously to world levels. As a result, the domestic price of crude has moved, in several stages, to its present level of $9.75 (compared to the cost of imported crude at or near Montreal — before the 1977 price changes — of $13.30). However, the disincentives provided by the Canadian domestic price ceiling are even greater than in the United States. At least the Americans have had the wisdom to allow newly discovered oil — or that from secondary and tertiary recovery — to sell at world price levels. Fields of marginal value at $11.28 could, as a result, be developed in the United States while these same marginal fields in Canada go undeveloped even though the oil could be sold for $11.28, not $9.75.

There is no doubt in my mind that our tax policies in the resource sector have long been misguided, and still are. The oil depletion allowance and current expensing provisions rest on no firm economic or social justification. There is no compelling evidence for taxing the resource sector at lower rates than other sectors. However, the wrangling between federal and provincial tax jurisdictions following 1973 price increases was too much for even an academic to bear!

In my view, federal actions aimed at ensuring at least a 19 per cent share of revenue from resources for all Canadians was eminently justifiable. After all, it was federal tax exemptions which helped build the sector.

At this point, when the federal-provincial war was most bitter, the taxation schemes acted as major disincentives to investment. While it is too early to see if the "correct" balance between royalties and taxes and industry revenue generation has been met, it is clear that these policies had a negative impact on supply.

In any event, one fact about the Canadian energy sector is incontestable: the prices consumers pay bear little relation to the long-run costs of the various energy sources they use. The price of oil is set by discussions among warring political jurisdictions. In another context I have called the annual deliberations about the price of oil in Canada the "*Real* Calgary Stampede".

The price of natural gas at the city gate is held at 85 per cent of the equivalent price of oil. Why not 80 per cent or 90 per cent? No one knows. We are presently discussing when and at what cost we will need the gas available in the Mackenzie Delta. The potential availability of western coal for eastern-Canadian markets is limited both by Alberta government policy and long-distance shipping costs. Electricity developments hinge on public acceptability of nuclear capacity, the environmental problems of coal-burning plants, and the approval of high-voltage transmission lines. It is difficult to know the true costs of electric power since much of the cost of developing the CANDU nuclear reactor is not included in the capital charges.

Political factors clearly exacerbate economic solutions to energy problems. Simply stated, the West has the resources (outside of uranium) and clearly wants its eastern brethren to pay world prices for these resources for several reasons. First, because when these reserves run out, westerners will have no resources left (except cash and investments of course). Second, because of a strong feeling that the West has subsidized the East for many years, westerners are quick to point out that all manufacturing is in the East and that tariffs have only taxed westerners to give jobs to Ontario. Now the shoe is on the other foot: Ontario is taxed to pay resource owners in Alberta, Saskatchewan, and B.C. The issue is not this simple of course: large publicly held resource companies are owned by residents of Ontario. Royalties captured by western-Canadian governments also help Ontario in so far as they are used to purchase Ontario-made equipment.

It is clear, however, that the distribution of wealth and political power will change markedly within the next two decades. But Alberta will "easternize". As the Alberta economy shifts to manufacturing, they too will want tariffs and the other trappings of inefficient domestic production. The East will then transfer wealth to the West, but political pressures will continue to maintain policies which will keep Ontario wealthy.

What about Québec? How does the new generation of energy prices affect that area? First, up to 1973, Quebeckers paid *less* for imported oil than residents of Ontario paid for domestic Albertan oil. There was talk of super ports in the St. Lawrence and large refinery expansions. Eastern Canada now has a vast over-supply of refining capacity since the sharp increase in oil prices curtailed demand growth (at least below the expectations of the early 1970s). Moreover, oil consumers in

Québec are now subsidized by some $1 billion per year—the actual price paid for imported oil is reduced by subsidies to the Canadian-controlled price and 250,000 barrels per day of western-Canadian oil are shipped to Montreal. An independent Québec would be forced to bear the additional costs of the real price of imported oil—as Canada increases its domestic price of oil to world levels this subsidy will diminish. An independent Québec would have large hydro capability and some uranium supplies, but likely little coal, and no oil or natural gas. As a result, an independent Québec would have energy problems similar to those of a central-European country.

SUMMARY: NORTH AMERICA IS EUROPEAN?

In the first part of this article, I described the asymmetric behaviour in consumption and reserve additions in various Western industrialized countries in response to higher oil prices. But, given the policies adopted by these countries, this is the only response that could be expected: western-European nations quickly moved to the new higher prices as well as expanding somewhat the role of nuclear power and coal. The country—Canada—which kept its domestic oil price the lowest in the Western world experienced the greatest increase in demand. The next lowest constrained price of oil was in the United States—and the second highest increase in demand followed: governments cannot escape the law of demand. Keep the price low, and conservation is idle talk. On the supply side, both economic logic and geological luck have had an effect on hydrocarbon reserves in Western economies. In economic terms, a combination of domestic price ceilings and higher taxes and royalties must act as a disincentive to additions to supply. A geological uncertainty argument would suggest that we are not fully aware of what remaining hydrocarbons lie in conventional formations in North America. On balance, I cannot say what proportion of the fall in our reserves in North America is attributable to economics or to geology. But in any event, economics is the handmaiden of geology: low prices almost guarantee that we will run out.

What if our reserves have already peaked? What if North America, rather than a have-oil area, becomes dependent on imports for the bulk of its oil consumption—as Europe once was?

I submit that we cannot stay with policies designed for

oil-rich exporting nations. We must come to terms with our limited geological luck and adopt European-type policies. This is especially true for the United States. A number of authors have blamed the oil crisis of 1973 on a combination of U.S. actions which led to an increased demand for oil imports and on divergent State-Department policies. In 1976, we saw an upsurge in U.S. oil imports combined with an inconsistent set of policies designed by a lame-duck administration.

The recent chink in OPEC armour exists for two reasons. First, there is general concern in Saudi Arabia that further large price increases will harm Western economies and therefore Saudi wealth. Second, there is no doubt that as the rise in world demand for OPEC oil strengthened the cartel, so must continued slackness in demand harm the cartel. So, in 1972 and 1973, a number of countries adopted realistic, responsible policies.

The United States is not among them. Canada is on the border—for are we an exporter or are we an importer? The economics of our energy policies in the next few years will help decide.

NOTE

1 P.W. MacAvoy and R. S. Pindyck, *The Economics of the Natural Gas Shortage (1960—1980)* (Amsterdam, 1975).

CHAPTER SIXTEEN

RESOURCE MANAGEMENT: A PUBLIC RESPONSIBILITY

CANADIANS HAVE BEEN HAD—and had badly—by their foreign-dominated petroleum industry. Just five short years ago, the oil industry in Canada was lulling Canadians to sleep by telling them that they had enough oil and gas for centuries to come.

Typical was this statement in Imperial Oil's Annual Report to its shareholders (mainly Exxon) in 1972:

> . . . the export of Canada's energy resources is being questioned; in effect we are being urged to "bank" our petroleum resources. Canada is not in any way deficient in energy resources. Our present energy reserves, using present technology, are sufficient for our requirements for several hundred years.

Today we face a $2 billion annual deficit and it's growing year by year. Today, the same oil companies which offered such soothing assurances in 1972 (in order to justify and maintain energy export levels) shrug off the "loss" of those mythical 1972 reserves. Now they intend to blackmail Canadians for more money as their price for oil exploration.

How could this happen? How is it possible that Canadians and their governments, federal and provincial, could be so ill-informed about such a vital resource?

The answer, of course, is that many years ago, our gov-

* Prepared for this volume.

JOHN F. KINZEL

ernments abandoned the management of petroleum resources to the private sector. Those responsible for energy policy were captive to the industry. Only the industry knew in 1972 what our real reserves were—and only the industry knows today. That's a poor foundation on which to build a rational plan for the use and development of these resources.

It is not my purpose to examine our energy policies here. Rather, I cite the oil dilemma in order to dramatize the importance of non-renewable resources to Canada's future, and to underline the need to manage them in the public interest. The Club of Rome may have overstated the case: the oil crisis may be more contrived than real in the short run. But there can be little doubt that the developed world is overspending its resource bank and that we had better take steps to husband what we have left.

If we look to the Canadian experience, there can also be little doubt, given our previous history, that the private sector cannot be relied on to manage our resources in the public interest. This is a job for government. The question then remains as to which level of government should manage our resources.

As things stand at present, the primary responsibility in this area clearly falls on provincial governments. There is no ambiguity in the BNA Act about which level of government has jurisdiction over the land and what lies beneath the surface: the management of resources and the returns to the public treasury in direct taxes for their extraction are the business of provincial governments.

But, just as clearly, there is a *national* interest to be served in the case of energy resources. It is less clear in the case, say, of potash. Nevertheless, there must be some means there to protect legitimate national concerns as well.

Some of these means are at hand in the BNA Act itself. The federal government is supreme in matters of interprovincial or international trade and commerce. The federal government also enjoys wider taxation powers than do the provinces and has overriding authority to maintain "peace, order and good government".

The problem has been that, as the provinces have asserted their rights of management, they have found themselves drawn into an adversary position with Ottawa. The federal government's reaction, in most cases, has been to assert its centralist power in competition with the provinces. This has heightened regional dissatisfaction, created damaging uncertainty, and diverted both levels of government from what should be their major objective in dealing with the resource industries—to wrest control of resources from largely foreign-owned resource companies and to place it firmly in the hands of governments responsible to the people. Let us look at two examples.

When the international price of oil shot up in 1973–74, both Alberta and Saskatchewan moved to increase oil royalties substantially. As owners of the resource, they considered it their right and duty to capture a large share of this windfall. Each, in its own way, changed its royalty structure.

The federal government reacted abruptly by changing the rules. The Turner Budget of 1974 decreed that royalties paid to a province could no longer be claimed by a resource company as an expense for corporate tax purposes. This meant that resource companies were required to pay federal tax on a royalty already paid to a province. This was not true, however, of royalties paid to a private company or a foreign government. Royalties paid to the CPR were still deductible; as were royalties paid to the State of Montana. Saskatchewan, Alberta, and British Columbia were treated differently.

This was a direct challenge to the right of the provinces to control and receive the benefits from the resources they own. Its net effect was to force the provinces to back down and reduce royalties.

In this case, disagreements between the western provinces and Ottawa did not centre on issues of resource management, but on the division of tax room. In management terms, they were counterproductive.

Similar dynamics were at play in the case of Saskatchewan and its battle with the potash industry. Prior to 1975, the potash industry was atypical of resource industries in Canada generally in only one respect: it was and is concentrated in a single province. All the companies operating in Saskatchewan were branches or subsidiaries of large corporations. Not one head office was located in Saskatchewan. Eighty-five per cent of the industry's productive capacity was owned outside Canada, predominantly in the United States. Some of the parents were very large indeed: International Minerals, Esmark, PPG Industries, Ideal Basic Industries, to name a few.

Despite all this corporate expertise, the Saskatchewan industry in the late 1960s found itself in serious trouble. Overly rapid expansion and a soft fertilizer market had pushed potash prices below the cost of production, and some mines were in danger of closing. The Liberal government of the late Ross Thatcher stepped in to regulate production and set a minimum price through "prorationing". All of the companies went along; except one which had a captive market and wanted to maintain full production. In 1972, after the NDP came to power, this company, Central Canada Potash, filed a suit challenging the constitutionality of prorationing.

At this point, the federal government took a step which, to my knowledge, was unprecedented in Canadian history: the Attorney General of Canada joined Central Canada as a co-plaintiff attacking provincial legislation. Here it was not acting as an intervener to argue a constitutional point—that is common enough—but as a co-plaintiff entitled to call witnesses and submit evidence to help Central Canada sustain damage claims against Saskatchewan. The federal government (together with a private resource company) argued in this fashion that authority to regulate production of a provincially owned resource did not rest with the government of Saskatchewan.

Again, it is difficult to see how this action contributed to the proper management of a resource in the public interest. In my opinion, the federal action was motivated by a desire to expand its centralist power at the expense of what have always been thought of as exclusively provincial rights.

These are only two of the most blatant examples of a series of aggressive actions by the federal government attacking provincial management of our resources. They contribute, in my view, to growing tensions in Confederation. Federalism is not enhanced when we find the federal government arrayed with resource companies against the provinces. What *are* enhanced and promoted are the narrow interests of the corporate mining world. If efforts by the provinces to manage their resources effectively are grounded on the shoals of constitutional jurisdiction, then all Canadians lose.

What we need, then, is a more creative federalist solution to the problem of resource management. This would recognize: (1) the primacy of provincial jurisdiction; (2) the reality of a legitimate national interest; and (3) the urgent need to exert effective public control over resource development and use.

This solution will not be found so long as the federal government adopts an adversary position towards provincial initiatives in resource management. Resource development *can* be an effective tool for regional economic development. Québec, in my view, is properly concerned that one of its important resources —asbestos—be processed in the province rather than elsewhere. Alberta and Saskatchewan are properly interested in channelling short-term oil revenues into investments which will diversify their economies over the long term. Not only should the *federal* government not oppose these actions, but it should support *provincial* objectives in areas which touch on federal jurisdiction— for example, marketing and export. The provinces and the federal government can certainly come to terms within a revived spirit of co-operative federalism if they will concentrate not on narrow jurisdictional issues but rather on means of serving the public interest: (1) by repatriating, to the greatest extent possible, Canadian control over our non-renewable resources; (2) by ensuring an appropriate return (economic rent) to the people of the provinces as owners of their resources; (3) by conserving resources, not only for this generation, but for the generations to follow; and (4) by protecting the environment.

Traditionally, provincial governments have used taxation and regulation as tools for managing resources. And these will undoubtedly continue to be the most commonly used methods. There is, however, another tool which is particularly appropriate for dealing with the management of some resource sectors, given Canada's history of excessive foreign control: selective public ownership.

First, if you are concerned about effective management, ultimate control can be exercised through ownership of an enterprise. When a province is faced with concerted opposition to its management policies by an entire industry, public ownership may be its only option. This is well understood in the Third World, but not as widely in North America. Second, the conversion of foreign ownership to domestic public ownership is the most direct way—perhaps the only effective way—to repatriate the key resource sectors in Canada. Third, public ownership in an industry provides governments with key knowledge about it which may not be available in any other way. The federal government, for example, owns a major uranium mining and refining company—Eldorado Nuclear. As a result, it has access to an intimate operating knowledge of the industry which would make it difficult for the private sector to pull the wool over its eyes. Had any government, federal or provincial, occupied a similar position in the oil industry, we would now be at least a decade closer to solving our energy problem in a rational way.

For these reasons, I suggest that selective public ownership *can* and *should* play a key role in provincial resource management. Provinces will doubtless differ in their interpretation of the "public interest" and in their selection of the management tools to be used. This may offend those to whom uniformity and certainty are virtues. To me they are not! Canadian history is replete with examples of provincial innovation as a catalyst for social and economic change. Saskatchewan gave us hospitalization and medicare, and Ontario the ultimate model for developing electric power in Ontario Hydro. In securing Canadian resources for tomorrow, let us learn from the provinces which dare to apply new tools—like selective public ownership.

PART FOUR

THREATS TO UNITY: THE SOCIAL ISSUES

DURING PERIODS of grave social or political crisis, short-term trends and issues dominate public consciousness. This is the case in Canada today. To many Canadians, our present political dilemma arises from nothing more complicated than Québec's apparent unwillingness to remain in Confederation. It appears to them that if we can find some "solution" or answer to the Québec Question we can go about our business much as we did before. When they think of the problems of national unity, then, they assume that "winning the referendum" is our chief task, and that after this has been done, Canadian political life can return to its accustomed grey dullness.

This way of thinking is both naive and dangerous. It is simplistic because it is not clear whether the Québec electorate wants to remain in Confederation or not. The support for some radical form of separatism in Québec— according to most polls —is small but significant. Moreover, it appears to be growing among young voters. Taken together, the support for some radical form of separatism and the "political independence within a sovereignty association" formula officially endorsed by the Parti Québécois, while still representing a minority opinion, is substantial. Since a "yes" or "no" vote on such a referendum (or, more properly, plebiscite) could not be binding either on the federal Parliament or on Québec's National Assembly, it seems that a majority vote for either or both of these alternatives may not be necessary and is certainly not sufficient to determine the outcome of the current debate.

Our blinkered habit of focusing only on the separation issue is also dangerous, because it assumes that present political alignments in Québec are static. They are not. No one—no matter how wise he or she may be in the ways of Canadian politics—is able to forecast what support either of these separatist alternatives will be able to command in the face of continued high rates of unemployment in Québec, further devaluation of the Canadian dollar, increased conflict over Bill 101, and so on. We simply do not know: we are operating, after all, in a situation with only the barest of precedents.

Beyond this, we know that the current debate over the structure of Confederation did not simply appear full-blown one morning, but that it has been going on behind the scenes for some time—and that it is by no means confined to the province of Québec. Other parts of Canada—other regions, other provinces—are also dissatisfied with how Confederation is working and also want fundamental changes in its form and substance. Thus while the Québec Question may have been the catalyst for our present deliberations, it is not their cause. This lies deeper.

A number of long-term trends will play an increasingly important role in forcing a later, heightened version of the kind of confrontation that we are experiencing now. First, Canada has a history of trying to resolve basic social disagreements through the use of force or the threat of force. This has been manifest not only in an everyday or routine preoccupation with issues related to social control (such as capital punishment or the regulation of prisons) but also in a repeated use of paramilitary and military forces in situations which pose no grave threat to public order. As examples one can cite the Estevan strike and the October Crisis of 1970. Second, both the provinces and the federal government have committed themselves to funding large-scale and expensive social programs with little thought for their effectiveness in achieving stated goals or for their long-term impact on public spending. This has caused almost confiscatory levels of taxation in some provinces, and a proliferation of overt and covert forms of taxes in all but a few of them. Some reduction of the general level of taxation and a rationalization of existing programs is clearly needed. Third, there is unimpeachable evidence that our educational system is not succeeding either in the narrow task of providing trained manpower to fill our current and future needs, or in its broader mission of creating an educated and informed public equipped to cope with the challenges which it will face in the future. This is because both our educational goals and the structure of our educational system need an overhaul. Finally, Canadians have a tradition of ignoring the interaction between technology and their environment. We have too easily assumed that the dynamics governing these interactions are either beyond our control or unavoidable. Given the mounting evidence that much of our industrial technology is obsolete or about to become so, and that our natural landscape is deteriorating rapidly, we can no longer afford to make these assumptions.

This fourth section of the book contains six articles which seek to underscore the connection between these basic social issues and our current national crisis. Tepperman examines the roots of our fascination with law and order, and argues that we have failed to provide a flexible and equitable system of justice. Chang dissects one of our major publicly supported social-service systems—health care—and finds that we have allowed it to become overly technological and inaccessible. Logan and Moore and Harvey scrutinize our educational system, and point to ways in which it can be changed to fulfil its broad mission and perform its social tasks better. Hare and, finally, Logan discuss two major threats to co-operation between scientists on the one hand, and government planners and industry on the other. While these kinds of concerns are unlikely to have an immediate and decisive impact on the form of Confederation we choose, these authors show how any political solution we adopt will be vulnerable to the stresses they produce.

CHAPTER SEVENTEEN

THE LAW IN CANADA: JUSTICE FOR WHOM?

RECENTLY, A COLLEAGUE reproached me for condemning the Canadian system of justice.[1] She did not disagree with my conclusion—that in comparison to Americans, Canadians enjoy relatively few civil liberties and human rights—but she argued that this difference was trivial when both legal systems were compared to the Chinese system of justice.

In retrospect this criticism seems entirely justified. It served to remind me that, from time to time, we must rise above the routine details of social life and ask the really tendentious questions: Are the institutions of Canadian society meeting our ideals? If they are not, why not? Is there justice for all Canadians? If not, who gets justice and how is unequal access to it maintained?

Since I am a sociologist and not a philosopher, I will begin with some thoughts on what it appears possible for us to do in this area. I shall then proceed to consider why we have not improved our system of justice in ways which are both possible and desirable—even if they are not ideal.

If we look at legal systems comparatively, we remember that what we have is only one of many possible kinds. There are at least as many types of systems as people have purposes for law.

PURPOSES OF LAW

The first purpose that comes to mind—and the one common to all legal systems—is the provision of certainty in social affairs.

* Prepared for this volume.

LORNE TEPPERMAN

Culture also provides this certainty to some extent, but, without law and the sanctions which a legal system can provide, social expectations would inevitably be violated. At the very least, confusion and insecurity would result.

In this basic sense, then, law is a traffic policeman which ensures that we move about in agreed-upon ways. Without regard to the specific content of a given law, certainty of this kind is probably necessary to our mental health. If it were absent, few social enterprises could be extended either in space or time.[2]

The second general purpose of law is one which is clearest in pre-literate societies. A long time ago, social scientists dispelled the myths that these societies were (or are) homogeneous and free from conflict. While conflicts in these groups do not tend to centre on basic values, they often do arise over basic rights and the difficulties arising from disputes over ambiguous rules. Bloody feuds, vendettas, and wars between kinship groups and tribes are extremely common in such societies.[3] Here, then, a second basic role of law comes into play: to mediate or arbitrate disputes, to prevent bloodshed, and to find compromises where legitimate questions have been raised about rights.

Historically, a third purpose of law has been to transmit morality. Emile Durkheim[4] saw this as the central role of law in pre-literate societies, which embodied what he called "mechanical solidarity". In such societies, he argued, members were largely agreed on the rules of proper behaviour, so that rule breaking constituted a threat to the tribal way of life. Punishment offered the group an opportunity to reaffirm its commitment to these rules, strengthening social cohesion. In both religious ritual and legal ritual, then, these communities celebrated their own values. The medium—whether ritual prayer or ritual punishment—was the message.

Durkheim thought the fourth purpose of law, as healer, was more characteristic of societies enjoying "organic solidarity". Where social evolution and a complex division of labour had brought about moral diversity, it was no longer possible to expect a monolithic commitment to customary rules. Deviance came to be seen as a practical, rather than a moral problem in advanced societies of this kind. Thus, the law would become less retributive or punitive in character and more concerned with making restitution—with healing wounds. It would seek to help the victims of wrong-doing and, eventually, to re-integrate the wrong-doer back into the community.

This "modern" conception suggests that the law should not simply, or even primarily, express morality. Rather, it should help people in a rather immediate and practical way. As a result, particular laws and legal practices should be evaluated according to their consequences, not their intentions.

Two of these purposes are, at least in Durkheim's mind, opposed to each other—the purposes of transmitting morality and of healing wounds. Common logic demands that one cannot both stand on principle and accommodate everyone's rights and expectations in a dispute. Accommodation demands flexibility. This is incompatible with a single, unchallengeable morality.

Related to the notion that law ought to heal wounds and remove harm—"restitutive justice" in Durkheim's words—is the notion that law ought to engineer social change. It is almost universally accepted, almost as a matter of definition, that one function of government is to promote social change. That the legal system—the same system that encourages certainty, resolves conflicts, teaches morality, or heals wounds—should also attempt to make social policy is less commonly agreed upon. Yet the potential for such a role is implicit both in the common law and in the continental legal systems. In the first, it is understood that case law and precedent might bring about unforeseen changes in accepted practice. In the second, the interpretation of a formal constitution by the courts may likewise lead to a new understanding of old rules and, hence, new policy.

Using courts to make law and bring about changes is part of the American system of "checks and balances". In this usage, the courts act as a counterforce against the executive and the Congress—and also as an initiator of change. We clearly saw this happen in the 1950s and 1960s in areas like civil rights and civil liberties.

Despite the efforts of so-called "strict constructionists" to keep legal questions at the level of technical debate, the last ten years have seen an increasing use of the courts as a public forum —even a public stage. The most dramatic recent Canadian example was the Morgenthaler case in Montreal.

Compared to the "socialist democracies" such as China, however, Canada has not gone very far at all in the utilization of courts for public debates and lectures. (There are many reasons for this—and I shall take up this topic again later.) Some socialist societies try to make the legal process highly visible at the "grass-roots" level and this makes some sense. Who is better able to evaluate the claims of contending parties than a local community? Who is in a better position to clarify the *local* understandings of written rules? Who can better ensure that everyone is dealt with equitably and fairly by legal officials?

The opposing view—which would seek to limit public participation in the legal process—argues that experts are needed who can master the large body of historical precedent and apply it without fickleness, the emotionality of the mass public, or expediency. This difference of opinion cannot be easily resolved.

I have left one of the most important purposes of law until last. This is the use of law in the service of class interests or, put more simply, to protect the property interest of the rich. Marx and Engels, of course, saw this as the primary role of law—and the purpose for which the State was devised.

The law continues to administer property even in countries where a great deal of property is publicly owned. But by far the greatest development of property law is to be found in capitalist countries. Here, lawyers' time is largely spent in drawing up contracts or carrying out litigation related to property. Rich individuals as well as large corporations employ legal specialists to conduct their business; plan estates, trusts, and foundations to avoid paying taxes; and numerous other tasks.

As a result of this important function of law in capitalist countries, Richard Quinney has concluded that "definitions of crime are composed of behaviours that conflict with the class interests of the dominant economic class", and that "definitions of crime are applied by the class that has the power to shape the enforcement and administration of criminal law".[5] In this instance, law enforcement primarily involves protecting property rights and establishing a climate in which investments will be safe. As a rule, legislation which protects working people has been much slower in coming about than laws protecting investors and employers. Historically, police were much more often called out on the side of owners and managers than of workers.

WHERE DOES CANADA STAND?

Judged against these general criteria the Canadian system of justice is unimpressive. As the Law Reform Commission recently pointed out, there is too much law and too much discretionary enforcement (and non-enforcement) of the law in Canada:

> There is too much law, too many offences and too many cases—
> they threaten the whole criminal justice system with collapse. No
> one can possibly know all these sections and offences. Yet, since
> ignorance of the law is no excuse, the citizen can never be sure he
> is not breaking the law.[6]

Surely this proliferation of rules produces uncertainty, not
certainty. Moreover, given this situation, policemen enjoy too
much discretion in deciding whom they can arrest, and on what
grounds:

> A peace officer may arrest without warrant (a) a person who has
> committed an indictable offense or who, on reasonable and prob-
> able grounds, he believes has committed an offense or is about to
> commit an indictable offense.[7]

The breadth of this definition makes virtually any arrest justifiable: it effectively prevents citizen recourse on the basis of false
arrest. Furthermore, citizens have been unable to establish civi-
lian review boards to oversee policemen to compensate for this
wide discretion.

Beyond this, Canadian judges enjoy wide discretion in the
kinds of penalties they can apply for proven breaches of the law.
The original purpose behind giving judges such discretion under
the law was to ensure flexibility in the service of equity, compas-
sion, appropriateness, and (in some cases) to set an example for
others contemplating crimes. In practice, discretion is also exercised in reprehensible ways: it typically works to the advantage
of well-turned-out upper- and middle-class people, and against
others—especially during periods of social unrest. John
Hogarth's recent work[8] on the sentencing practices of magis-
trates in Ontario makes clear that discretion allows too wide a
play for human foibles and frailties.

But nowhere is discretion exercised more often or more
unpredictably than by Crown prosecutors. It is the Crown prosecutor who prepares a case brought by the police for presenta-
tion before a judge. He or she negotiates guilty pleas in a process
known as "plea bargaining". In this process the Crown prosecutor persuades a defendant to enter a guilty plea through strategic
discussion and compromise with the defence attorney.[9] This
mechanism is unconstrained by law, invisible to the judge, the

media, and the public, and ineligible for an appeal (since it is unofficial and undocumented). It results in "automatic convictions". Like other kinds of discretion, more often than not this works against the unprotected, the uneducated, the poor, and the naive. Canadian law offers little in the way of civil liberties which might substitute for other forms of protection. Yet Pierre Berton points out that Canadians have been so thoroughly acculturated by American television that they do not know they lack many rights Americans enjoy. He notes a few of the more important differences:

- The police are under no obligation to inform you that you have the right to remain silent and that you have the right to counsel.
- If you insist on seeing a lawyer and the police refuse to allow you to see one, any voluntary statement you make to them without a lawyer present, is still admissible in court.
- Evidence, even if gathered illegally, can still be admissible in a Canadian court of law . . . .

There's no doubt at all that the American mass media have again convinced large numbers of Canadians that there's very little difference between the two countries. In this case, as in others, the confusion has worked to our personal detriment.[10]

Thus the Canadian system is both unpredictable in practice and biased. It offers few protections against official abuses of power such as those by the RCMP recently uncovered. The system is also antiquated, having gone largely unchanged in this century. It has often been very punitive—as we can see from continuing high rates of imprisonment. John Hogarth notes that:

There are many factors which may explain the relatively high rate of imprisonment. First of all, the law itself is rather punitive. The Canadian Criminal Code was drafted in the 19th century when deterrence and retribution were the predominant goals of the criminal justice system. Because of the legislative inactivity since that time the present criminal law and sentencing practice continue to reflect these themes. Sentencing laws in Canada are characterized by high maximum penalties . . . restrictions on the use of probation, no provision for conditional or unconditional discharge, and a failure to provide fines as a specific punishment for certain less serious offences. The absence of alternative methods for dealing with social problems such as alcoholism and drug addiction, except through the criminal justice system, tends to swell the prison population. Lack of community resources, particularly probation services in many provinces, forces the courts to use institutional sentences more often than they would desire. It may also be that Canadians, compared to Scandinavians and others, are rather more intolerant of social deviance, and this may be reflected in the policies and practices of the courts in dealing with criminal offenders.[11]

CHARACTERISTICS OF THE CANADIAN SYSTEM

PAROCHIALISM

Durkheim would attribute the historical tendency towards punishment to Canada's traditionalism, social homogeneity and, consequently, parochialism. David Chandler's analysis of the recent vote on capital punishment confirms this.

MPs from culturally and socially homogeneous ridings were found to be more likely than others to vote in favour of retaining capital punishment. In such communities one finds religious and political conservatism and an "expressive orientation to law": a view of law as a declaration of communal principles rather than a means of engineering social control. It was precisely because the retentionists ignored the efficacy of capital punishment in preventing crime, and the abolitionists cared most about its efficacy, that the debate on this question was so long and confusing. The final decision of Parliament to abolish capital punishment was very close: 130 votes in favour of abolition and 124 opposed. The closeness of this victory suggests we have not heard the last of this debate.[12]

Canadian courts, in general, have not only failed to take a leading role in change, they appear to have avoided such a role on principle. Peter Russell has noted the widely held belief that Canadian courts do not legislate as American courts do, and that "in essence, courts have no power".[13] This lack of initiative has resulted from some naiveté, he argues, although this same naiveté may have allowed the highest courts to follow a truly non-political, unifying course in Canadian history. "The inertial role of the Canadian judiciary differs from the American system where courts have lately been used as a platform for debating major ethical and political issues. In an analysis of the trials of Louis Riel, the leaders of the Winnipeg General Strike, and the Quebec separatists, among others, McNaught observes that the courts have 'resisted any effort to make them the agents of social change. . . . Judicial insistence on the legitimacy of established authority . . . has often, of course, worked to the advantage of social-economic elites.'"[14]

INSUFFICIENT PUBLIC SPIRIT

Indeed, the Canadian judiciary, both federal and provincial, has become increasingly professional in composition and decreasingly public spirited.[15] Fewer political hacks are being given positions on the bench today than previously and that is gratifying, to be sure. But one would wish that more civic-minded lawyers would bring their special skills, their political savvy, and their moral concern to debates over social policy.

Recently, both Osgoode Hall and the University of Toronto Law School have come to define their roles more broadly: they have attempted to link legal training to research in other disciplines such as the social sciences and to associate legal practices with community needs.

These developments have been advanced particularly by Martin Friedland, Dean of the University of Toronto Law School, whose research concluded, in general terms, that the public does not often receive accurate information or sound advice—let alone prompt, sympathetic guidance—when it seeks free legal assistance. Legal forms and language, he also discovered, are almost totally incomprehensible to the average citizen. These must be simplified he argues, if law is to become a matter for public debate and consideration.

HOW DO WE COMPARE WITH OTHER SYSTEMS?

If we had to render judgment, then, on the over-all contribution of the Canadian law to public well-being, it would be quite mixed. The Canadian legal system does ensure a fair degree of safety against personal hurt and property loss, but little guarantee against the depredations of the marketplace. There is, for example, little consumer protection, environmental protection, protection against organized crime, or against many common kinds of injury (e.g., discrimination on grounds of age, sex, or race). In this respect Canada is not very different from other capitalist countries.

Our system also, however, does not curtail massive legal

and governmental bureaucracies' powers to arrest, try, convict, and punish citizens for any number of petty wrongs. Civil liberties and human rights are poorly ensured and there is little public or expert debate on how this ought to be changed. Indeed the public is kept pretty much away from inspecting or affecting the law, and public opinion is rarely sought. There is little communication, as well, between the legal profession and legislators. Lawyers rarely, if ever, seem to consider the effects of what they do upon social policy and the public good.

One way to compare our system with others is to classify systems according to (a) who makes decisions and (b) how much discretion they have in doing this.

As Figure 17:1 (at the end of this essay) shows, at the extreme where the community exercises absolute control over legal decisions—and rarely deviates from the customary rule—we have what might be called "tribal repression". The (Chinese) "participatory system" appears to make such a system more flexible, while maintaining a high level of communal participation. "Inquisitional justice" combines the inflexibility of tribal justice with a kind of elite professionalism. Finally, "Solomonic paternalism" allows a small body of real or self-conceived expert decision makers to render well-intentioned and often unpredictable judgments.

I submit that the Canadian system is most like what we have called "Solomonic paternalism". This is certainly preferable to "inquisitional justice"—after all, for all its predictability, who would speak on behalf of the Spanish Inquisition? Moreover, the paternalistic system is more appropriate to a modern, changing society than tribal justice; it is more flexible. But important issues about our system must be debated. Who should provide justice? And for whom should it be provided? What do we want our legal system to accomplish? And how likely is it that important changes will come about?

IS THE PAST OUR FUTURE?

Predicting the future is always fraught with difficulty. Modern life is complex, and what is hard to understand today is even harder to project into the future. In the past, even the most sophisticated social-science methods have often proved inadequate to predict the future because of major socio-economic shifts going on. As a result, the prediction of social change is no better, and probably often much worse, than attempts to predict the weather.

But we do try to predict the weather, and we are often faced with no alternative but to try to do the same for social events as well. In these terms—and recognizing inherent limitations—what is the future of the Canadian justice system likely to be? To answer this question requires that we understand what kind of modern, changing society Canada is in comparison with its neighbours.

Comparisons between Canada and the United States suggest many differences, but a few are especially germane. First, as John Porter[16] has said, Canada is a "vertical mosaic" of ethnic groups. This means that Canada consists of a large number of local or regional enclaves of unassimilated ethnic groups and that our ethnic "mosaic" has a vertical or "class" dimension. According to Porter, each particular ethnic group holds a specific status in Canadian society from which it is largely unable to escape because of limited educational opportunities. Thus, not only do particular groups come to Canada to perform particular jobs or tasks, but they largely retain their "entrance statuses" later on.

Another characteristic of Canada is its economic dependence on the United States. Direct American investment in Canada is large enough to justify the belief that the Canadian economy is "owned" by foreigners. This, in turn, results in a lack of political and cultural as well as economic autonomy. Trade, travel, communication, and immigration across the Canada –U.S. border are also extremely common, making Canadian separateness, like sovereignty, little more than a fiction. This fiction may not be maintained in the future.

In this sense, Canada is a "peripheral" nation whose disappearance from the world stage would scarcely cause a ripple. By contrast, the United States is the world's wealthiest and most powerful nation. As Chirot[17] has shown, Canada's dependence is, in large part, the reason the vertical mosaic described above came into being: peripheral nations often consist of regions with unequal development and hierarchically arranged culture groups. There are few incentives, in peripheral nations, for national unification and cultural assimilation, and many incentives for direct exchange between particular regions (or groups) and "core" societies—in this case the United States.

The third feature of Canadian society which distinguishes it from the United States is its relative conservatism, its traditionalism, and its enthusiasm for elites. This, too, is derived from and fed by its peripheral status—although it is rooted in the characteristics of our founding cultures and in the dominant orientations of our immigrants since the Loyalists.[18]

A fourth characteristic is the special history of class structure in this country. Although Canadian cities and urban working classes developed early, a substantial middle class arose relatively later than it did in other countries[19] because of our financial dependence on Britain and, later, the United States. As a result, it was *not* an indigenous but a *foreign* bourgeoisie which financed and directed industrialization in Canada. Besides the lack of local capital, the restriction of higher education to the favoured few restricted the growth of a middle class until quite recently.

THE SOCIAL ROOTS OF LEGAL PRACTICES

Each of these features helps to explain the historic development and perpetuation of "Solomonic paternalism" in Canada. The preference for professional elites as decision makers over elected elites or community participation can be directly traced to the English legal system which Canada adopted after Confederation. However, our continuing failure to limit the power of these elites —to restrict their authority or to organize their recruitment and socialization more democratically—must be traced back to the Canadian "vertical mosaic". In large part because of the regional, linguistic, and ethnic fragmentation of Canadian society, little consciousness of class position and class interest has ever developed here. Most Canadians are slow to interpret the law and the way it operates in terms of class interest, and (except for the rich) they are slow to demand legal changes in the service of their own class interests. By contrast, Canadian elites manage to hang on to their own positions, as recent work such as Clement's *Canadian Corporate Elite*[20] shows.

This public willingness to leave so much discretion to legal elites is partly explained by the trust Canadians have customarily reposed in elite judgment. But it also reflects a lack of education and information about the law on the part of Canadians; a widespread lack of self-confidence and socio-political efficacy;

and an almost total ignorance about the legal system. Canada's peripheral position in the world and an accompanying colonial mentality have fed an inclination to await innovation from outside, rather than promote it from within. Canadians are rather passive: things happen to them, and they try to survive, as Margaret Atwood has suggested. Canadian history documents few successful exploits on a world scale—whether political, economic, technological, or humanitarian. And such memorable history as Canadians have gets largely ignored by the schools and the mass media in favour of American and British history— or at least it was until recently. The result is a nation of people who know little about themselves and do not think of themselves as a nation of innovators—if they think of themselves as a nation at all.

Historically, it was neither the aristocracy nor the peasantry nor the working class which played a central role in modernizing the Western democracies: it was the bourgeoisie. Since the Canadian bourgeoisie was late in developing and remained small, it failed to establish that tradition of leadership in social planning characteristic of the middle classes in Scandinavia, England, and even the United States.

I submit that these historical and societal factors have, taken together, produced a social consciousness which reflects a love for authority, for the community, and for endurance, in opposition to the individual and his protest.[21] "Canada must be the only country in the world where a policeman is used as a national symbol," Atwood notes [22] in commenting upon the symbolic as well as practical importance the Mounties have had for us. "Canada has from the beginning defined itself as a place where revolutions are really rebellions against lawful authority —which . . . is seen as the social form of a divine order."[23] What may have allowed a garrison mentality to triumph over a living and therefore changing community, and allowed conservation to triumph over change, was the kind of development our national security demanded in the nineteenth century. This historical theme was the suppression of rebellion and the stifling of political protest. In reading Canadian literature, Atwood discovers:

> Canadian history defeats attempts to construct traditional society-saving or society-changing heroes. . . . All Canadian revolutions are failed revolutions, and our writer . . . will find himself almost inevitably writing a drama in which an individual defend-

ing the rights of a small group finds himself up against faceless
authority—the Establishment, embodied usually by the Mounties
—and is overcome by it.[24]

If these relatively enduring aspects of the Canadian national
character serve to explain Canada's present system of law, what
is the prospect for change in the future? One must conclude that
the prospects are moderate, for two reasons. First the fact that
many Canadians, increasingly educated and increasingly impatient with elitism, are beginning to question their legal system
and read books such as the present one, suggests some support
for change from within. And the forces of change within Canada
will undoubtedly be intensified by concerns over Québec separation and other forms of regional unrest. It may be too much to
expect that change of the legal system will come about through
demands for change from the working class; more probably they
will come in response to pressure by the more enlightened segments of the legal and political community itself.

As is often the case, these changes may occur as a partial
and perhaps misguided attempt not only to rectify old wrongs,
but to prevent a more severe disturbance of the existing system
that could result from a failure to make reforms. However, this
is, I think, less likely than a scenario in which Canada will follow
the lead of its dominant partners in culture, trade, and government—the United States, Britain, and perhaps even the Soviet
Union and China. Canada will remain a small fish, a follower
rather than a leader; and as new experiments in democratizing
justice are made elsewhere they will be tried, ever so hesitantly,
in Canada. Because they are humane and make sense, these reforms will be kept. Yet, in fairness, this scenario is also rather
unlikely: significant changes in American and British law have
failed to produce a counterpart in the Canadian system. Canada
is not, in this sense, a predictable follower of innovation.

In the foreseeable future we can expect the small-scale
changes already in progress to continue, with cumulative results
that are significant though not earth-shaking. Legal assistance to
the poor will become more widely available, reducing the disadvantage historically suffered by poor people before the law. Law
students will continue to broaden their perspectives—learning
more about their social responsibilities—as seems to be common among current students in other professions. The public
will continue to become educated, informed, and inquisitive,

putting ever more pressure on legal professionals and bureaucrats for accountability. The media will become ever more aggressive, more often exposing the ways the legal system works,
and in whose interest. These small changes may accumulate and
force implementation of some of the many valuable recommendations made in the past by the Law Reform Commission, the
LeDain Commission and other bodies that call for change that
does not come.

No major reduction of social, economic, or political inequality is foreseeable in Canadian society. And because the
delivery of justice is shaped by this inequality, we should not
expect justice to become much more equally available than it is
today. It will continue to serve those it presently serves—the rich
and powerful, the educated and well-connected. Rich and poor
alike will continue to enjoy the right to sleep under bridges; and
white-collar crimes will continue to go largely undiscovered and
unprosecuted. With luck, the RCMP will be brought under legislative control. Property will continue to get the protection it
seeks. No one will be able to murder with impunity, but crimes
against property will still be riskier for poor than for rich people.
And the certainty of unequal justice in an unequal society is a
soothing social regularity, if nothing else.

Figure 17:1 Types of Systems of Justice

| | | Who makes the decisions? | |
		legal professionals	the community
How much discretion (flexibility) is allowed in decision making?	much	Solomonic paternalism	participatory justice (Chinese)
	little	inquisitional justice	tribal repression

NOTES

1   Which I did in: Lorne Tepperman, *Crime Control: The Urge Towards Authority* (Toronto, 1977).

2   It was this aspect of the law that most interested Max Weber, who became famous for his studies of bureaucracy. Max Weber, *Law in Economy and Society*, Edward Shils (trans.) and Max Rheinstein (ed.) (New York, 1967).

3   Particularly good documentation of such a feud may be found in the Icelandic *Njal's Saga*.

4   Emile Durkheim, *The Division of Labor in Society*, George Simpson (trans.) (New York, 1964).

5   Richard Quinney, "The social reality of crime", in Richard Henshel and Robert A. Silverman (eds.), *Perception in Criminology* (Toronto, 1975), pp. 381, 382.

6   Report of the Law Reform Commission, 1976.

7   Criminal Code of Canada, Section 435.

8   John Hogarth, *Sentencing as a Human Process* (Toronto, 1971).

9   Brian A. Grosman, *The Prosecutor: An Enquiry into the Exercise of Discretion* (Toronto, 1969).

10   Pierre Berton, "It's the cops", *Quest*, Vol. 5, no. 2 (1976), pp. 8, 10.

11   Hogarth, *Sentencing as a Human Process*, pp. 40, 41.

12   See Tepperman, *Crime Control*, Chapter 3, for an extended discussion of this debate.

13   Peter Russell, "Judicial power in Canada's political culture", in Martin L. Friedland (ed.), *Courts and Trials* (Toronto, 1975), p. 76.

14   Kenneth McNaught, "Political trials and the Canadian political tradition", in ibid., p. 160.

15   David Smith and Lorne Tepperman, "Changes in the Canadian business and legal elites, 1870-1970", *Canadian Review of Sociology and Anthropology*, Vol. 11, no. 2 (1974), pp. 97-109.

16   John Porter, *The Vertical Mosaic: An Analysis of Social Class and Power in Canada* (Toronto, 1965).

17   Daniel Chirot, *Social Change in the Twentieth Century* (New York, 1977).

18   See S. M. Lipset, *The First New Nation* (New York, 1963), and *Revolution and Counterrevolution: Change and Persistence in Social Structures*, revised ed. (New York, 1970), for a discussion of this.

19   Leo A. Johnson, "The development of class in Canada in the twentieth century", in Michiel Horn and Ronald Sabourin (eds.), *Studies in Canadian Social History* (Toronto, 1974).

20   Wallace Clement, *The Canadian Corporate Elite: An Analysis of Economic Power* (Toronto, 1975).

21   For a further elaboration of these ideas, see Tepperman, *Crime Control*, Chapter 4.

22   Margaret Atwood, *Survival* (Toronto, 1972), p. 171.

23   Ibid.

24   Ibid., p. 170.

CHAPTER EIGHTEEN

PAYING FOR HEALTH

SINCE ITS INCEPTION in Saskatchewan in 1963, every province in Canada has followed suit in providing pre-paid medical insurance to its population. Since then, the health bill has grown almost fivefold (to $11 billion in 1975)[1] without, however, any significant improvement in mortality or life expectancy. In this article, I will briefly examine trends in the costs of health care and the benefits we are getting from our investment. I will examine the goals that we should be moving towards in health, and suggest ways of restructuring the system so we can reach them.

THE GROWTH OF THE HEALTH-CARE SYSTEM

In 1960, the health bill for Canada was $2.1 billion or $118 per capita. In 1975, the total cost had risen to $11.5 billion or $503 per capita.[2] During this period, the number of hospital beds rose from 5.51 to 6.8 per 1000. From 1961 to 1971, the cost per day for hospitalization increased from $23 to $61. Today, an acute bed costs almost $200 per day. Hospital care accounts for 46.4 per cent of our health budget; professional services for 24.2 per cent. Physicians get 18 per cent.[3] In all, some 88 per cent of the health budget is allotted to acute or chronic care; while less than 3.5 per cent is directed towards preventive medicine.[4]

Surgical rates and payments have increased dramatically as well. In Saskatchewan, which has been more successful than most provinces in controlling costs, major surgery increased from 68 per 1000 in 1971 to 73 per 1000 in 1976.[5] Services per patient increased by 22 per cent between 1971 to 1976, while

* Prepared for this volume.

ERNEST CHANG

the number of physicians also increased by 22 per cent in the same period.[6] Payments for office visits increased, over this time, from $8 million to $20 million, and average payments to physicians have increased at a faster rate than average income, going from $42,000 to $60,000.[7]

WHAT ARE WE GETTING?

Given this fivefold rise in health expenditures, and dramatic increases in servicing of patients, utilization of hospital beds, and surgical procedures, have we benefited?

Sadly, the impact appears to be minimal at best. Morbidity rates and life expectancies for almost all groups have changed little in the past fifteen years.[8] Heart disease, cancer, accidents, and suicide are still the major causes of death in Canada, and the heavy investment in technology and capital-intensive institutions (hospitals, testing laboratories, etc.) has had little effect on them. Instead, we are becoming increasingly aware of inequalities in the geographic and socio-economic distribution of health facilities which have led to gross inequities in access to a high quality of care.

We have also come to realize that many diseases originate in the stresses of urban living, while many others are attributable to environmental and industrial pollution. Low levels of nutrition, inadequate leisure, and poor personal habits are widespread, and these lead directly to many health problems. Yet our health system is poorly equipped to deal with them: few preventive programs based on the "medical model" of these lifestyle illnesses have been very successful. Few physicians or nurses are trained to counsel or advise on recreation or nutrition. Public health education—in schools and in the public forum—is inadequate. The present system has also been ineffective in dealing with health problems (such as drug addiction) which arise from unemployment, inadequate housing or education, improper socialization, and social frustration. And, in many instances, it is these "chronic" problems which have been absorbing the lion's share of our new health resources. In many parts of Canada, for instance, almost as many people are treated each year for psychological as for somatic illnesses.

IMPLICATIONS

We have a very expensive and technologically intensive health-care system which, at the same time, is insensitive to the specific problems of many people. It focuses on the detection and treatment of illness, rather than on the promotion of personal and social well-being. This is the *first* contradiction in our health system—one which leads inevitably to the creation of facilities in which large amounts of money are spent on extremely sophisticated equipment for dealing with rare diseases. Increasingly, such facilities have become irrelevant to the health of the public as a whole.

Most physicians today work under a method of payment which provides an incentive towards bringing the patient back for further treatment. This built-in bias is a second major contradiction in the health system: fee-for-service systems encourage over-servicing and over-payment.

A third contradiction in the system is the powerlessness of patients in the face of the authority of a medical establishment dominated by physicians. This leads to a passive obedience on the part of the patient which is often inadvisable given the inadequate training of many physicians in counselling and in the treatment of social and situational problems.

Underlying each of these problems is the major contradiction of health care in Canada today: that the attempt is being made to meet the social goal of providing equal and appropriate health service to all Canadians by using a private-enterprise system. Given this emphasis on private medicine at public expense, it is hardly surprising that structures encouraging a high degree of capital accumulation would evolve, e.g., specialty hospitals, complex laboratory and diagnostic equipment, sophisticated surgical procedures, and elaborate medical treatments. It is even less surprising, of course, that this system should be biased towards over-servicing and over-treatment of a middle-class clientele.

The technological view of medicine, coupled with competition, has contributed in no small way to fragmentation of services, inefficiency, and duplication of facilities. The contradictions inherent in this system may well lead to its dissolution. As costs spiral and few benefits are obvious, the Canadian public is becoming impatient. With the end of federal revenue sharing in the health area, the temptation will be for some provinces to opt out of insured medicine altogether.

WHAT WE SHOULD PAY FOR

If health is not simply the absence of illness, then we must formulate a policy of encouraging the positive well-being of people. As such, we must address the total environment in which we live. If we could eliminate industrial carcinogens and drastically reduce the sources of urban stress, we could go a long way towards finding answers to problems such as heart disease, cancer, and emotional disorders. These illnesses *must* be attacked through preventive means.

I submit that a consistent and rational health-care system reflecting the goal of universal access to appropriate care cannot be based on notions of "private enterprise". Rather, it must be a publicly funded system of *public* medicine and *public* health. It must stress directions in medicine which hold out the greatest possibilities for improving the health of Canadians as a whole. It must reduce the technical emphasis in medicine today and more efficiently allocate health personnel to problems. It must encourage patients to participate fully in decisions with respect to their own health care. It must, in short, employ a *social* rather than a *medical* model of health.

REORGANIZATION OF THE HEALTH SYSTEM

Central to these changes must be a redefinition of primary, secondary, and tertiary care.

Primary contact between the health system and a person ought to take place at two levels. At the institutional level, it should occur through educational programs in schools, workplaces, and the public media. At the personal level, a system of primary health-care workers should be developed to deal with a broad range of personal, social, and medical needs.

Secondary care should be confined to the strictly technical work done by specialist doctors and other health technicians today—dentists, speech therapists, etc. Those persons requiring bed care or convalescence should, as much as possible, be treated in their homes. Routine hospitalization would be provided in community hospitals.

Tertiary care is highly specialized and technological and would be available in a few metropolitan areas for the infrequent cases which truly benefit from it. These centres should be viewed as provincial rather than community resources.

The goals of this reorganization are simple. The first is to reduce the wasteful and inappropriate use of professionals by developing a new primary-care worker. This person will be responsible for providing positive health education and counselling, home care and support, common medical treatment and referral. Education about well-baby care, nutrition and obesity, hygiene, dental care, leisure, recreation, and fitness should be available to every household on a personal basis. Home-care services are vital if the convalescent, disabled, and elderly are to remain within their homes. Personal and family counselling, assistance in employment and retraining are areas in which many people need help. The treatment of upper respiratory infections, cuts and sprains, and other simple ailments, as well as the administration of immunization and allergy shots should also be handled by the primary health worker who must also know when to refer people with disorders potentially requiring more specialized care. Medical workers are today so overburdened with other roles that they cannot practise good technical medicine.

The second goal would be to move health care away from its current heavy emphasis on institutionalization. As things now stand, chronic patients are virtually forced into hospitals, senior citizens into nursing homes, and people with emotional disturbances into psychiatric hospitals. We recently learned, for instance, that Ontario's Ministry of Health would pay out over $1600 per month to keep a terminal cancer patient in hospital, but was unwilling to subsidize the $20 per month rental of a nursing bed so he could stay with his family. Similarly, places with adequate home-care programs—like Britain—have *half* the institutionalization rate for senior citizens that most provinces in Canada do. Psychiatric patients—as we recently discovered in Ontario—are frequently committed *not* because they are a danger to themselves or others, but simply because they have no place else to go. By providing community-based alternatives to these institutions, not only could we provide more appropriate therapy, but we could significantly reduce health-care costs as well.

Our final goal would be to create an attitude towards health on the part of people generally which would make them more self-reliant, critical consumers of the care they were receiving, and more health conscious, generally. Without accomplishing this, it will be impossible to ensure that any reorganization of the health system will have much impact on how things are done.

HEALTH CARE AS SOCIAL POLICY

General programs and policies should seek to establish the social and educational environment essential to personal health. This would imply full employment, sensible, affordable housing, tough safety legislation, universal compensation programs, strict control of toxic wastes, and the reversal of environmental pollution. In schools and through the public media, it suggests education concerning nutrition, lifestyle and personal development, hygiene, fitness and recreation, and the health-care process itself. Agricultural policy, food-processing and distribution mechanisms, and a host of other issues would have to be examined to ensure that an adequate supply of the goods necessary for life and health are available to all.

These ends cannot come about in a system based on finding private solutions to public problems: private enterprise inevitably has its own interests at heart. It has been detrimental to the quality of health care in the past, and has added greatly to escalating costs. The pharmaceutical industry with its enormous mark-up on drugs is one example. Private nursing homes are another. We must recognize that health—as something which is by its very nature social— must be dealt with by the public sector.

A truly global health industry exists today. It profits from a worldwide demand for health care, but unfortunately it does not recognize the *social* goals of health care. To extricate this health industry from the private sector will be a long and difficult task, but some beginnings can be made.

First, premiums for health insurance should be abolished: they are regressive and undercut the right to health care. Second, the retail pharmaceutical industry should be controlled through the provision of drugs by community clinics. The cost of drugs should be borne out of general revenue, and should be free to those who require treatment. Third, private practice should be abolished for health professionals: physicians, dentists, pharmacists, optometrists, orthodontists, etc. For those services already insured, this removes the bias towards over-servicing. For those not insured, this will remove the regressive aspect of making services least accessible to those with the lowest incomes. Health professionals, salaried at arbitrated rates, employed by community centres, may initially experience a loss of status and independence, but will be more responsive and responsible to the community they serve.

What I have described is a decentralized and community-oriented health-care system—one which, it is to be hoped, will be more sensitive to local and personal needs. In removing centralized controls and profit making, I recognize that it becomes difficult to know whether minimum standards of health will be provided in all communities. The need for a well-constructed and reliable information system is therefore obvious: a system which will provide up-to-date information concerning mortality and morbidity, utilization rates, and patterns of practice in all communities. Such an information system does not yet exist, anywhere, and is essential if this model of health is ever to be adopted. The technology exists.

CONCLUSION

In examining the health-care system, we see that costs have escalated while benefits have not. The built-in contradictions of our current system lie in the pursuit of social goals of universal access to appropriate health care using a private, capital-intensive, and technological medicine.

A more appropriate model of health care, based on prevention and a societal view of health and illness has been presented. This model calls for changes in the structure of primary and secondary health institutions, and a reorientation in the kinds of services provided to the public. The rationalization of the health system will mean the progressive removal of private enterprise from the health sector, which will in turn lead to vastly different work conditions for health professionals.

Whether or not such a system can be implemented at all in Canada is by no means clear. Private enterprise is so pervasive that it may be questioned whether alternative mechanisms for achieving social goals can be created without a complete upheaval. What is clear, however, is that the price we are paying for health care is too high, and the product is inferior. An alternative method of providing health care exists, one which follows rationally from accepted social objectives. It is more reasonable, more positive, and more likely to succeed. It deserves exploration.

NOTES

1 Health and Welfare Canada, *Health Field Indicators* (December 1976).
2 Ibid.
3 Statistics Canada, *Perspectives Canada* (July 1974).
4 Ibid.
5 Saskatchewan Medical Care Insurance Commission, *Annual Report, 1976*.
6 Ibid.
7 Ibid.
8 Health and Welfare Canada, *Health Field Indicators*.

CHAPTER NINETEEN

CANADIAN EDUCATION, A NATIONAL DISGRACE

THE CANADIAN EDUCATIONAL SYSTEM is a failure. This fault is reflected not only in the large number of students who drop out of it, but also in those who ostensibly succeed within it: while we produce some technically trained people who perform their specialized tasks competently, we have not, as a rule, created individuals who are aware of or sensitive to problems in their own lives and those of their friends and family, or to the complexities of our society and environment. As a result, we have produced two or three generations of consumers and wasters embroiled in an alienation and malaise that was once atypical of Canadian society. We have created a materially comfortable life, but we are uncomfortable. We have developed the means for mass communication, but we cannot communicate. We have created a complex transportation system across Canada, yet we cannot reach each other. We have built dozens of institutions of higher education and yet we are still a country of two solitudes—basically unilingual—unable to speak each other's language. In short, our educational system has failed us. It is a national disgrace.

Hundreds of explanations of this failure have been offered. Numerous causes have been isolated. Countless solutions have been proposed. The size of classrooms has been increased and

* Prepared for this volume.

ROBERT K. LOGAN & GALE MOORE

decreased, programs added and dropped, student-teacher ratios decreased and increased, and so forth. Nothing seems to have changed—the problems remain. The main reason for this is that no one has asked the basic questions: What is the purpose of our education system? Why was it organized? What should it accomplish?

We submit that "the figure" of the school has been isolated from the social context or "ground" in which it exists. As a result, too much attention has been focused on the school itself and not enough on the relation between the school and the social, economic, and political realities of our society.

We shall attempt in this article to explain the shortcomings of our educational system by examining the social and political context in which it has historically operated in Canada, and shall indicate possible directions for the future. Before proceeding with our analysis we should make it clear that in some respects the school system is quite successful. Our schools, by and large, provide adequate technical training. Their chief problem is that they do little else. They perform only a partial job by not preparing their students to cope with the realities of Canadian life.

The underlying reason that our schools perform only a partial job today is that they were originally intended to do only a partial job: they were never designed to teach values or to provide pupils with experiences in the real world. At the very beginning of the industrial revolution—when public education was first being organized—this component of a child's education was provided by family and church. At the same time, children learned about the world outside school by helping on the farm or in their father's workshop. Indeed, many children themselves worked in factories, mines, etc.

As the industrial revolution progressed, the percentage of the population engaged in farming or cottage industry decreased markedly. As a result, children became increasingly more isolated from their parents' economic activities—particularly with mass compulsory public education. Today, the world of work is basically a black box to most children: a place to which their parents go in the morning and from which they return in the evening. Many schools attempt to correct this situation through field trips intended to give their pupils a first-hand view of the working world. These trips usually last only a few hours, and the factory or farm visited seems like Disneyland: there is little or no opportunity for significant interaction with these environments.

Despite everyone's good intentions, our children are basically insulated from the working world by their school experiences.

In addition to being isolated in this fashion, children do not receive the education in values once provided by the family and church. The industrial revolution fragmented many extended families in Western society into nuclear families. Now nuclear families themselves are breaking down into single-parent families. With children spending more time in day-care centres, the moral suasion of parents is further reduced. Churches are trying to retain their influence, but the number of families directly or powerfully affected by them is decreasing.

Our school system was originally designed to provide an abstract education and understanding of the world to augment the training children received at home. Today's educational system never adjusted its program to compensate for the breakdown in pupils' moral and real-life education. This has produced a gap in our knowledge of how to use technology, when it should be used or not used, and why. The evidence for this is all around us. Instead, it has continued along as before. The abstract training provided by our schools has acted as no impediment to Canadians' treating their lakes and streams and atmosphere as dumping grounds for pollutants. Our callousness towards problems of industrial health and safety; our destruction of prime agricultural land for the sake of urban growth and development; and our pell-mell consumption of non-renewable resources with little or no regard for future generations continues unabated. Our schools could and should be making our children aware of these issues. They should no longer train technocrats capable of this kind of behaviour. But, as a rule, they do not recognize this as their job.

Because of its emphasis on teaching abstract, linear thinking, our school system has literally been training only one-half of the brain and hence has literally produced "half-wits". Neurophysiologists such as Bogen believe that, while there is a certain degree of redundancy and overlap between the two hemispheres, essentially the left and right hemispheres of the brain act as *loci* for the representation of different specialized tasks: the right hemisphere is the focus for the artistic, intuitive, spiritual, holistic, pattern-recognizing, and creative sides of our personalities; while the left is the focus for rationalistic, linear, logical, mathematical, and literacy functions.

A recent study by McLuhan and Logan[1] hypothesizes that

the widespread use of an abstract alphabet brought the left side of the brain into greater dominance in Western culture, and contributed to Western development of codified law, monotheism, science, abstract mathematics, and logic. By abstracting aspects of human experience from one another, they argue, these developments laid the basis for individualism. Our schools, as a result, primarily specialized in training the left side of the brain, ignoring the use of the right. This explains, in part, why we are able to train individuals who have the capacity to perform specialized tasks, but who are completely blind to the complex interactions of individuals, societies, and the environment. The only way to remedy this situation is for our schools to change their emphases, and to promote activities which encourage use of the right hemisphere as well.

By placing their emphasis on those skills and tasks which call upon the activities represented in the left hemisphere to the exclusion of those represented in the right, our school system has promoted a way of thinking and acting which accentuates the disjunctive, segmented, and linear aspects of our society. It enables engineers, for example, to design nuclear power plants without developing a satisfactory means of disposing of nuclear wastes, or to design a pulp-and-paper plant which poisons rivers, fish, and people.

The technologists we train in our schools, with rare exceptions, have not been taught to perceive and deal with complex environmental patterns—nor have they been sensitized to the need to do so (neither have the humanists for that matter). No one has an overview. We have lost control of our destiny.

It is the activities of the right side of the brain, largely ignored in our education system, which are responsible for pattern recognition. Persons with right-brain damage cannot recognize faces. If asked to draw a face they put all the elements of a face—eyes, ears, nose, and mouth—into their drawing, but they are unable to reconstruct the pattern of the face. It is the right side of the brain that enables one to develop an overview, to create and recognize patterns.

Our society operates as though the right side of its "collective brain" is damaged. Using our left brains and left-oriented training we have created elements of technology which work extremely well on their own. Unfortunately, these elements of technology do not fit into the sort of integrated pattern which is a basic need of our society. Technology too frequently achieves one task at the expense of another. It provides us with great mobility through the private car but destroys the countryside through which we wish to drive.

Because we lack an overview, because we are unable to create a holistic pattern, we are continually frustrated in our attempts to create a society which satisfies both our material and our spiritual needs. What we lack in Canada as in other industrialized countries is the capacity to think not just systematically but systemically, to consider—to use Buckminster Fuller's metaphor—our planet a spaceship.

An example of the narrowness of a left-oriented training program and of our lack of systemic thinking is to be found in our health-care program. Medical education, unfortunately, places more emphasis on diseases and their cures than on promotion of health or preventive medicine. Medical schools train physicians and medical auxiliaries to be, at best, higher technicians. Broader or more global aspects of health are ignored. Our elementary and secondary schools *do* have courses dealing explicitly with health problems, first aid, nutrition, health and sex education, driver education, and swimming (preventive drowning). But these deal almost exclusively with *physical* health: very little, if any, attention is being paid to mental or emotional health. Students are warned, from time to time, of the dangers of alcohol, tobacco, and drugs without an explanation of the psychological factors which lead to addiction. This, unfortunately, is the extent of most school programs in the area. Environmental questions related to health are almost totally ignored.

To be prepared for the eventual stresses of life, the student should be introduced to some of the basic skills and strategies necessary for promoting and maintaining his or her physical and emotional health. Students should be made acquainted with the nature of anxiety and stress, and made to realize that these are aspects of life which cannot be avoided, but which *can* be coped with and overcome. They should be prepared for the natural reactions that develop when one feels rejected or as though he or she has failed—taught, in short, the strategies required for dealing with life.

Another very important area which is also largely ignored is interpersonal relations. This is typically treated cursorally—with advice to the student to dress neatly, be polite when applying for a job, and so on. Sex education courses largely confine themselves to the mechanical functions of the body. Classroom treatment of interpersonal relations is inadequate. This is not surprising because teachers themselves are either not trained— or are only superficially trained—to deal with these issues. Given the complexity of relationships in our multilingual, multicultural, and multiracial society, the sooner these deficiencies are corrected the better. Young people should be helped to discover the nature of interpersonal relations in different situations (one to one, family, small groups, work, social situations). Learning to appreciate, to understand, and to get along with other people is as important a skill as the three R's. In fact, the three R's should be the four R's: reading, 'riting, 'rithmetic, and relating.

Particular attention should be paid to the most important relationship of all in our society: that of parent and child. What is more important in the long term for society than child rearing? If we taught students something about the emotional needs of *their* children, and how they might satisfy those needs, the next generation of youngsters would be happier and healthier.

Another example of the narrowness of Canadian education is the lack of understanding we have for one another's regional cultures and lifestyles. Ways must be found to change this, not only through increased classroom activities (left brain) but through exchange programs to give young people first-hand experience of other parts of Canada (right brain).

Steps must also be taken to ensure that the next generation of Canadians learns both of our official languages. With all the resources we make available to the education establishment, the least we can expect is that it teach a second language to our children. This is absolutely taken for granted in Europe and other parts of the world. The North American pattern is the exception, not the rule. At a minimum, a facility in both French and English should be required for *any* university degree—or even perhaps a high-school diploma. The teaching of a second language should not be regarded as merely a solution to a political problem, but as an educational opportunity which helps to establish a unique identity for Canadians on the North American continent.

Another feature of our education system which weakens its effectiveness is the fact that it is fractured. Thousands of schoolchildren moving from one part of Canada to another suffer education discontinuity from uneven standards and curricula throughout the country. This lack of a common educational experience contributes to our splintered national image. While we recognize the importance of local input into the educational systems of Canada's various regions, we believe that a core curriculum for the entire country would provide a "thread" to bind us together intellectually (and, hopefully, culturally as well), and would promote national unity.

Canada is not a uniform nation, and our diversity should be encouraged by our education system. We see no contradiction in a core curriculum which provides a common educational experience in mathematics, physical sciences, biological sciences, language skills, life skills, Canadian history, geography, federal politics, and national literature and culture, but which leaves room for specialization in local and regional history, geography, politics, literature, and culture. The latter are matters over which provinces require autonomy, but there is no need to develop Ontario physics, Nova Scotian chemistry, or Albertan mathematics. Certain topics would benefit from a uniform treatment, so that students could easily move from the secondary school of one province to the university of another. Canadian history, literature, and geography would be enriched with material from all the regions of Canada. Perhaps, in this way, North and South, East and West, English and French may understand each other better. Also, perhaps, we shall be able to develop a "sense of Canada", to use Premier Blakeney's term.

Finally we come to perhaps the most serious indictment of our educational system: its failure to prepare our young people to cope with contemporary economic realities. Unemployment among youth is one of the pressing social problems we face today. We cannot fault our schools for the problems of an economic system which does not provide jobs or opportunity. But many of today's youth are handicapped in ways that their predecessors, perhaps, were not. There are many reasons for this. First there is alienation due to scale. Our institutions and government are large and often out of touch with those they are designed to serve. Technology, which with one hand gives us many comforts and conveniences, threatens to destroy us when used only for economic ends. Advertising floods our senses from all directions, creating both markets for products which are not only unnecessary, but, frequently, harmful, and increased expectations which our economic system cannot meet. Television has also played a part, engendering passivity and encouraging a voyeuristic attitude towards life. This, in turn, leads to cynicism and a tendency to dissociate abstract learning from real life.

All these factors contribute to alienation, which is heightened further by the moral, religious, and family breakdown we mentioned earlier. The chief failure of our educational system, we think, has been its inability to recognize these factors and, through modified curriculum and counselling, help students to understand the forces acting on them in contemporary society. (Counselling to acquaint our youngsters with the institutions of our society—with banks, insurance companies, large corporations, small businesses, the social-service network, the apparatus of government services, agencies, and departments, the legal system, the medical system, the arts—would not come amiss in this respect. The only institution of society in which they seem to receive much training at present is competitive sports which, by and large, teaches them to be the passive consumers of spectator sports.)

In sum, an important part of the educational experience of our youth is missing: we send young people into the world largely unprepared for the stresses and challenges of adult life. Our society, i.e., literate Western industrial society, is almost unique in not providing a rite of passage which enables the young to negotiate safely their transition into adulthood and beyond. Our educational system, successful in providing our students with many experiences and skills, is ultimately a failure because no social or personal context is provided to show the practical meaning of these disparate skills and experiences.

We have outlined a number of problem areas of our education system which we attribute to a lack of systemic thinking—a lack of an overview. The inability of our schools to develop this type of thinking is, at present, self-perpetuating. In order to remedy this tragic situation, more attention must be given to the integrating skills of the right brain. Placing greater emphasis on music and the tactile arts will help but will not be sufficient. New methods of training the right side of the brain must be discovered. We believe this can be achieved by integrating the teaching of abstract skills with their applications. The medium is the message. If mathematics and science are taught in isolation from their applications, the student learns to use these tools without considering their impact. The myth that science and technology are value-free must be exploded and the dangers to the environment and to society of technologically induced change must be revealed. The mentality that allows our rivers, streams, lakes, and oceans, our atmosphere, and our land to be used as dumping grounds for garbage and pollutants is a reflection of the abstract, linear, disjunctive nature of our educational system.

We must break new ground. We must look to new models of education. Perhaps the native people of Canada who originally lived in harmony with their environment can be a source of ideas and inspiration for us. Skills were never taught in isolation from their application. Education itself was totally integrated into the everyday life of the society. In short they had, not schools, but learning.

Many of the social and economic goals that we are presently struggling to achieve were built automatically into the native peoples' way of life. They managed their limited resources wisely without waste or pollution. They had a decentralized economy, full employment, no inflation, no fiscal or balance-of-trade problems. They developed appropriate technology (small was beautiful). They did not suffer from alienation and, despite their rugged struggle for survival, they had time for a rich spiritual life.

We do not wish to romanticize their existence. They suffered from starvation, disease, and war. Very few Canadians would be prepared to accept the hardships and discomforts of that life. Nevertheless we must admit that many of our present-day aspirations, as enunciated, for example, by the federal government in its working paper *The Way Ahead*, match many of the elements of native life mentioned above. Perhaps by blending aspects of native education with those of our present system we will be able to achieve a happy mix that will allow us to train individuals who are technically competent and at the same time have the capacity to deal with the complexities of our society, our technology, and our environment.

NOTE

1   H. Marshall McLuhan and Robert K. Logan, "Alphabet, Mother of Invention", *Etcetera*, forthcoming.

CHAPTER TWENTY

EDUCATION FOR WHAT?

DURING THE 1960s, Canada's educational system entered a period of dramatic growth in both enrolments and expenditures. Rapid enrolment growth was particularly concentrated at the pre-grade-one, secondary, and post-secondary levels, with average annual enrolment growth rates during the 1960s of 8 per cent at the secondary level, and 11 per cent for full-time post-secondary students. Total full-time enrolments at *all* levels of the educational system rose from 4.4 million in 1960–61 to 6.4 million in 1970–71. This meant that by the end of the 1960s full-time students comprised 30 per cent of the total population.

These burgeoning enrolments necessitated ever-increasing levels of expenditure to provide teachers and facilities. During the 1960s, teaching staff in Canada increased from about 175,000 to nearly 320,000—and many existing teachers went back to school to improve their qualifications. Billions of dollars were spent during the same period. Expenditures rose from about 1.7 billion in 1960 to an estimated 7.4 billion in 1970. This represented 8.8 per cent of our GNP in that year.

University enrolments increased by 213 per cent between 1961 and 1971; an average annual growth rate of 11 per cent. In addition to growth, the Canadian educational system was subjected to diversification and other reforms during the 1960s. It was during this period that community colleges were introduced across the country. Curriculum and organizational reforms were carried out at all levels of the system—mainly in the direction of providing freer choice for students, giving them a greater say in decision making (particularly in post-secondary institutions), and freeing them from some aspects of competition and "the fear of failure" (particularly in primary schools).

* Prepared for this volume.

EDWARD B. HARVEY

Massive processes of institutional transformation seldom go smoothly and are rarely unqualified successes. The experience with education in Canada during the 1960s was no exception. Today, in the mid-1970s, the discussion of educational issues and institutions is less optimistic than it was in the 1960s. Some people are asking what it is we have received for our massive expenditures. We hear about unemployed and under-employed university graduates; and about secondary-school graduates who can't read or write properly. We hear about young people who are bitterly frustrated because their excursion into higher education has not provided a ticket to secure, well-paid, higher-level, white-collar employment. Does any or all of this suggest that the educational expansion and reforms of the 1960s were somehow a failure? I think not. It does, however, raise some questions that need to be explored.

- What are the sources of some of the current and future problems we will experience in our educational institutions?
- To what extent are the sources of certain of these problems located in institutions other than educational institutions or in changing relationships between education and these institutions?
- To what extent are some of the apparent shortcomings of educational institutions caused by unrealistic expectations about what educational institutions can accomplish? What sort of education-related goals are realistic? What policies are required to foster the attainment of such goals? What mechanisms should be used to evaluate performance in terms of such goals? What sorts of objectives should we be trying to accomplish through our educational institutions which we are not presently trying to do?

In exploring these questions, it is useful to re-examine some of the thinking that underlay the decisions and policies that resulted in the educational expansion of the 1960s. Clearly, a major source of pressure was demographic: the upsurge in the birth rate between 1945 and 1959 (the post-war "baby boom") meant that there would have been great enrolment pressure on our educational institutions, even if there had been no upward shift in participation rates in education. These rates *did* rise, however.

During the late 1950s and early 1960s there was considerable acceptance in policy circles of "human capital" theory and the associated assumption that investment in more educated manpower would ultimately lead to economic growth. Prior to the educational expansion of the 1960s, Canada relied heavily on immigration to meet its highly qualified manpower needs. Given the potentially volatile nature of such immigration, one goal of the expansion of educational faciltities was the establishment of domestic manpower self-sufficiency.

Also during the 1960s there were rising social demands for education in general, and for higher education in particular in Canada. The times were affluent and many parents wanted their children to have benefits that they had not experienced. Moreover, universities and colleges during the 1960s became more than educational institutions: they became one of the principal locations of a youth-oriented lifestyle that many young people wanted to pursue.

The 1960s were also a time when, in many Western industrial nations, policies were designed to increase equality of opportunity in such areas as education, health, and social security. The expansion of education, particularly higher education, in conjunction with various loan and bursary schemes, was an important addition to institutional arrangements for social and economic mobility in Canadian society. Finally, as the members of the baby-boom generation reached labour-force age, our economy would be hard pressed to provide sufficient jobs. Higher education, in particular, appeared to provide a useful "holding pattern" which would relieve some of these pressures, albeit temporarily.

With these factors in mind, let us look at some of the current and future pressure points in the educational system, and also at how this system relates to other major institutional arrangements in Canada.

THE EDUCATIONAL SYSTEM

The 1960s were a period of boom for the educational system. The 1970s are, by strong contrast, a period of constraint and adjustment. Competing spending priorities in such areas as transportation, housing, and the environment have dampened the rate at which educational expenditures were increasing during the 1960s. Moreover, as the last of the baby-boom cohort move through the educational system they leave behind them surplus capacity. Costs for operating this capacity, including physical plant and teachers' salaries, can be expected to increase given even moderate levels of inflation. Secondary schools are now being affected by declining enrolments and this impact will reach the university level by around 1983. The demographic side will be further complicated by migration patterns which will exacerbate the problem of declining enrolments in some areas, and moderate it in others.

Dealing with surplus capacity is a complicated problem. Teacher/pupil ratios can be revised in the direction of smaller classes. However, this is not likely to be a popular move with a public increasingly concerned about education costs. And there are limits to the extent to which economies can be realized with physical plant. That leaves teachers' salaries as one potential source of adjustment. Teachers' organizations are well aware of this and, increasingly, militant bargaining has resulted in more emphasis on job security in employment contracts.

Interestingly enough, despite a depressed labour market for university graduates throughout the 1970s, both part-time and full-time university enrolment in Canada have continued to increase during this period. (This phenomenon will be expanded upon later.) Despite the fact that enrolments have held up well, it seems unlikely that there will be further significant increases over the next few years in the participation rate in higher education of eighteen to twenty-three year olds. University planners are increasingly seeking alternatives in part-time study and adult education. It seems unlikely, however, that these alternatives can offset entirely the impact of the decline in the traditional source population for university enrolments.

The problem of surplus capacity in the educational system is complicated by another important consideration. To some extent, the surplus capacity is temporary. Even if the birth rate remains low, the fact that so many young women were born during the baby boom means that we can expect that a large number of babies will be born as these young women form families. This is the so-called "the boom has an echo" effect and will, in cyclical fashion, eventually increase enrolments.

More employers are coming to believe that the short-term savings of laying off staff are more than offset by the costs of obtaining and training staff when they are needed again. A rigorous analysis of this issue certainly needs to be applied to the field of education manpower. The issue is larger than questions of costs alone. An important part of the problem is how to keep our educational institutions vital and creative places in an environment of restraint.

In the universities, for example, there is little or no new hiring. University faculties will age and the benefits arising from new, young colleagues will be rare. Some evidence suggests that creativity and productivity decline with age; other data suggest that this is not the case. Clearly, firm conclusions cannot yet be drawn and further study is required. None the less, in general terms it is clear that different mechanisms are needed to maintain the intellectual health of our educational institutions during a period of restraint and, indeed, anxiety than were appropriate during a period of growth and optimism.

One prospect does seem reasonably firm: the demand for *continuing* education will increase for at least two reasons. A substantial proportion of the baby-boom generation will seek, through such education, the challenges and satisfactions that may be increasingly difficult to realize in the world of work. Increased competition in the world of work, as well as inhibited satisfactions, may also increase the demand for career-oriented adult education designed to confer some degree of competitive advantage in an increasingly tight race for advancement and achievement.

EDUCATIONAL SYSTEMS AND THE LABOUR MARKET

There is growing evidence of an institutional problem in the linkage between the educational system and the labour market. The principal symptoms are high youth unemployment, laments from employers that young people lack the basic skills that would make them attractive employees, and the growing frustration of young people that education (particularly higher education) has not delivered secure, well-paid, prestigious employment. The problem of unemployed or under-employed university graduates has served to dramatize the employment problems of youth in Canada—particularly since in earlier times such higher education virtually served as a ticket to a good job and a good life.

However, despite the bad news from the labour market, young people do not appear to be deserting educational institutions. In fact, dropping out from high school has started to decline. During the 1970s, both full-time and part-time enrolments in colleges and universities have continued to *increase*.

Some patterns of adjustment have been observed. In universities, for example, young people have started to shift their choices towards courses such as business and commerce and engineering which appear to have more certain vocational futures. However, as I have pointed out in some recent projection studies, such decisions are typically based on current labour-market information—not the situation that will obtain four or five years hence when the students graduate. The collective result of such individual choices may simply be to increase the future supply in various fields with a resulting decline in occupational opportunities. Typically, this then triggers a decline in enrolments. With the resulting manpower shortages, opportunities increase and enrolments increase, starting the cycle once again. These so-called "cobweb" effects are virtually impossible to avoid in labour markets that operate with far-from-perfect information and which attach a high degree of importance to the freedom of individual choice.

As Richard Freeman has documented in a recent book, *The Overeducated American*, the depressed market for university and college manpower in the United States has been accompanied by a decline in enrolments. It is interesting to speculate why such declines have not occurred in Canada.

I suspect several factors. First, given the general weakness of our manufacturing sector, there is not, as in the United States, a wide range of relatively well-paid and attractive jobs. For young people in Canada the choice may assume a sharper edge: stay in school or accept a really unattractive job. There is also the tendency to believe that the bad labour-market news applies to others and not oneself. Finally, students are well aware that employers use educational credentials as a screening mechanism. For these and other reasons I do not see the bottom falling out of enrolments in the foreseeable future. While adjustments can be made in the extent to which education in general—and higher education in particular—meets manpower requirements, it is unrealistic to expect (and in my view undesirable as well) that educational institutions will simply become a means of producing the required labour supply. This relates to my point that we need to become more explicit about what it is we expect our educational institutions to accomplish so that we can fine-tune our policy and planning initiatives and also become more realistic in our expectations. It is somewhat fashionable to say that in the light of high youth unemployment, for example, educational institutions have somehow "failed".

This simplistic view fails to take into account the many fundamental structural changes that are taking place in Western industrial societies which are directly contributing to youth employment problems. Employment opportunities for youth have been adversely affected by growing rigidity in our labour markets. In particular, an increasing proportion of the labour force is protected by one form of contract or agreement or another. The white-collar component of the labour force has always traditionally enjoyed greater job security than other types of employment and, of course, this component of the labour force has been expanding most rapidly in recent years. For reasons of social justice, however, it is difficult to deny other workers the benefits enjoyed by those in white-collar employment. Hence, there has been a growing strong trend towards greater employment security for *all* classes of workers.

Compared to the twenty-five years of rapid and sustained economic growth following the Second World War, the Canadian economy has entered an era of slower growth in productivity. There have also been changes in the technology and scale of industry that have reduced or eliminated employment opportunities for young people. The branch-plant nature of our economy further inhibits the extent to which we enjoy flexibility in our use of manpower policy as an instrument of job creation. Over the past few years there has been a narrowing in the wage differential between older and younger workers which has generally served to make younger workers less attractive to employers. Bluntly put, the question is why pay as much for less experience? Young people have also been significantly affected by competition in the labour market from women returning to work. Finally, we have to remember that the attitudes young people hold with respect to work have changed. It is not that the "work ethic" has passed away. Rather, it is unrealistic to expect young people who have experienced the affluence of the 1960s, and who are the best-educated cohort in Canadian history, to accept poor jobs. This experience of education and relative affluence is a major source of the gap between the generations, and no amount of urging a return to the "work ethic" will alter the reality of this change.

In my view, education is less a cause of the employment

problems of youth than it is a potentially valuable institutionalized means of ameliorating some of these difficulties. I do
not, however, mean this in the sense of education as a short-term
instrument of labour-market policy.

Let me expand: because of their numbers, and a generally
more constrained economic environment ahead, the young people of the baby-boom cohort face a lifetime of stiff competition.
Simply put, there will be two or three people competing for every
good job. The prospects for promotion and compensation will
be distinctly slower. Yet the affluent and optimistic models of
the 1960s are still strong and the search for satisfaction and
fulfilment are powerful components of the baby-boom generation's world view. Education may not have delivered what they
expected, but they have none the less acquired a taste for it. The
educational system can increasingly become an institutionalized
means of creating such satisfactions.

On a more pragmatic level, many well-educated young
people will accept jobs below their expectation levels and in
doing so will displace less well-trained workers. If we continue
to believe that it is politically important that all individuals have
some experience of work in society, then educational institutions
will have an important role to play in the retraining of people as
well as a more general role of creating and disseminating new
thoughts about our national direction and goals.

Lastly, although jobs that require post-secondary education are increasing more rapidly than jobs that do not, the supply
of people trained for such jobs far outstrips the number of such
jobs that can be created. Many blue-collar jobs that do not
require post-secondary education are not growing so rapidly,
but here there is some evidence that the growth in labour supply
may fall short of even that more modest growth in the number of
jobs. Clearly, our high schools, in particular, are still turning out
young people who value post-secondary education and are seeking white-collar employment. This white-collar glut is out of
phase with the realities of opportunities today and in the foreseeable future.

Although I have argued against treating educational institutions as mechanisms of manpower supply, it does not mean
that there should be no adjustments in this respect *within* our
educational institutions. I cannot go into all the details here, but
there is a need for a fundamental re-appraisal of the linkage
between educational systems and the labour market, and for a

specification of the goals that we can, realistically, expect educational institutions to serve in a society like Canada.

SOCIAL AND ECONOMIC MOBILITY

As Vilfredo Pareto observed, it is in the interests of a society's well-being and adaptive capability to ensure some degree of circulation of its elites. Although subject to some national differences, education in Western industrial societies has typically been a significant means to higher social and economic achievements. Certainly the expansion of higher education in Canada in the 1960s, in conjunction with government loan and bursary schemes, was designed to expand the avenues leading to social and economic opportunities.

In a recent study I found that our system of higher education has, between 1969 and 1975, become more open to such previously under-represented groups as women and students from lower socio-economic backgrounds. Despite the real gains that have been made, however, there appears to be a growing feeling—particularly among the young people who have pursued higher education—that such education has failed to deliver on their expectations for social and economic mobility. In another study conducted with Lorna Marsden, we found that the occupational mobility prospects for university graduates have declined in the 1970s compared to the mid-1960s. These data also suggest that the rate of return on investment in higher education has also declined during the same period.

There is no contradiction here. Compared, for example, with the 1950s, access to higher education in Canada is nowadays more open and equal. Compared to the high point of the mid-1960s, the then-strong relationship between higher education and upward social mobility has weakened. We experienced an unusual configuration of events in the 1960s: educational expansion, an employment boom, rapid and sustained economic growth, a youth-oriented culture, a generally high degree of optimism. This configuration perhaps made higher education appear to be more of an avenue for mobility than, in fact, it was or could be.

Nowadays, higher levels of education have become a necessary but not sufficient condition for social and economic mobility: there is no longer an automatic linkage between a good education and a good job. Does having such education mean that an individual is better equipped for a satisfying and full life? I suggest that it does and that we need to create definitions of mobility other than the rather narrow indicators of occupational attainment and salary earned.

This line of argument implies that we cannot only judge the benefits of public investment in education in terms of the economic benefits arising from such education. Economic benefits are important, of course, and certain limits must be kept in mind, but it would seem that education serves society in other important ways. It helps to create people who are better able to participate in society and who know how to identify and solve problems. Education also contributes to a greater degree of tolerance for alternative points of view. These qualities are increasingly important to us as a nation as we continue to shape our consensus under increasingly difficult circumstances of scarcity and uncertainty. We must also bear in mind that there is more to social security and well-being than food and clothing and shelter. Industrial society is bureaucratic. It is technological. Things change rapidly. Our urban centres foster isolation and alienation. An educated population is an important pre-condition for the creation of new social frameworks and the maintenance of both the social and political health of a society and the well-being of the individual and the family unit. All of these "good outcomes", which are at least in part created by our educational institutions, are notoriously difficult to measure. They are, however, important in the determination of policy and planning priorities. Because the measurement task is difficult, we should assign a stronger and more evident priority to its solution.

EXPECTATIONS AND OPPORTUNITIES

The specific problems I raised with respect to education, employment, and mobility in Canadian society all point towards a more general and pervasive problem: the crisis of rising expectations. As we moved into the 1970s, many things changed. We have become accustomed to affluence, but now we must become accustomed to a less-welcome addition to our economic and social environment—scarcity. It is not just a matter of oil. The 1970s have witnessed the emergence of a new world economic order. Third World nations have become impatient: they are tired of waiting for their share of world economic benefits. This has been reflected in the growing number of cartels. A wide range of products can be mentioned: oil, coffee, copper, bauxite, etc. In Canada, our balance-of-payments situation shows an alarming deterioration as we continue to import more at the same time as we are pricing ourselves out of world export markets. The urbanization and industrialization of the last three decades has created a proliferation of values, groups, and interests in our society. Many interest groups are increasingly well-organized and articulate in their pursuit of the resources and benefits that are no longer growing at the same rate as they did in the past. The ever-upward cycle of inflationary wage settlements was one of the most alarming symptoms of this disease. The disease resulted in strong medicine—the wage and price controls of 1975. We are at a fundamental crossroads in the shaping of our national destiny and our future consensus. Do our educational institutions have a role to play in these broad matters of shaping the future?

POLICY AND PLANNING FOR THE FUTURE

As the 1960s came to a close there were a number of commissions held across Canada on the status and prospects of post-secondary education. These commissions reflected the fact that a turning point had been reached. The rapid expansion of the preceding years was beginning to slow. Public concern over costs was on the rise. It was an appropriate time to review what had been accomplished and what the future might hold.

These processes of change are continuing as our educational institutions evolve through the 1970s. The concern with education costs is apparent in both government and the attitudes of the general public. This concern is reflected in new policies and guidelines restricting further physical-plant expansion and the hiring of new teaching staff. Demographically related declines in enrolments are receiving greater attention, have been and will continue to be studied, and are reflected in the growing concern with job security in the contract negotiations of teaching staff across the country. The student unrest of the 1960s seems for the most part like a dim memory now. Young people nowadays appear to be much more concerned with getting a good job if at all possible and their educational decisions increasingly reflect this reality. Many of the reforms of the 1960s have now become a permanent part of our educational institutions. Still, some backlash against some of these reforms can be observed in recent times, particularly among those who are arguing for a return to the teaching of basic skills in the school system. Finally, although enrolments are declining in some parts of the educational system, the demand for adult education is growing apace and increasing numbers of people are anxious to be involved in part-time study of one kind or another.

These comments outline in very broad terms some of the current and continuing changes in our educational system. There is clearly also some need for a continuing reassessment of how our educational institutions relate to the other major institutions of our society. There is, for example, a continuing concern with youth unemployment or under-employment and the implications this holds for the present state of our educational-system—labour-market linkages. Indeed, the transition from school to work is receiving increasing attention these days and various proposals and alternatives are being discussed. The federal government has embarked upon an ambitious program of occupational forecasting which is unquestionably valuable, but the problem still remains of translating these results into a form useful to the guidance and counselling functions within the school system. Work/study programs have been discussed as another means of ameliorating some of the school-to-work transition difficulties; however, employers are not totally convinced of the merits of such programs and complex questions also arise where unionized labour is involved. Various post-doctoral programs have been used in an attempt to ameliorate the employment problems of some of our most highly qualified young graduates, but such programs are at best stop-gap measures. In this connection, the expansion of industrial research and development activity in Canada would appear to be a promising strategy, both in terms of the benefits it would confer upon our manufacturing industry and of the creation of meaningful career opportunities for at least some of our young graduates. It might be noted that the trend of industrial research and development activity in Canada has remained virtually static since 1970, despite a growth in real GNP of 25 per cent.

As suggested earlier in this article, our educational institutions also confer upon our society a number of non-economic benefits. There is sometimes a tendency to treat the non-economic benefits of education as unmeasurable and, therefore, not relevant to policy and planning. A more reasonable approach is to continue to confront these questions of measurement, as many in the social-indicators movement are doing nowadays, and arrive at indicators useful for policy and planning. Some of the non-economic benefits arising from education, particularly higher education, clearly benefit the individual although their contribution to a social product is less clear. It is reasonable to treat certain kinds of education as "consumption goods", goods consumed principally for the satisfaction of the consumer and therefore paid for by the consumer rather than subsidized from the public purse. However, there are other non-economic benefits arising from education which appear worthy of public subsidization. I referred to some of these earlier.

More specifically, what roles lie ahead for our educational institutions? As Senator Maurice Lamontagne has pointed out, the basic consensus of Canadian society is becoming increasingly fragmented at a time of increasing interdependence. The bargaining trade-offs between interest groups carry greater potential for social turbulence as the bargaining environment is increasingly affected by scarcities and uncertainties. Clearly, both of these unwelcome realities are going to be with us in the future. Our educational institutions can surely assume a more active posture as agents of and contributors to the ongoing forging of a national consensus and play a greater part in debating the urgent social and political issues of our time—including national unity. As we prepare to enter post-controls Canada there is a growing awareness that we need to develop new consultative institutions to develop our goals and future directions in an environment less prone to suspicion, conflict, and confrontation.

Our educational institutions have both a direct and indirect role to play in this regard. Indirectly, educational institutions can contribute to the ability of our population to enter into such ongoing social and political dialogue. Our institutions of higher education can help to create an involved rather than an alienated society. More directly, it is to be hoped that our educational leaders will take an even greater interest in the task of shaping our educational institutions; for are they not a most significant component of the over-all institutional framework within which we identify and grapple with the major social, economic, and political problems of our nation?

There is no room here to enter into a financial or technical analysis of the policies or planning arrangements that might serve these goals. However, some general future directions for development can be identified. Unfortunately, our educational institutions have some long distance to go to free themselves from the image of being age-graded institutions. Most people still live linear lives of school, work, and retirement, with leisure time sandwiched into weekends or yearly holidays. We need to continue to work towards the development of arrangements that will allow individuals greater flexibility in their lives. The concept of sabbatical leave should not be restricted to academics. Many people in other lines of work are inhibited from such possibilities; for example, because of liquidity problems they feel they cannot afford to take time away from work.

With regard to these kinds of problems, the distinguished Swedish economist, Gosta Rehn, has advanced ingenious policy proposals for intra-life-cycle drawing rights—in effect, arrangements by which we could make transfer payments to one part of our life against another. Our educational institutions can be an increasingly important part of the framework of institutions in which people learn, work, and contribute to the future quality of life in our society. To realize the full scope of that challenge, we need to reassess constantly the goals of our educational institutions from the perspective of our larger national priorities and our over-all institutional arrangements. To maximize the efficacy of educational institutions in the pursuit of these goals, we need to develop the kinds of arrangements which maximize the freedom with which people can participate in such institutions.

CHAPTER TWENTY-ONE

ENVIRONMENT, RESOURCES, AND CONFEDERATION

IF QUÉBEC SEPARATES, we lose more than people. We lose territories, contiguity, physical intactness. Canada is a vast, integral block of land—apart from the Arctic islands, Vancouver Island, and Newfoundland. With Québec gone, the country's mainland will be sundered into two parts like Pakistan before the Bangladesh separation: we shall be split across the middle. History provides forbidding examples of what happens to physically divided nations.

Not, of course, that the split need be a physical barrier. The CPR main line to New Brunswick crosses Maine to avoid the long way around that state's northern promontory (which the CNR's two main lines have to detour). The shortest rail route from New England and the Hudson Valley to Detroit and Chicago lies across southern Ontario. U.S. freight and Amtrak trains still use this short-cut over the lines of the former Michigan Central. No doubt we could arrange similar access to the Atlantic provinces across Québec territories, or through the United States. Europeans do it; and René Lévesque has often pointed admiringly at the EEC's flexible arrangements. But we can't be sure.

It is strange how little discussion has surfaced over issues of this sort. Public debate since November 15, 1976 has been about people and institutions, not the physical implications of separation. Canadians seem little aware of their geography and environment—or perhaps they take it for granted. Obviously we *can't* take such things for granted if an alien state is suddenly thrust across our lines of communication. Atlantic Canada is already too far away—geographically, economically, and psy-

* Prepared for this volume.

F. KENNETH HARE

chologically—from central Canada. An interposed block of alien land would make the link even weaker.

Nor do the consequences stop at such a splintering: there are endless unanswered questions about environment and resources. If a split comes we shall have to find answers in a hurry. What, for example, about Québec's claim to Labrador? Since the Judicial Committee of the Privy Council (of the United Kingdom) handed down its 1927 judgment, the Atlantic coast of Labrador (to which Newfoundland laid claim) has included a large part of the interior because the Ashuanipi–Hamilton drainage basin extends into the central plateau. The committee supported Newfoundland's claim, and Labrador, thus enlarged, has been that province's *de facto* territory ever since. But Québec has never accepted this judgment—and several statements by Péquiste ministers suggest that the issue will re-surface.

If it does, and if Québec takes a 200-mile economic limit for the sea as standard, presumably it might lay claim to the resources of the western Labrador Sea. It will certainly regard the St. Lawrence as a Québec river down to Anticosti Island, and will presumably claim a share in the resources and management of the Gulf of St. Lawrence, Hudson Strait, Hudson Bay, and James Bay. The present provincial government does not possess the skills, the ships, nor even the inclination to manage these water bodies. But will considerations of sea-bed hydrocarbons and of sovereignty force Québec to do so?

Will it also attempt to manage the airspace above its territories?

At present the networks of telecommunications, meteorological and geophysical observatories, and navigational aids are largely federal. Québec's meteorological service, for example, exists largely to support its resource industries, notably hydro power and forestry. It would be swamped by the need to absorb the main networks and forecast responsibilities. The federal service within Québec is largely Francophone, but it is by no means clear that this service and its individual professionals could simply be diverted to a new Québec government: all these areas are typically handled by tightly integrated national systems.

The same unknowns present themselves in hundreds of other bread-and-butter ways. It would be prohibitively expensive for an independent Québec government to assume the full cost of environmental and resource management, given its already overstretched provincial budget. Québec is huge—and the cost of such management depends on area, not human population. Its six million people would be shouldering the cost of administering and developing almost 600,000 square miles of territory—an area equal to that of the British Isles, France, Spain, and West Germany combined.

In fact, what would happen, unless Québec asked Canada to continue to provide these territorial, aerial, and marine services, would be that shortages of cash and skilled manpower would lead to a vast deterioration of the natural environment. Québec is already well behind Ontario in much of its environmental management and it would fall further behind.

To anyone like myself, who has spent his life working towards a better understanding, use, and sustained yield of Canada's natural endowment, such developments would seem absurd, tragic, *saugrenus*. I wrote my doctoral thesis at the Université de Montréal on the climate of the eastern-Canadian Arctic and sub-Arctic, much of which is the great peninsula of Labrador—Ungava. Nationalism and separatism were alive then, especially in the universities. But they were directed inwards—towards the society of southern Québec—where Maurice Duplessis paid little regard to the north.

More recently, of course, Québec has reached out towards her northern territories. French or Innuit names have replaced familiar terms like Port Harrison, Great Whale River, and Knob Lake, and the James Bay development is one of the largest ventures in publicly organized resource development ever attempted. But this has placed a prodigious strain on provincial finances, and will continue to do so. The fact is that all 23,000,000 Canadians can hardly marshal the resources needed for such immense enterprises.

Nationalism is never rational, but it remains, as George Orwell predicted, the most compelling political force of the present century. So I don't expect these arguments to deter M. Lévesque or his colleagues. But at least they should be debated publicly on both sides. Canada is not just a nation, a grouping of peoples and their institutions. It is also a gigantic physical reality on the world map, rich in resources, but calling for the strength of a giant to manage and develop. An independent Québec would be a pygmy, not a giant.

CHAPTER TWENTY-TWO

A LONG-TERM POLICY FOR FEDERAL FUNDING OF SCIENTIFIC RESEARCH

THE INCREASE[1] IN the total federal expenditures on scientific activities for the fiscal year 1977–78 was only 5.5 per cent. This represents an effective cutback of spending on science (when inflation is taken into account) and reverses the trend of the recent past which saw a moderate but steady increase of support for scientific activities. The 15 per cent increase[2] of the total federal science budget the year before, for example, was well above the inflation level.

As Graham Mainwood has argued: "Perhaps one of the strangest dilemmas of recent years is the decline in the status of science in the midst of an ever increasing dependence of society on science and the technologies that it has developed."[3]

The cutback in the budget may not seriously have hampered our scientific program yet, but it has left a number of scientists wondering whether our society will once again assign a low priority to science.

Perhaps the most tragic aspect of the cutbacks is the missed and/or delayed opportunities to solve many of the pressing problems now facing Canada that they represent. At no other time in our history, with the possible exception of the period of the world wars, have we needed the services of our scientists as much as we do now.

* Prepared for this volume.

ROBERT K. LOGAN

We are on the brink of an energy crisis which threatens our very survival. With present petroleum reserves expected to last only ten years, we should be involved in a crash program to develop alternative and renewable energy sources. With nearly one-third of the government's funds being spent on health, we should be increasing our support of medical research—particularly of preventive medicine—as well as discovering ways of combating the pollution of our environment. With world-wide food shortages, research to increase the bountifulness of both the land and the sea should also be receiving full support. The severe economic problems of continued inflation and unemployment cry out for research which will improve communication and transportation as well as create new employment opportunities. Against countries with cheap labour, Canada can no longer compete in world markets in industries such as furniture manufacturing and textiles which utilize nineteenth-century technology. We should be taking advantage of our well-educated population to create industrial opportunities which exploit leading-edge technology. We are not doing so. "It is an absolutely criminal waste of our talent that there are only 400 jobs for the 2,000 PhDs we train each year in the sciences."[4] This trend is part of a general pattern, but it's especially acute here. Canada's support of science relative to its GNP compares very poorly with that of other affluent Western countries.[5]

We can no longer rely on others to develop the scientific breakthroughs that will solve our problems. We can no longer allow others to take the lead in research if we wish to be economically competitive with other nations in world markets. We can no longer rely on others because of the unique problems we face in Canada: because of our extreme northern climate, our geographically large land mass, our uneven distribution of population, our vast forest lands; because we have the longest coastline in the world; and so on. Our unique geographical features should be sufficient motivation for us to do pioneering work in the fields of northern research, forestry, space heating of interiors, decentralized energy production, oceanography and communication, and long-distance transportation.

In view of the urgent need in Canada for more scientific research, I suggest that the over-all budget for scientific activities should be increased by 10 per cent in the coming fiscal year, and that this *increase* should be directed towards mission-oriented research consistent with our national goals. A council of scientists, economists, and government officials should be established to assess the needs of Canada and to define more precisely the type of research projects to be encouraged and supported. The government must develop a long-range plan and an over-all strategy for science research—as the Senate Science Committee chaired by Senator Maurice Lamontagne recently recommended.[6]

By keeping the budget for pure research fixed, the government is essentially reducing its support relative to inflation. The effect of this will be to prune the pure-research effort and remove less-competitive researchers from this area. This will most seriously effect our pure-research effort. Since the over-all budget for research is not being cut, those whose pure research is curtailed can always move into mission-oriented research. The pure-research budget should not remain fixed year after year— that is to ensure that pure research will eventually wither away. While it is the mission-oriented research that should experience greater growth at this time we must always maintain a certain level of support for pure research. Pure research provides the foundation for applied research and it also renews the scientific community both intellectually and spiritually.

In return for the additional support to the science community that an increased science budget would provide, the government should ask the scientists spending their government funds to purchase Canadian products where scientifically and economically feasible. This goal can best be achieved, perhaps, by requiring grant holders to abide by the Federal Purchasing Guidelines. One could then justify more support for science in terms of the employment that would be generated through increased purchases of Canadian supplies and services, as well as the direct employment of scientists.

A "Buy Canadian" policy might serve to stimulate the founding of new businesses. Potential suppliers and manufacturers could be assured of a captive market if they created equipment or services which were economically and scientifically competitive with their foreign counterparts. The Ministry of State for Science and Technology should do a study to determine how many jobs could be created by requiring grant holders to abide by the Federal Purchasing Guidelines, and whether an industrial strategy could be developed in the science supply and service sector.

Institution of the "Buy Canadian" campaign among scientists would serve as a gentle reminder to them of their respon-

sibilities to society and might motivate them to involve themselves more in mission-oriented research. More mission-oriented
research would contribute to the knowledge necessary for developing new industries and, again, new employment opportunities. An increase in the science budget can, therefore, be justified politically as a scheme for creating employment in Canada
through direct employment of scientists, through the growth of
the science supply and service industry, and through the creation
of new knowledge which could eventually lead to new jobs.

A discussion of a long-term policy for federal funding of
scientific research might, at first, seem somewhat removed from
our present political *impasse* . However, let us consider the fact
that Canadian support of scientific research compares very
poorly with that of other Western countries. "Recent surveys
indicate that in the period 1967–1975, support for scientific
research in universities in various countries has increased relative
to that in 1969 as follows: U.S.A. by 45%; United Kingdom by
60%; Japan (to 1973) 80%; France by 100%, and W. Germany
by 150% . . . in Canada . . . by only a trivial 10–15%."[7] The
reason for the reduced support of science in Canada, I feel, is
that our energy and resources are drained by our perpetual political crises. It is therefore incumbent upon us to settle our political differences so that we can begin to turn our attention to other
vital concerns—in which our very physical survival may be at
stake.

NOTES

1 Ministry of State for Science and Technology, *Federal Science Programs*
   1977-78 (Ottawa), Catalogue St 21-3/1978, p. 8.
2 Ibid.
3 Graham W. Mainwood, *Canadian Science Policy*, Canadian Association
   of University Teachers (CAUT) Bulletin, Association Canadienne des
   Professeurs d'Université (ACPU) (March 1977), p. 7.
4 Patricia Bell, paraphrasing Dr. Fraser Mustard, Dean of the Faculty of
   Health Services, McMaster University. See "Cutbacks in funding by
   Ottawa assailed by health researchers", *The Globe and Mail* (Toronto),
   October 25, 1977.
5 Mainwood, *Canadian Science Policy*, p. 7; and Brian E. Conway,
   "Research Funding in the Pure Sciences", CAUT Bulletin, ACPU (March
   1977), p. 10.
6 "Science policy efforts wasted, Senators feel", *The Globe and Mail*
   (Toronto), October 27, 1977.
7 Conway, "Research Funding in the Pure Sciences", p. 10.

PART FIVE

THE THIRD OPTION

IN THIS FINAL SECTION we present three articles designed to help free Canadians from the kinds of stereotyped ways of thinking which have so often stood in the way of our solving our problems in the past. They are not intended as a "blueprint" for actions we can take in the short term—although they do propose concrete suggestions in many cases. Rather, we intended them, first, as an antidote to the sort of rigid scenarios which now seem to pass for a creative rethinking of our current constitutional and social arrangements; and, second, as a spur to all of us to think seriously and deeply about our national goals and priorities.

In part, what we have tried to do here is to show the reader that few of our current options are so clear that they should be adopted without further public scrutiny. Senator Lamontagne, for instance, suggests that there is a robust institutionalized basis for the positions currently being adopted by senior governments in Canada which would soon break down if policy makers were forced to confront one another directly rather than issue pronouncements. We believe that this is true. One of the underlying theoretical bases for this collection has been the assumption that important grounds for common action in the face of our current crises may be found in our common attempt to understand and cope with forces which are impinging on us from outside our borders. Because we are a country of regions, we tend to assume that many problems are unique to our own areas. If we can come to understand that we are all experiencing similar difficulties, though in different ways—and that their genesis lies in Canada's place in the world political economy—we will be more willing to compromise with one another in order to face them together.

We are also trying to suggest new means of conceptualizing the nature of Confederation itself. Logan suggests, by analogy, that we have been drawn into highly mechanistic models of what constitutes a nation-state which are neither necessary nor desirable. By proposing a new type of social physics which we can use in defining our ties to one another, he suggests ways of thinking about our problems which will expand the number of options open to us. All our alternatives are not zero-sum where one party —be it a province, or the provinces, or the federal government— "wins" and the others "lose". From his perspective we can see that there are a number of forms of association we could enter into which would benefit us all and which would not necessitate a loss in power or control to any social group or government.

Finally, we have tried to draw together and synthesize the thinking of each of the authors who have contributed to this collection and to propose a framework in which each of their suggestions for new policy directions can be carried out. As the reader is no doubt aware, this is no easy task because we are not in total agreement with one another on a number of points. Nevertheless, in the course of writing the final essay in this collection, "Towards a New Unity Through Diversity: Canada's Third Option", we were struck by the similarities between articles written by authors with markedly different political affiliations and social perspectives. We have tried to capture these points of convergence and present them to you in the form of a systematic program for dealing with those aspects of our national crisis which are most amenable to direct and pragmatic action. We do not pretend that this program will cure all our current ills—or even that it comprehensively defines the nature of our problems. We hope, however, that it may provide a catalyst for discussions which will provide some answers.

CHAPTER TWENTY-THREE

CONSENSUS IN THE NEW SOCIETY

THE EMERGENCE OF A NEW SOCIETY

A NEW SOCIETY has emerged in Canada and in other advanced countries since the Second World War. Its basic features are becoming more and more precise.

This new society is increasingly urban, and affluent, better-educated, and post-industrial. In our country, 44.3 per cent of the population was rural in 1941 and 76.1 per cent was urban in 1971. Between 1950 and 1975, gross national product per capita in constant dollars almost doubled, rising from $2,460 to $4,783. Since the Second World War, Canada has built one of the most generous and elaborate systems of social security in the world. Expenditures devoted to education, in constant dollars, increased from $2.2 billion in 1960 to $7.8 billion in 1970. The percentage of total employment in service-producing industries rose from 42.5 per cent in 1950 to 64.3 per cent in 1975. Incidentally, those changes were accompanied by a decisive shift of our federalism towards government decentralization: the share of total government revenues directly spent by the federal government declined from 73 per cent in 1945 to 40 per cent in 1975.

Before the last war, the prevailing situation was misery in the midst of plenty; today, it is affluence in the midst of growing scarcities. Canadians used to believe that their country was en-

* Paper submitted to a Liberal Party Policy Conference workshop, Toronto, March 1977. Published here in modified form by kind permission of the author.

MAURICE LAMONTAGNE

dowed with boundless resources. We are now forced to reassess our physical potential.

Our agricultural frontier is close and an increasing amount of good arable land is withdrawn every day from agriculture. Higher productivity of presently developed land is possible, but only with much greater use of mechanization, artificial fertilizers, and pesticides, all of which require more capital and great amounts of energy and mineral resources, and lead to problems of soil and environmental quality. The mining committee report to the 1973 National Economic Outlook Conference emphasized that the era of "easy ore" was over for Canadian mining. It warned that most of the deposits which are easy to discover have been found and that new ore would have to come from more expensive frontier areas and greater depths. A former spokesman for the pulp-and-paper industry recently estimated that in the early 1980s our supposedly inexhaustible supply of trees would be taxed to capacity. In the area of energy, our best hydraulic sites have been developed. In 1971, the then Minister of Energy, Mines, and Resources was asserting that Canada had over 900 years of natural gas left and just under 400 years of oil. Today, Canada has already become a net importer of oil. Those few illustrations are presented as a warning that even Canadians should not build their future on blind hopes, and that their traditional patterns of economic growth may be threatened sooner than expected. Our new society must learn to become a "conserver" society.

In the immediate postwar period, it was relatively easy to identify specific national goals; today, our national objectives have become almost innumerable and interdependent. In 1945, when the White Paper on employment and income was published, we simply did not want to go back to the tragic situation created by the Great Depression. The goal was to maintain full employment and to fight against social insecurity. Today, as the discussion paper entitled *The Way Ahead* shows, the old problems of unemployment and poverty are still with us, but new ones have developed. Chronic inflation, balance-of-payments difficulties, growing scarcities, urban overcrowding, environmental pollution, frustrated expectations, cultural alienation, social maladjustments, and violence constitute some of the elements of the mounting crisis affecting most post-industrial societies. To this list should be added such world threats as nuclear wars, population explosion, changes in weather conditions, and acute famines.

These problems often require solutions which appear to be incompatible. They are intertwined and they cannot be successfully attacked separately, although they all seem to be related to quantitative growth addiction. Harlan Cleveland states: "We are only just beginning to see that all these well-researched 'problems' are so exquisitely tangled together that action on any one of them requires thinking about all of them—that is, thinking about the whole predicament."[1] Even a specific problem like chronic inflation, which is the result of collective irresponsibility, requires concerted action. In other words, the new society in terms of its problems and their solutions has become interdependent.

The old society was vertical in the sense that decision making and the exercise of power were hierarchic, but based on widely shared values. The new society is horizontal, as a much greater number of people participate in the collective decision-making process, but since these people belong to different groups which all insist on satisfying their own divergent interests and aspirations, the new society has also become fragmented and factious.

In the past the family, largely dominated by parents, was a powerful integrating force. Churches had a great deal of influence and religion gave a fatalistic meaning to poverty and other sources of adversity. Firms were comparatively small, but management could largely determine its conditions on the labour market and it was not inhibited by consumer or environmentalist groups or by government intervention. The role of the state was restricted, but governments, once elected, could operate without too much outside interference. In other words, as Harlan Cleveland puts it: "In the vertical, pre-systems society, dogma, doctrine and dictation were the normal style of leadership."[2] As a result decision making, being the privilege of the few and restricted in scope, was a relatively simple process.

The transition between the old and the new society witnessed the development of a horizontal society, characterized by the involvement of an increasing number of people in the collective decision-making process either through the market mechanism or universal suffrage. But this "random" society could not last very long. As people were better educated, they became less fatalistic and more conscious of their own priorities and of their power to assert them. They also gradually realized that the so-called free market and the ballot box were poor mechanisms for effective participation and the successful assertion of newly felt expectations.

When the fight for the right of association was won, horizontal societies ceased to be "random" societies and became fragmented societies. Indeed, people discovered that association meant power and that in order to achieve effective membership in participatory democracy they had to join a group. As a result, a multitude of movements, associations, and citizens' committees have developed to serve special interests or causes. Today, it is almost impossible to list them all. Here lies one of the fundamental contradictions of the new society: while, as mentioned before, it is interdependent in terms of its problems and their solutions, it is fragmented in terms of its organization.

THE BREAKUP OF CONSENSUS

A basic difficulty raised by the existence of "thousands of organizations" is that they often attempt to serve divergent and conflicting goals and interests. In this context, fragmented societies give rise to factionalism. James Reston wrote in 1975: "If you watch the news on television these days you can hardly avoid the feeling that the United States is a nation of selfish actions, lobbies, and squabbling tribes that have lost their concern for the national interest and even abandoned the tradition of public civility.... There is a rise of factionalism in America, something beyond the old battles between management and labor, but a feeling even among teachers, policemen, fire-fighters and other 'public servants' that they can protect their own interest only by fighting the public they are supposed to serve."[3]

It is interesting to compare this analysis with the description of the decline of the ancient Roman republic given by the historian Henry Pelham: "Italy was living through the fever of moral disintegration and incoherence which assails all civilized societies that are rich in the manifold resources of culture and enjoyment, but tolerate few or no restraints on the feverish struggle of contending appetite....There was no longer any body of sound public opinion to which, in the last resort, appeal could be made."[4]

With the rise of factionalism, the new society tends to become more turbulent and unstable. This tendency is reinforced by the media which devote disproportionate attention to the least stable and the more marginal factions. Television puts the emphasis on the news of conflict: good news is no news; the worst news becomes the best news. We have daily experience of the far-reaching effects which flow from interruptions of key services easily organized by small determined groups.

Moreover, the rise of factionalism has been accompanied by the widening of the scope of the collective decision-making process resulting from the extension of human control and expectations. Sir Geoffrey Vickers has illustrated this trend: "There would today be no sense in arguing that there ought to be more or less rain; but there is plenty of sense in arguing that there ought to be more houses. And as soon as we come to control rainfall, we shall certainly begin to argue about how much ought to fall on whom. The greater the span of human power, the greater the field of human responsibility is deemed to be, and the wider, in consequence, becomes the area in which ethical arguments can be used."[5] And there is a reciprocal relationship between factionalism and human conflict: factionalism leads to human conflict and, as the field of potential human conflict widens, factionalism tends to spread.

Obviously, the various factions of the new society cannot win all their battles or achieve their conflicting objectives at the same time. Hence their frustrations, which lead them to appeal to the state to resolve private conflicts—which they resent as unfair government interference if the decision is not in their favour. Ultimately, the state becomes the scapegoat of the collective complex of guilt transfer, but it cannot solve conflicts to everybody's satisfaction when society will "tolerate few or no restraints on the feverish struggle of contending appetites".

Not being able to keep all factions equally satisfied, governments try at best to keep them equally dissatisfied. They become fire brigades, solving crises as they arise without the benefit of planning. At worst, since it is becoming increasingly difficult to get consensus for and easier to receive support against something, they tend to provide negative leadership.

Peter Drucker claims that governments have become big, fat and flabby, ineffective, expensive, and sick "just at the time when we need a strong, healthy, and vigorous government".[6] It is true that the state in the new society has become big and weak.

In addition to being the object of increasing guilt transfers from the private sector, it is within itself the victim of factionalism. Growing bureaucracies fight against each other to preserve or extend their respective territories. Time-consuming legislative processes are too often dominated by the negative operations of the adversary forces. Federalism, in spite of its advantages, introduces another element of factionalism. The whole international community has become horizontal, fragmented, and dominated by "the tyranny of the majority".

As a result, in all Western societies, the state is losing its credibility and there is a mounting crisis of government leadership. Governments, when they are not quickly defeated, barely hang on to power, and post-election honeymoons are shorter than ever, but this decline in government credibility, leadership, and stability appears to be a symptom, or at most an element, of the crisis rather than its cause. We perhaps need strong government, but do we really want it? Moreover, in the private sector as well, followship has replaced leadership. Private leaders are too often mere spokesmen for the marginal interests of their respective factions; they refuse or are unable to provide strong and healthy leadership in the public interest and, without it, factionalism cannot produce the "body of sound public opinion" which is required in a democracy to support vigorous government leadership. In other words, strong leadership in the private sector leads to weak leadership in the public sector.

This picture of our situation may be unduly bleak and pessimistic. I believe that it is, in substance, realistic. If it is, it means that Canadian society, like others in the Western world, cannot successfully face current challenges and still less those which lie ahead. In this sense, the new society is an unprepared society. Basically, it is the victim of a breakup of consensus at a time when its problems and their solutions are becoming increasingly interdependent.

THE NEED FOR CONSENSUS

The new society faces three basic alternative avenues for the future:
- it can continue to evolve as it emerged and let trends be its destiny;
- it can let the state take over and impose extensive controls and detailed regulations;

- it can choose concerted action based on effective co-
operation both within the private and the public sectors
and between them.

These three basic avenues can be briefly described as resting
respectively on freedom and independence, on compulsion and
dependence, and on self-reliance and interdependence.

In essence, these are the three alternatives outlined by
Prime Minister Trudeau when he attempted to launch a public
debate on the new society in December 1975. Unfortunately, he
received only an emotional response from those who wanted to
go back to the old society and to resurrect nineteenth-century
laissez-faire. The ensuing controversy was sterile, unrealistic,
and even dangerous, because, in attempting to reconstruct an
idealized past which had never existed in Canada, it could have
diverted our attention from the opportunities and the threats of
the future. Fortunately, this initial emotional response did not
last very long and Canadians today are prepared to look more
objectively at the three basic options offered to us.

More and more people are convinced that the first avenue
is undesirable. They feel almost instinctively that the new
societies in the Western world, including ours, are engaged on a
dangerous course, and that if we let trends be our destiny, we
will face mounting problems, deeper dissensions, a growing
paralysis of the collective decision-making process, and eventual
chaos. We are already exposed to physical, economic, social, and
institutional limits to quantitative growth. For instance, if our
demand for energy continues to grow at current rates and if we
persist in relying mainly on traditional sources of supply, the
cost in terms of capital requirements, external trade deficits, and
environmental problems will be enormous. Other areas of our
national life, such as transportation, housing, and labour negotiations, raise similar or other threats which will all be reflected in
higher costs and chronic inflation.

One alternative to the business-as-usual attitude is government dictation and more bureaucratic controls from the top.
It is obvious that Canadians are not prepared to follow this
second avenue. The strong opposition voiced by important
groups to the relatively mild program of price and income controls clearly reveals this prevailing view. Government dictation
in a democratic society composed of opposing factions cannot
last very long. Moreover, such an approach would require much
greater power in the hands of the federal government at a time
when public opinion seems to favour more decentralization. We

may still have to accept this option not by choice but by necessity, only as a last resort to meet a crisis situation—which should be avoided by all means.

In this perspective, only the third avenue is desirable. All industrialized countries are at a major turning point. This transition period can be described as the post-industrial revolution and, if we are not very careful, it can be in many respects more turbulent than the era which followed the industrial revolution in Europe. Eventually, we will have to develop new lifestyles better adjusted to the new environment. In the immediate future, if we want to minimize turbulence and government dictation, we will have to break the solitudes of factionalism, mainly at the level of public and private leadership, to build a sound body of public opinion and a broad consensus in order to achieve effective concerted action.

During this age of distemper and dissent, there is no more urgent need than to organize the basis for consent and consensus. A growing number of observers recognize this essential need. To meet it, Alvin Toffler calls for "a continuing plebiscite on the future".[7] Sir Geoffrey Vickers contends that the containment and resolution of conflict depend more and more on persuasion and dialogue.[8] But we have not paid much attention to the organization of the dialogue. Private and public decision makers in the different segments of our society have very little opportunity to meet and discuss their common problems, and, when they do, it is often because they face a crisis which divides them. This is not the ideal climate for consensus or even for consent. The public at large is too often placed in a position where it remains outside of the decision-making process and it can only react to decisions already taken.

HOW TO BUILD CONSENSUS

In building consensus, as Claude Gruson states: " . . . the organization of the debate holds a crucial place. It is this debate which must identify conflicts, prepare the bases of agreements and delimit disagreements, and which must in any case allow each interested party to understand the nature of the problems raised, to design the solutions which appear the best to him, to measure his agreement and disagreement with the solution being implemented, and to evaluate the political importance of this agreement or disagreement."[9]

Various attempts have been made in Canada to organize the debate. A few years ago, the Economic Council initiated a series of annual economic conferences with participation by business and labour representatives. Unfortunately, after two meetings, this initiative had to be abandoned at the request of the council members representing labour. John Turner, when he was Minister of Finance, had elaborate consultations on voluntary price-and-income guidelines but failed to get agreement. More recently, the manifesto issued by the Canadian Labour Congress sought greater participation in policy decision making. In October 1976, when it issued its discussion paper entitled *The Way Ahead: A Framework for Discussion*, the Canadian government expressed its intention to "initiate a formal process of discussion, dialogue, and consultation with all elements of Canadian society: provincial governments, representatives of business, labor and consumer organizations, other special interest groups, and individual Canadians." Since then, such provinces as Ontario and Québec have started a similar process.

These new attempts will be useful and may provide a more orderly basis for the post-control period. It would be surprising, however, if they were to lead to the degree of mutual understanding and consensus required by the continuing challenges of the new society. To meet this highly complex objective, we will very likely need new and more effective institutional arrangements.

A NEW INSTITUTION: HORIZONS CANADA

To overcome the solitudes of factionalism, nothing less than an intellectual and moral conversion will be needed. Groups and their leaders will have to start to ask themselves what they can do for the country. This is essentially what interdependence means. Such a shift in attitudes and motivations will not be easy to achieve. It may prove less difficult to change our respective perception of future opportunities and threats and to develop an intellectual consensus which might lead to a moral conversion. But even this more limited objective will require a better-structured process of dialogue than that apparently contemplated by governments in Canada at present. This process should at least meet the following conditions.
- The debate or dialogue should be organized on neutral grounds and not exclusively under government auspices.

Governments in our new societies have lost a great deal of their credibility. They are often viewed as just other factions with their own vested interests. They should, of course, actively participate in the debate, but they should not accept the exclusive responsibility for initiating and controlling it.

- The participants in the formal debate should constitute a good sample of public and private decision makers representing the various segments of Canadian society. If consultations are fragmented, participants will not be able to enlarge their shared views of problems and solutions. If they are too restricted, participants may not represent the respective views of their groups.

- The debate must be held in public. Even if the number of participants directly engaged in the formal process must be limited for practical reasons, the public at large has a vital interest in the debate and must be informed of its content and its results. The public nature of the dialogue would also have a healthy influence on its direct participants and improve the level and the results of the discussions.

- The dialogue must be organized on a continuing basis and involve periodic meetings on specific topics allowing sufficient time for serious and detailed discussion. Our society faces a multiplicity of complex challenges requiring collective consideration and concerted action. The agenda for tomorrow is heavy. It will not be adequately covered by sporadic meetings lasting two or three hours in an otherwise busy daily schedule. Participants should have ample opportunity to get involved in the debate.

- Meetings should be well planned and prepared in advance by providing participants with "objective" information on the problems to be discussed and the pros and cons of alternative solutions. If the dialogue is to allow each interested party to understand the nature of the problems raised, to prepare the bases of agreements and delimit disagreements on solutions, the best technology and techniques should be used to gather information and make it available in advance to participants so as to enable them to refer to the same facts and options during their discussions.

We do not have the institutional arrangements required to meet those conditions of success for the building of consensus. A new institution that could be called Horizons Canada should be set up for this purpose. It should be a private service organization designed, financed, and controlled by a representative group of public and private decision makers to ensure its independence and objectivity. It should not engage in research, but its relatively small staff should be composed of experts in information technology and techniques and of people who can digest the results of research conducted elsewhere in various areas and transcribe them in usable form for decision makers.

The main mission of Horizons Canada would be to keep decision makers better informed on existing and future opportunities and threats and to help them reduce the areas of dissent and enlarge the areas of agreement on the important issues faced by Canadian society. It would have two main kinds of activities. First, it would serve as the relaying station of a national information network. Second, it would act as a rallying station and organize periodic meetings of decision makers with the hope of gradually developing a greater national consensus.

There is a growing vacuum at the centre of our collective decision-making process. Horizons Canada or a similar institution could fill that vacuum. However, even if it were properly launched and managed, it could not accomplish miracles. Its mission will be difficult and to accomplish it successfully, it will not be able directly to involve many people. At the beginning at least, it may appear too elitist. But it could become a seed operation and start an amplification process and an institutional chain reaction.

THE CREATION OF OTHER
PARTICIPATORY INSTITUTIONS

Horizons Canada, limited as it would be to national issues, should and could lead to the creation of other similar or complementary institutions at the regional and local levels. It could be of great assistance to such organizations, but also be reinforced by them.

The Americans have led the way in this respect and we should profit from their experience. Since 1970, several types of participatory and anticipatory institutions have been created in the United States at the state level, such as Alternatives for Washington, Hawaii 2000, Iowa 2000, the Commission on Minnesota's Future. These experiments have been reviewed recently in an article entitled "Anticipatory Democracy" published in *The Futurist* by David Baker in October 1976.

Baker claims that these organizations have common features: they focus on all aspects of the future, they exist outside normal governmental structures, and they emphasize citizen involvement. He argues that these groups have experienced their greatest success in educating participants about current state problems, projecting alternatives in various sectors of state activity, and devising general goals for state action. The creation of such groups should be encouraged at least in the five broad regions of Canada.

In the United States and to a lesser extent in Canada, local and community groups involving citizens' participation have also emerged. They usually have more specific goals and specialized activities than the broader organizations mentioned above, and, thus, they vary greatly in their composition and structures. The most interesting ones have been launched as a result of social innovations designed to meet community needs. They may concentrate on care for the handicapped, local cultural and recreational activities, urban agriculture, waste-utilization systems, or local use of solar energy. These are just a few illustrations of the activities of such community groups. Governments should encourage the creation of community groups and share in the financing of their activities when this assistance is needed.

In most cases, the existence and the programs of such organizations are not widely publicized, although their social experiments could easily be applied in many other communities. An inventory of the success stories of these groups should be kept and made known to other communities. In the United States, the Institute for Local Self-Reliance was incorporated in Washington in 1974 as a tax-exempt, non-profit organization. In 1976, it began to publish a bi-monthly newsletter called *Self-Reliance*. Its main purpose is to compile an inventory of private institutions dealing with local issues and to report on their programs and activities, thereby providing most valuable services. A similar institute supplying these services should be created in Canada.

The movement towards self-reliance offers great hope. It represents an excellent opportunity for citizens to reach a consensus on concrete issues of immediate concern to them and to organize concerted action to deal with them according to their own needs and aspirations. The movement can also help reduce the tasks of governments and simplify the public decision-making process. Moreover, as citizens learn to achieve consensus on community problems, they may find it easier to agree on larger regional and national issues.

Parliamentary institutions were originally designed as the focus of collective decisions and were assigned the relatively simple task of maintaining the rules of the random game in atomic societies. The rise of factionalism involving the multiplication of monopolistic and other pressure groups has created new important centres of collective decisions in the private sector and seriously distorted the random game. These new centres, serving their own conflicting interests, have created an oligarchic society and a jungle game which our parliamentary institutions, based on the adversary system, on checks rather than balances, were not designed to rule alone.

Thus a vacuum has developed. To fill it, we must create new and parallel participatory and anticipatory institutions at various private levels, designed to build consensus on public-interest issues and to facilitate concerted action to deal with these issues. Otherwise, governments and parliaments will continue to try to fill the gap, but in the process they will become more over-burdened, more bureaucratic, and more inefficient and they will not be able to face current and future challenges successfully.

CONCLUSION

Many people adopt a fatalist—pessimist or optimist—attitude towards the new society. The pessimists see the future as a series of mounting crises and man as a purely egoistic animal practising "life-boat ethics". They foresee an end to present trends, but they claim that it will happen by catastrophe rather than by calculation. At the other extreme, the optimists believe that our problems could easily be solved if we could rely on the "technological fix" and return to the good old days.

We should resist the temptation of choosing between these two extremes. We should refuse to be petrified by the pessimists or tranquilized by the optimists. We should adopt the attitude of the realist and look at our new society as presenting opportunities which should be maximized and threats which should be minimized. We should have faith in human beings and in their capacity to respond positively and creatively to collective challenges when they are given the opportunity to perceive them clearly and together. As we begin to build a new broad consensus in our society, we should be inspired by the thoughts of a great realist, Jean Monnet, the father of the European Community, who wrote recently in his *Mémoires*:

> Events have taught me that human nature is found weak and unpredictable when rules are missing and institutions are failing.
>
> It is certain that the egoism of man and nations finds its source in most cases in an inadequate knowledge of the problem raised, everyone being inclined to see only the aspect of his immediate interest.
>
> Men, when they are placed in certain conditions, see that they have common interests and then they tend to come to an agreement. These conditions are that they discuss the same problem with the will and even the obligation to give it a solution acceptable to all.[10]

Jean Monnet's long experience with very different human beings having apparently conflicting interests and his great achievements in getting them to reach consensus on highly complex and thorny issues, should give credence to his message. Let us accept it. Since our present institutions are failing and new rules are missing, since our knowledge of issues is inadequate and often biased, let us create new participatory and anticipatory institutions which will enable individuals and groups to see that they have common interests and to discuss the same problems—with the will and even the obligation to give them solutions acceptable to all.

NOTES

1 Harlan Cleveland, "How Do You Get Everybody in on the Act and Still Get Some Action?", *Educational Record*, Vol. 55, no. 3 (1974).

2 Ibid.

3 James Reston, "Failure to realize democracy's common interests", *Ottawa Journal*, September 9, 1975.

4 Henry Pelham, "Rome", in *Encyclopaedia Britannica* (1963), Vol. 19, 490.

5 Geoffrey Vickers, *Making Institutions Work* (London, 1973), pp. 12-13.

6 Peter Drucker, *Age of Discontinuity* (New York, 1968), p. 212.

7 Alvin Toffler, *Future Shock* (New York, 1970), p. 422.

8 Vickers, *Making Institutions Work*, p. 30.

9 Claude Gruson, "Réplique aux objecteurs de croissance", *Expansion* (juillet-août 1972).

10 Jean Monnet, *Mémoires* (Paris, 1976).

CHAPTER TWENTY-FOUR

QUÉBEC AND CANADA, QUANTUM STATES? THE INS & OUTS OF CONFEDERATION

CANADIANS ARE now engaged in a nationwide discussion in which the future of Confederation is being debated.

As a theoretical physicist studying the basic interactions of elementary particles I feel that some of the metaphors and images from my profession might provide a useful model for those looking for an alternative to the status quo. Metaphors of course are not a description of reality, but they can often be helpful in providing new and useful ways of perceiving old problems.

Simple notions of physics have influenced political thinking in the past. Newton's cause-and-effect description of the universe using precise mathematical equations served as a paradigm or framework for social and political thinkers. Adam Smith's formulation of economic theory in terms of supply and demand was patterned on Newton's notion of homeostatic or balancing forces. Similarly the division of government into the executive, legislative, and judicial branches in the American constitution with its system of checks and balances, forces and counterforces, was based on the political thinking of Rousseau and Locke who in turn had been influenced greatly by the mechanical model of Newton's universe.

The Newtonian picture, in which the exact position and

* Prepared for this volume.

ROBERT K. LOGAN

velocity of every particle of the universe could be determined, broke down when scientists began to study the atom and its constituents: the proton, the neutron, the electron, and the photon. Every attempt to measure the position or velocity of an elementary particle changes its state due to its extremely small size. It is, therefore, not possible simultaneously to know both the position and velocity of a subatomic particle as had been the case in a Newtonian world of large objects. This formulation of the Heisenberg uncertainty principle implies that one can no longer definitively state if an electron is inside or outside an atom, since precise measurement is no longer possible. The electron, therefore, must be considered to be both inside and outside the atom at the same time.

Perhaps this is a useful image for looking at models of Confederation and the various options available to Canada. In one scenario (sometimes referred to as option one) Québec remains inside of Confederation. There are no fundamental constitutional changes or reallocation of functions. In option two, Québec forms a sovereign state outside of Confederation with the possibility of association. In the third option, as it is usually formulated, Québec remains inside Confederation but the nature of Confederation changes.

Each of these formulations of Confederation is Newtonian since Québec is either inside or outside of Canada. In a quantum-mechanical formulation of Confederation, Québec would be simultaneously in both states just as an electron is simultaneously inside and outside the atom.

This model allows for more flexible arrangements between Québec and Canada. There is a sense in which Québec should be totally part of Confederation and one in which it should be separate. The same is true for all the other regions of Canada. They too should be both in and out of Confederation, not, perhaps, in the same way as Québec, but in a way best suited to their needs. This is not to suggest special status for Québec, but, rather, special status for all the provinces.

This quantum model should not be mistaken for "sovereignty-association" which entails the actual separation of Québec from Canada followed by association. Such an arrangement is impractical because the very trauma of separation would make association difficult if not impossible. What is being proposed is a rearrangement within Confederation which corresponds more to present needs and which entails provinces or possibly regions acting both inside and outside Confederation at the same time.

The provinces should act within Confederation when a function can only be performed at the national level or where co-ordination avoids costly and inefficient duplication of activities. Protection of our arctic coastline is not an activity that can be carried out by a single province or even a group of provinces. It must be carried out by the national government. The same applies to a number of other activities including foreign relations, monetary policy, postal service, national defence, patents and copyrights, and so on.

There are a number of activities such as health, welfare, and education which are essentially provincial in nature but which can, nevertheless, be administered more effectively if some aspects of these fields are co-ordinated nationally. The delivery of health-care services is without a doubt a provincial matter; however, national co-ordination of research, epidemic control, and vaccination programs is essential to avoid costly duplications. The same type of reasoning applies for such activities as commerce, labour relations, welfare, and education. Because of the large number of activities that are both local and national in nature no simple formula can be provided which will cover all cases. Each area will have to be renegotiated between the provincial and the federal authorities. The general principle governing the reapportioning of authority should be as follows: the provinces should be responsible for those activities which do not require national co-ordination, such as delivery of local health, welfare, education, transportation, and communication services and the regulation of local economic, civil, residential, and recreation activities. The federal or national government should be responsible for those activities which require national co-ordination such as interprovincial transportation, communication, and commerce; research in science, health, welfare, education; and the development of a national industrial strategy.

The use of the quantum-mechanical metaphor was not intended to provide a detailed formulation of Confederation, but rather to suggest a model in which the subunits, the provinces, would maintain a flexible and constantly changing relation with the whole. We live in an era of rapid change which requires periodic reapportioning of responsibilities between central and local authorities rather than a fixed and static relation.

After 110 years with a constitution which has not undergone any significant changes, Canadians should once again examine their constitutional arrangements. In searching for an accommodation that is tailored to our pluralistic needs we must realize that some compromise between what is practical and what is ideal will have to be made. The Heisenberg uncertainty principle states that it is impossible to determine simultaneously the exact position and velocity of a subatomic particle. By analogy, a political system cannot simultaneously be perfectly practical and perfectly ideal.

Practicality in a political system is achieved at the cost of idealism, and *vice versa*. A political system which is ideal but not practical cannot achieve very much and one which is very practical but not principled is not worth having. A compromise between the extremes of idealism and practicality must be found. Decentralization of authority in order that people have control over their local affairs is a political ideal that few could challenge. This principle unfortunately does not always lead to practical consequences. If each of the regions of Canada became autonomous independent states, we would lose the advantages we presently realize by working and co-operating together.

Our present political system is obviously in need of repair. But the solution to our problems does not lie in the separation of Canada into two separate countries. We must find ways of remedying the present injustices in our political structure while maintaining the unity of Canada. In searching for this solution we should not be constrained by an either/or type of mentality. Bearing in mind the quantum-mechanical model of the atom let us search for ways in which Québec and the other regions can be both inside and outside Confederation at the same time. Let us search for a Canada which is flexible enough to accommodate the legitimate aspirations of each of its regions, but united and strong enough to maintain and protect that pluralism which makes us unique.

CHAPTER TWENTY-FIVE

TOWARDS A NEW UNITY THROUGH DIVERSITY: CANADA'S THIRD OPTION

PIECEMEAL SOLUTIONS AND HOLISTIC PROBLEMS

IN THIS COLLECTION, we and the other authors have tried to isolate for the reader the root causes of some of our specific problems. We and they have proposed solutions for many of them. But no set of "solutions" of this kind is likely to succeed without the recognition that "piecemeal" solutions will not work. How can we revitalize and restructure our medical system, without examining medical education—and higher education in general—at the same time? Can we really reorient medicine towards communities and health, as opposed to illness, without redesigning medical training? Can we wean physicians away from "capital intensive" medicine without changing the way in which medicine is provided, the types of settings in which it is practised, and the way in which we pay for it? Chang argues that many of the functions now performed in the private sector could be undertaken by Crown agencies more expeditiously and cheaply. But Berkowitz and Corman point out that Canadians have not seriously examined the implications of state intervention in the economy and cannot agree on the uses to which it

S. D. BERKOWITZ & ROBERT K. LOGAN

should be put. Given our current constitutional arrangements, could we forge agreements between Ottawa and the provinces which would allow Crown corporations in health to work efficiently and in the public interest when almost every other federal-provincial effort has been rife with bickering and bureaucratic competition? And can these particular impediments to co-operation be overcome without settling a host of other issues which have plagued federal-provincial relations in the past?

We suggest that, in all cases, the answer to these questions should be "no". The Canadian constitution, both in the sense of a fundamental law and as a set of social and political compromises, is not working well. The British North America Act—with its built-in parochialism and institutionalized conflict—needs to be altered substantially and a new constitution, more in tune with our social history and legal traditions, forged in its stead.

Canada now stands at a watershed in its history. On one side we find the old "tried-and-true" mechanisms and agreements which brought us to the brink of civil war in 1970, to a constitutional crisis and the threat of dissolution in 1976, to an *impasse* over the control of natural resources and communications between Ottawa and the West, and to permanent economic depression in the Atlantic provinces. These arrangements are not likely to survive the decade and it is whimsical and dangerous to behave as if they will. On the other side we face rough and uncharted terrain; but here there is always the possibility that we may learn from the past, avoid its pitfalls, and reshape our destiny.

It is generally assumed by those who oppose this position that "changing the constitution" is synonymous with "giving more concessions to Québec" or, more neutrally, with "greater provincial autonomy". But it is self-defeating to think of constitutional reform in this way. In some areas, certainly, the fundamental and *de facto* primacy of provincial governments should be recognized. As things stand now for instance, cultural development, local communications (telephone, cable TV), primary and secondary education, and resource development should fall under provincial jurisdiction. The centralization of policy making in many of these areas in Ottawa has led to jurisdictional disputes and popular alienation from government. However, some functions now almost exclusively under provincial jurisdiction—for instance, higher education—can and should be funded and managed by both the federal and provincial governments. And some areas—securities regulation, for instance—ought to be centralized entirely.

In each case, the touchstone for allotting responsibility to either of our two senior levels of government—or to other bodies, regulatory agencies, municipal governments, rural councils, etc.—ought to be the extent to which a given constitutional arrangement, old or new, would promote the widest possible participation by the people most directly affected by a given policy, and ensure the most consistent and rational development of the area. This would mean, in practice, that Canadian elites, who are used to getting their own way with little opposition, would be forced to justify themselves in the public arena, and to face real competition from "outsiders".

PRACTICAL EXAMPLES

We do not pretend to have come up with a final, ideal set of arrangements which will solve all of Canada's present and future ills. Indeed, it would be foolhardy to try to do so. But there are several areas where we think the direction Canada ought to take is clear.

As we mentioned earlier, one area of government responsibility which we feel ought to be centralized (or "nationalized") is securities regulation. It is a truism that capital markets in Canada are far shallower and less responsive than those elsewhere. This is often explained by reference to the "innate conservatism" of Canadian investors or a downright unpatriotic tendency to put money into American companies rather than domestic ones. As evidence of this, it is pointed out that small investors, in particular, tend to buy life insurance policies which barely keep up with inflation rather than "take a chance" by buying equity in small and "untried" firms. But as we recently saw in the case of the Vancouver exchange, some Canadians do, routinely, invest in small stocks—with results that make Loto Canada look risk-free by comparison. Stock watering, spurious claims, and precious little public disclosure are and have been common on our exchanges. Regulation of these markets is inadequate and, as we have seen in several recent cases, foreign investors know this and have used Canadian "fronts" to avoid it. We should not, therefore, expect Canadians to place their savings in small or less-known securities, or be surprised when the bulk of our equity investments tend to move away from worthwhile projects in Canada and towards their counterparts in the United States. Is it not one of the least debatable and clearest functions of the state in western countries to see that the marketplace is operated in a fair and honest fashion? Yet, for all the wrangling going on between federal and provincial governments over jurisdictions, we have not seen a great deal of disagreement over authority in this area. We submit that Canada's failure to establish a well-regulated and open securities market is a prime example of how the BNA Act institutionalizes the *wrong* kinds of conflict, while leaving important areas in the wrong hands.

Another area where the arrangement of federal and provincial responsibilities needs to be reconsidered is higher education. Elementary and secondary education are rightly under provincial jurisdiction because their effects are primarily on local communities and local labour markets. But university-level training—because it is extremely expensive and because the labour market it trains people for is not really confined within provincial boundaries—would benefit from being shared between the federal and provincial governments. It was wasteful and inconsistent, for instance, to have Saskatchewan closing down one of its engineering programs (as it did a couple of years ago) just as Alberta's need for engineers was increasing. Similar examples of "provincialism" can be found in almost every field requiring advanced training.

One way to bring about joint management of higher education would be to create a "national university system". Under this plan, five or six regional university centres—Dalhousie, say, and the smaller colleges in the Halifax area, Université de Montréal–McGill–UQ à Montréal, Toronto–York, the University of Alberta, and UBC–SFU—would be designated as "national universities". Funds for basic support services (e.g., libraries, computers, large-scale research equipment) and for graduate training would come out of funds at the federal level. Students would be able to transfer freely between these centres for graduate training, and bursaries would be fully portable. Exchanges of faculty would be set up on a routine basis and a general circulation among them could be encouraged through graduate admissions procedures.

The principal result of a change of this kind would be to break down the insularity of Canadian university life and the consequent inflexibilities in our system of job allocation. Why should we have unemployment among engineers in Ontario and jobs going begging in Alberta? Why should we ask the Canadian taxpayer to pay for the duplication of expensive research tools in each major city in the country? And why should Ontario and B.C. taxpayers, through the cost of the University of Toronto and UBC's libraries, subsidize the entire inter-library loan system while we maintain the fiction that we are supporting a "national library" in Ottawa for such purposes?

Note, in this instance, that we have *not* advocated simple rearrangement of paper responsibilities or a simple division of tax revenues. If co-operative efforts of this kind are going to work, we must get away from our old ways of formulating and implementing policies in areas like higher education, break our old cycle of oscillation from over-concentration to under-concentration of responsibilities in Ottawa or the provincial capitals, and begin to think of these problems in new ways.

REORIENTATION

What we are suggesting here—and what many of our authors have suggested earlier—is not so much a simple "reorganization" as a *reorientation* of our governmental and social institutions. John Harney thinks that this could best be realized through some form of looser confederal structure. But we must first agree on some general goals and principles, some practical mechanisms and evolutionary structures, before a drastic redrawing of our political institutions can be undertaken.

Many Canadian problems arise from a lack of clarity in the designation of responsibilities rather than a peculiar or particular division of powers. This, as Felt notes, has led to the construction of parallel bureaucracies at the federal and provincial levels—and a consequent competition between them.

One way to deal realistically with this problem of duplication is to decentralize the federal bureaucracy itself and develop ties between it and provincial bodies. Would it be so impractical, for instance, given the new forms of communications technology now available, to locate the main branch of the Department of Agriculture in Regina? Or a Department of Northern Development in Yellowknife? Provincial government operations, by contrast, might be fruitfully co-ordinated on a regional basis. Does it make much sense, for instance, to plan energy policy in Regina and Winnipeg and Edmonton at the same time? Shouldn't energy development be rationalized across imaginary political boundaries? Waverman has pointed out some of the deleterious consequences of *not* doing this.

THREE OPTIONS

In making these changes, we should always bear in mind what we are trying to accomplish. Constitutionally, there are three basic types of option open to us. One option is the present form of Confederation, which has worked reasonably well over the past 110 years, but which now shows signs of breaking down. And this choice would still require us to do something to satisfy the aspirations of those, within and without Québec, who are unhappy with things as they stand. A version of the status quo presents almost as many difficulties as making drastic changes would.

A second option is for Québec and English Canada to go their separate ways. This would present enormous problems for many Canadians—for the Anglophones in Québec, for the Francophones outside of Québec, and for the native peoples. And this course of action could well lead to the further balkanization of the country and its eventual acquisition by the United States. If presented with a better set of options, most Canadians —including many Québécois who now think of themselves as *indépendentistes* — would reject this course.

Canada's third option is to redesign our constitutional and social arrangements—not half-heartedly or timidly—but with the clear intent of making fundamental changes. This course would be perceptibly different from a simple (and almost inevitable) change in the status quo (the first option) if a systematic and co-ordinated plan for change were to be developed and implemented over time. By this means processes would be deliberately set in motion which would, in themselves, generate further change. Planned change would occur on a broad front—not in one or two areas. And popular consensus at each stage of the process would have to be gained for the next stage to proceed.

A PLAN FOR SOCIAL CHANGE

Changes of the sort which would be included in a "third option" of this type would not be merely formal or jurisdictional but would be functional in Scott's sense. They would be part of a plan for broad-scale social change. Such a program should include both short-term and long-term goals and priorities. In broad outline—and incorporating some of the ideas of contributors to this collection—we propose the following beginning points for such an undertaking.

CANADA TO BECOME FULLY BILINGUAL

Trading the language rights of one minority group for those of another in a different province is no solution to the current language crisis. Rather we should redouble our efforts to achieve bilingualism in practice. The way to do this with a minimum of dislocation and resentment might be to place primary emphasis (a) on the education of new cohorts in both official languages, and (b) on French education in English Canada (since many Québécois are bilingual already).

As a minimum short-term goal, this would imply that by 1980 all schoolchildren—in order to graduate from secondary school—would be required to be at least (a) fluent in one official language and (b) have a practical reading and speaking knowledge of the other. By 1985, this should become a grade-six graduation requirement. By 1990, secondary school students should be studying at least one of their non-language subjects in each official language. By 1995, at least a third of the instruction should be in the non-dominant language within the area where the school is located. By 1995, as well, approximately a third of the instruction at the university level should be in the non-dominant language.

This policy reflects not only the political exigencies of the moment and the historical rights of Canada's two principal language groups, but a basic precondition for the growth and development of a distinctly Canadian culture within the North American context. The "separate but equal" development of language and cultural groups in this country has created language ghettos and limitations on cultural horizons which have held back the development of both English-Canadian and French-Canadian culture, and ensured the domination of both by the powerful commercial imperium to the south. Neither the status quo nor a "sovereignty association" will deal adequately with this fact: unless and until all Canadians can speak to one another, read what each other has written, and share each other's insights, both English-Canadian and French-Canadian culture are doomed. National bilingualism is not simply a political expedient for dealing with "separatism", but is essential to national cultural survival.

Similarly, if Canada is to avoid the chief consequences of ethnic homogenization—the atomization, normlessness, and social disintegration characteristic of so many American cities—we must promote a robust sense of affinity among parts of our population and between generations. In practical terms, this means that our educational system must become an active participant in the process of national unification and not just a passive observer.

Similarly, in the area of job and employment opportunities, by 1985 all new appointees to the federal civil service should be required to have a reading and practical speaking knowledge of both official languages. Further, by 1985, no fewer than one-third of all new appointees in each provincial civil service should be required to meet this criterion. For appointments at managerial and supervisory levels, this requirement should apply to all new recruits.

Almost all of the largest and most powerful economic enterprises in Canada are federally chartered. Each of them should be required to provide, by January 1, 1979, a "bilingual plan" which would involve (a) producing their written communications in both official languages, (b) requiring all employees in direct contact with the public to be bilingual, (c) ensuring that at least one-third of all operating employees are bilingual, and (d) requiring managers to be bilingual. The federal government would have to set firm deadlines in each industry for implementation of this program. In general, all transportation, communications, or service establishments should have a clear plan underway no later than 1980. Large provincially chartered firms should be required to follow suit. By 1985, all places of employment of more than thirty employees should be required to have such a plan in operation.

CANADA TO INSTITUTIONALIZE CULTURAL RIGHTS

One of Canada's chief strengths lies in its cultural and social diversity. But this strength has often been dissipated in fruitless ethnic and group conflicts which are aggravated by our constitutional arrangements and problem-solving strategies. All groups in Canada would benefit from removal of these sources of friction.

Many groups within our population are torn between the desire to preserve elements of their historic or antecedent cultures and the need to integrate these into the larger Canadian society. Of these groups, at least three—French Canadians, native peoples, and non-British immigrants and their descendents—should have constitutionally guaranteed cultural rights.

Specifically, French Canadians should have tax-supported cultural centres in every province in Canada, French language newspapers, a negotiated portion of all cultural support funds, and special federal bursaries for students of French origin from outside Québec to study in predominantly Francophone universities. A national Crown corporation should be chartered to publish and distribute technical and scholarly books with limited markets which would not normally be translated into French. In addition, a special semi-autonomous foundation should be set up which would be charged with providing grants for French cultural groups and projects, research on topics related to French history and culture in Canada, and French cultural education outside the school system. To ensure that these programs are not simply tokenism, a clear proportion of all tax revenues should be allotted for their support.

Similar activities should be begun or extended with respect to Canada's native peoples. In addition, full-fledged provincial governments should be established in the Northwest Territories and the Yukon and in designated areas in northern Ontario and Québec where there is a predominantly native population. Adjacent areas of the provinces of Manitoba, Saskatchewan, Alberta, and British Columbia should be annexed to these new provincial governments where appropriate.

In both these new provinces and Québec, the provincial governments should exercise conjoint power with the federal government to set and maintain quotas for immigration from outside Canada.

Within these newly designated provinces, all land which has not been specifically alienated should be considered native-group property; all surface rights to this land should be retained in band or group right unless alienated; all sub-surface mineral rights should be vested in the provincial Crown; and all claims, licensing arrangements, rents, etc. currently in force between individuals, groups, and corporations and the federal government should be transferred to these new provincial governments.

While these new provincial governments are being established, the bulk of infrastructure development costs should be borne out of federal tax revenue. All monies from the adjustment payments for resource pipeline construction and similar projects should be geared towards establishing this infrastructure—and these funds should be administered by elected quasi-governments in each of the areas designated for the new provincial jurisdictions. In each case, a clear timetable for the transfer of power to these new provincial governments should be negotiated with the quasi-governments.

Too often in the past, the attitude adopted by European society towards our native peoples has been highly paternalistic. Ultimately, we believe, the preservation of native cultures and the protection of native rights must arise out of independent political power and responsibility. Earlier in this book, John Harney suggested the creation of semi-autonomous self-governing areas in the north. We feel that arrangements of this kind would likely be too inflexible to accommodate to changes which will surely go on in these areas in the next few decades. If provincial governments were set up in these same areas, however, native peoples would have more freedom to shape their own destiny in the same fashion that southerners do at present.

Beyond this, we think that in southern areas native reserves should be incorporated as co-operatives or corporations without share capital and allowed to manage their own affairs. Treaty rights and obligations between native groups and the federal government should be vested in these corporations as a whole or transferred to non-resident treaty Indians. All federal and provincial programs currently being managed by departments of Indian affairs, federally and provincially, should be placed under the control of native groups, and these departments, *per se*, abolished.

In some ways, the problem of maintaining a cultural identity is not as acute for non-British immigrant groups as it is for French Canadians and native peoples. Specific ethnic, language, religious, and nationality newspapers, clubs, associations, cultural centres, radio and television stations, and so on, exist and are growing. Moreover, in each case, these cultures continue to thrive in the countries of origin of these immigrant groups.

The danger is, however, that as time passes, if immigration does not continue from any given national homeland, ethnic communities in Canada will become isolated. This will recreate, for each of these groups, a situation similar to that experienced by French Canadians outside Québec until quite recently. In order to guard against this, third-language instruction should be guaranteed to each of these groups, where appropriate, as a matter of right; tax support for cultural and religious programs should be provided on an equitable basis; an ethnic languages press should be established to reprint or publish materials which would not normally be commercially feasible given market limitations; and a national foundation should be established to support research and teaching on ethnic affairs.

Within the public and separate schools, multicultural education programs should be established for all children to learn about each of the immigrant cultures represented within Canada as a whole. These programs should be designed with the active participation of representatives of ethnic communities themselves, and the relevant material integrated into the general curriculum.

In the area of broadcasting, all stations currently licensed by the federal government should be required to provide ethnic language broadcasting in areas where numbers warrant it, cultural programming in English or French specifically dealing with ethnic groups in Canada, and general educational programming on the history of immigration and immigrants in this country.

CANADIAN CULTURE TO BE STRENGTHENED

In a broader or more general sense, a number of initiatives should be immediately undertaken to protect and enhance our national and regional cultures.

As we said earlier, it is widely argued that regional isolation and regional disparities are a pervasive and growing threat to national unity. Moreover, the *practical* effect of many of our national policies (or lack of them) has been to enhance regional differences and stimulate regional conflict.

To offset these effects in the area of culture, we argue that a number of programs should be begun or strengthened to sustain and integrate a national consciousness. Specifically, we feel the federal government should enact legislation to limit severely programming of non-Canadian origin on Canadian radio and television stations. In Ontario, a Royal Commission was charged with examining the impact of violence in the media on public consciousness. During the hearings before this commission, a number of persons or groups testified that the vast majority of violent programming was foreign in origin. We are concerned not only with the impact of this violent material, but with a range of other cultural values which are being conveyed via the media to Canadian audiences. These, in the aggregate, cannot help but distort and weaken Canadians' self-awareness.

In their place—and this follows a suggestion by McLuhan

and Nevitt in this volume—we propose a massive initiative by federal and provincial governments to support Canadian development in the area of broadcasting, film, and related media. Canada has, in the National Film Board, one of the best professional film organizations in the world. Its budget should be substantially increased and a new tax instituted on the showing of films of foreign origin. The revenues from this tax would be earmarked for the NFB. Provincial programs in support of film and related media, and joint ventures with provincial Crown agencies in the area should be encouraged by the federal government. In addition—since many film production and distribution companies in Canada are both foreign-owned and vertically integrated—we would also need anti-combines legislation to prohibit this practice. Private film production by Canadian-owned firms should be encouraged through direct subsidies to production costs and additional tax write-offs.

In the area of publishing—in addition to the steps we mentioned earlier—Canada should create a national universities press to publish, either directly or through joint-ventured operations with private Canadian-owned firms, scholarly works of Canadian origin or interest. As a rule, all such works should be published in both official languages. Non-scholarly books should continue to be funded as they are at present, but a special tax on mass-market paperbacks of non-Canadian origin should be instituted to discourage their penetration of the Canadian market.

In the plastic and visual arts, we feel that the principal problem at the present time is that Canadian art markets are highly regionalized. In order to help overcome this, we propose the creation of a national network of art galleries, through a consortium of provincial Crown agencies, to encourage the wider distribution of works of art produced within various regions. In addition, we propose the creation of a National Visual Arts Board charged with arranging for the showing, distribution, and sale of works of art by Canadian artists to buyers in other countries.

REORIENTATION OF THE CANADIAN INDUSTRIAL AND FINANCIAL STRUCTURE

As Berkowitz and Corman noted earlier, the Canadian industrial structure is dominated by foreign ownership. This, we argued, is also the proximate cause of much of the historic pattern of regional inequality and uneven development of our industrial base.

In order to offset these effects, we propose the nationalization or provincialization of all natural monopoly areas (communications, utilities, etc.) where these are currently in foreign hands. In industries, such as petroleum production, where virtual oligopolies exist, we suggest that federal or provincial governments enact legislation which limits foreign ownership to no more than one-half of the outstanding common stock of the corporate subsidiaries chartered in Canada. In no case, we feel, should foreign ownership of a Canadian subsidiary exceed 70 per cent of the outstanding common stock.

Although rules of this kind might, at first reading, appear drastic or excessive, legislation of this kind is not unusual in the world context. Japan, for instance, severely restricts entry of foreign capital into its markets and a number of other western industrial countries place limits on foreign investments in key sectors. At the moment, a great deal of Canadian bank capital is invested abroad due to the relative shallowness of the Canadian equity market. By forcing foreign-owned firms to trade publicly or divest themselves of their ownership of Canadian firms, we could strengthen this capital market and retain more equity investment at home.

In the financial area—which has traditionally been dominated by Canadian firms—there is recent evidence of foreign incursions into the consumer credit market. Since this market exists in a grey area which quickly shades off into traditional banking, we argue that the same restrictions on foreign ownership which apply to Chartered banks should be applied to these firms as well.

In general, various proprietary and legislative means needed to ensure the processing of Canadian raw materials in this country. In the areas where we enjoy a competitive advantage, we would welcome world-scale Crown corporations to undertake the extraction and processing of these raw materials where private capital seems reluctant to do so. In addition, in cases where Canadian resources are not being used to greatest advantage—as, for instance, where lumber-quality timber is being used in pulp production—the productive use of these resources should be a condition or standard for the granting of leases for the use of Crown lands, or integrated Crown corporations should be established to increase the efficient and productive use of these resources.

Specifically with regard to existing regional inequalities, we believe that Felt is correct and that GAIN programs should be rapidly phased in to replace the welter of cumbersome programs of income support and maintenance which currently exist. Moreover, we concur that showpiece industrial development is not likely to substantially reduce existing reservoirs of unemployment. Medium-scale technological development, consortia of provincial Crown corporations, and similar strategies suggested by Berkowitz and Corman are more likely to be effective in bringing this about in the long run. In the short term, GAIN programs, if sufficiently well funded, should generate considerable amounts of employment in the private sector.

SCIENCE POLICY AND TECHNOLOGY TO BE RATIONALIZED

One of the key difficulties in Canada today, as we and other authors in this collection have noted, is the absence of any clearly defined policy for orchestrating the relationship between our labour supply, our educational system, and technological development. Earlier in this chapter, however, we suggested that further integration of our system of higher education might be advanced through conjoint federal and provincial responsibility for the management of a national university system. This would also have the positive effect of allowing for the more careful regulation of our technical manpower supply. If initiatives of this kind were coupled with the development of "centres of excellence" in selected branches of this system, we believe that Canada would be able more effectively to harness its technical skills for promoting regionally specific development in high-technology areas.

Most observers of technologically advanced industries in Canada agree that our national potential in this area is not being fully exploited because our largely foreign-owned high-technology sector is insufficiently developed to absorb many technological innovations which have originated here. We propose a three-pronged attack on this situation. First, all capital development grants from federal or provincial governments in the high-technology area should be restricted to Canadian-owned firms. Second, federal and provincial government agencies should initiate a "buy Canadian" policy for all capital equipment purchased with public funds except where it can be explicitly shown that Canadian alternatives do not exist. And third, the federal and provincial governments should jointly create and fund a bridging capital corporation to provide start-up loans for high-technology companies with advanced and demonstrable ideas with reasonable commercial potential. At present, both federal and provincial programs, in our experience, effectively preclude small companies of this kind from participating in them. Further, many of the ideas advanced by Berkowitz and Corman for joint federal and provincial marketing agencies would be useful in getting these small firms over the initial hurdles.

The theoretical basis of these suggestions, of course, is, as Logan suggested earlier, that our science policy should be linked to an industrial strategy; and *vice versa*. Because of the thinness of our research efforts in many areas, we face the perennial risk that much of the money we currently spend on research will simply get lost in the shuffle. By focusing our pure research in various "centres of excellence" and increasing our commitment to mission-oriented research in the universities and private sector, we stand at least some chance of getting short- and medium-term economic spin-offs from this activity.

OUR SOCIAL-WELFARE SYSTEM TO BE RESTRUCTURED

As many have suggested, Canada's social-welfare system is in grave need of restructuring. Earlier we mentioned the benefits which we feel will flow from moving away from the present hodgepodge of income-support programs towards a GAIN scheme. Similar attempts to de-bureaucratize other areas of our social-welfare system can, we believe, be attempted.

The keystone of this new policy can be summarized in the term "self-reliance". By this we mean that the aim of our initiatives in the broad area of social welfare should be to place the primary responsibility for administering programs, deciding policy directions, and ensuring the health and welfare of the public on the individuals, groups, and communities most directly affected by these decisions.

At first, this strategy would seem to contradict the need that many of us feel to ensure the careful administration of tax-supported programs. But as Dukszta and Berkowitz have demonstrated in the area of health care, it is possible both to decentralize decision making and to ensure accountability — and to do so with a minimum of bureaucratic red tape. Schemes of the kind they propose would benefit other areas of social-welfare planning as well.

Our current social-welfare programs reflect the defects of our process of public policy planning. In particular, we rely far too much on officially defined "experts" and "expertise". Chang has pointed to the over-dependence on technology and the staggering health-care costs which this has led to in medicine. Greater emphasis on community-based strategies in health, and preventive medicine, and the greater use of local knowledge and experience — as, for instance, in the use of native "shamans" as part of the medical system — is desirable both because it gears these services more closely to community needs, and because it de-mystifies medicine in general. De-mystification or "de-expertising" other areas of our social-welfare system would probably help these services to be more humane and realistic as well.

ENVIRONMENTAL PROTECTION TO BE STRENGTHENED

As Hare has indicated, if Québec separated from the rest of Canada our efforts to understand and protect our environment would suffer a considerable setback. Because of the small size of our population relative to the land mass we administer, our resources for protecting or even monitoring our environment are stretched as it is: networks of contact among scientists doing environmental research are sparse and fragile; research money is thinly spread over the gamut of relevant disciplines; information systems are poorly integrated and relatively undeveloped; and, in the arctic in particular, much basic work has not even been begun.

Part, then, of any commitment to a united Canada must be a redoubling of our efforts to take care of the land mass we occupy. Ultimately, we must change our wasteful and often destructive approach to the environment. As an alternative, we need to promote a kind of "prudent materialism" in which Canadians should learn to be less wasteful of our non-renewable and renewable resources; to employ less energy-intensive small- and medium-scale technology where this is economically feasible; to develop stiffer controls over materials discharged into the environment; and to undertake substantial research into renewable sources for the energy and materials which we now derive from non-renewable ones.

FORMAL CONSTITUTION TO BE DEVISED WHICH IS AIMED
AT A CLEAR ALLOCATION OF FUNCTIONAL RESPONSIBILITY

Over the last several years, senior governments in Canada have spent an increasing amount of their time arguing about jurisdictional issues. Given the severe and complex problems we now face, this is a luxury we can ill afford. Some rational means of ensuring greater co-operation between and among provincial and federal governments must be found.

To our way of thinking, the roots of these conflicts are clear enough. When Canada was largely undeveloped, the activities undertaken by both the federal and provincial governments were relatively restricted, and there was, consequently, little scope for conflict. As each of the provinces "grew up", it tended to expand its services—in response, in most cases, to popular pressure—into all areas where it was not specifically prohibited from doing so by the BNA Act. In provinces which were relatively populous or well-to-do, these activities gradually came to encompass almost the entire range of those functions—apart from defence, monetary regulation, etc.—which are normally performed by sovereign nation-states. Ottawa, for its part, was quickly expanding the range of its programs as well.

At both levels, bureaucracies grew rapidly to administer the new services being provided by government. This, in turn, created a group within each provincial government—and in Ottawa as well—with a vested interest in preserving its jurisdiction in one area or another. In time, these bureaucracies and the ministers attached to them began jockeying for tax room to support their activities while jealously guarding their areas of jurisdiction.

In some ways, it has been quite useful to have eleven national governments. In particular, it provides flexibility. Consider, for instance, the relative ease with which Canada adopted an insured medical system—after Saskatchewan proved it was feasible—as compared to the difficulties attendant on bringing in universal health insurance in the United States. Canadians would be foolish to give up this flexibility entirely.

Flexibility is convenient—when it does not degenerate into inconsistency. Consider our energy policy. In some cases the price of fossil fuels has been held at arbitrarily low levels. This, as Waverman pointed out, encourages consumption. As he futher notes, this has also meant that Alberta and Saskatchewan have been forced to accept a less-than-economic price for their reserves. In other cases, local monopolies have overbuilt their electrical generating capacity, sold their power cheaply to commercial users, and forced homeowners and tenants to pay artificially high prices for power.

In areas like energy policy, which can affect the quality of life in different parts of the country so dramatically, it seems foolhardy to rely on cumbersome methods like federal-provincial conferences to reconcile different interests. Moreover, given Ottawa's tendency to make policy in areas like this unilaterally, the provinces are probably correct in insisting on being consulted on the matter. As Kinzel observed earlier, Ottawa has not always been sensitive to provincial interests in the past.

What we probably need is some entirely new mechanism for making decisions of this kind. Given our traditions and a desire to retain provincial input, one device we might experiment with would be a permanent joint federal-provincial board to set long-range goals in areas like energy policy, or, to name another point of friction, freight rates. Institutionalizing such an arrangement, rather than bargaining about issues one at a time, would dissolve much of the aura of a high-stakes poker game which surrounds such events and allow reasonable trade-offs to occur (a less rapid rise in energy prices, for instance, in exchange for lowered freight rates). Moreover, because it would be the responsibility of this board to set long-term goals—and up to the provinces to establish short-term priorities in terms of them —the likelihood of highly politicized confrontations between levels of government would be reduced.

In some instances where jurisdictions are now ambiguous, a simple permanent division of responsibilities would reduce tensions. Dukszta and Berkowitz proposed just such an arrangement in health care—in which the federal government would undertake primary responsibility in areas like the monitoring of infectious disease, and provincial governments would act in others—which could be used as a test case for additional divisions of responsibility. Given that both federal and provincial governments are under pressure now to reduce costs, there ought to be strong popular support for moves of this kind.

What we are suggesting, then, is that since both the federal government and the provinces have defined "health care" and similar areas as their responsibilities, some rational division of functions within these areas would limit the arena for conflict and provide higher standards of service to the public by allowing each level of government to focus its activities more precisely than it does at present. Moreover, by gradually phasing in these divisions of responsibility—according to a master agreement worked out in advance—it would be possible, over a period of time, to experiment with different configurations of authority and find out which work best in practice.

Implementing a program for social change of the type we propose here would not be easy. Each of the areas we addressed —language policy, cultural rights, a national cultural policy, an industrial strategy, science policy, our social-welfare system, environmental protection, and formal constitutional changes—is fraught with problems which would make agreement difficult. And the risks of intense conflict during the period when policies in these areas are being established is great. However, we would argue that the risks implicit in continuing present trends are even graver. There is no risk-free course for us to pursue and, on balance, we probably have a better chance of finding solutions to many of our present dilemmas if we discuss them frankly and openly. The risk in the present situation is that our conflicts and disagreements in the past will blind us to the urgency of our current situation, leave us paralysed to act, and thus push us into disaster in the future.

If this book has opened up new avenues to explore in our quest for Canadian unity, then we and the other authors will have succeeded. If the reader now has come to agree with the course of action which we propose in this final chapter, we are, of course, pleased. If he or she disagrees with us—but does so on the basis of an enlarged understanding of the broader issues at stake—then this collection will have served its purpose as well. Beyond this, however, we hope we have convinced all our readers that Canada's diversity, flexibility, and historic tolerance for divergent points of view is her strength and her greatest asset as a nation. If all Canadians can now resolve to seek a new unity in this diversity, then we will find solutions to our present crises which will endure. Our current risks and challenges are great— but so are our opportunities. History will not forgive us if we ignore them.

GUIDE TO ACTIVITIES AND ORGANIZATIONS CONCERNED WITH CANADIAN UNITY

WE SHALL ASSUME that if our readers have read this far in our book they are concerned about Canada and might wish to translate their concern into action. For those that are interested in joining with others in debating or discussing the future of Confederation, we have provided at the end of this section a list of groups or associations which are presently concerned with some aspect of the Canadian unity issue. Some of the groups were in existence long before the PQ government came to power in 1976. Other groups have sprung into action in direct reaction to this event. We believe, like Senator Lamontagne, that mass citizen participation in the development of a consensus throughout Canada is the only way our country will survive intact. It was this belief that led us to draft the following proposals which were submitted by us and other members of the Club of Gnu, University of Toronto, to the federal Cabinet on the historic occasion of their first full Cabinet meeting held outside Ottawa on February 17, 1977.

- That a Parliamentary Constitutional Commission be established consisting of Senators, federal MPs and members of provincial legislatures from all parties and provinces to examine the present state of Confederation and to make recommendations for changes in our present constitutional arrangements.
- That Regional Constitutional Conventions be convened in each region to deliberate and to meet with the Parliamentary Constitutional Commission. Each of these regional conventions should consist of Canadians from *all* across the country including ethnic

and native leaders and territorial representatives. To ensure the widest possible participation, their travel expenses should be subsidized by the federal government.

- That Constitutional Workshops be convened on a regular basis over an extended period of time to allow for discussion of local, regional, and national problems directly between citizens. These discussions could be linked electronically. These workshops could also provide the necessary background for the Regional Constitutional Conventions.

- That the federal government encourage and support the formation of "Canada Forums" in which Canadians meet on a regular basis to discuss the patriation of the Constitution and to generate ideas on new forms and mechanisms for ensuring cultural, economic, and political growth and maturity in the future. These discussions will enrich the activities of the Constitutional Workshops, Conventions, and the Commission mentioned above.

- That the federal government call upon the existing social institutions such as the churches, schools, service clubs, social clubs, ethnic organizations, trade unions, professional societies, and business organizations to support, encourage, and participate in the activities of the Canada Forums.

- That research into the technical aspects of Confederation such as economics, energy, transportation, etc. be immediately undertaken through existing institutions (universities, labour unions, institutes, etc.). That this technical research be reported in such a way as to make it useful to those citizens who will be participating in the processes described above. As part of this research program, an independent National Opinion Institute should be established at an existing research facility (responsible not to the government but to the Parliamentary Constitutional Commission) to undertake frequent topical studies, polls, and nonbinding referenda on popular reaction to various issues that arise in the process of patriating our Constitution.

- That federally owned communication and transportation facilities be made available for all of the activities described above so that as many Canadians as possible can interact and communicate with one another. These include the federal telephone network which can be made available after business hours, CBC/Radio Canada radio and television prime program time, and the Air-Canada/Canadian National system for transporting delegates to meetings. Military facilities and personnel should also be made available where they can contribute to these processes.

These mechanisms or others like them were not intended solely as means of promoting discussions of patriation and reform of the constitution. Similar processes, we argued, could be used to initiate discussions relevant to Canadian unity going beyond strictly constitutional issues. Their purpose is to provide a range of opportunities for Canadians to discuss and re-experience Confederation. Other mechanisms along these same lines could, of course, be tried as well.

These proposals were based on the assumption that the direction in which Canada proceeds in the future is too important, and that the issues involved are too complex, to be decided by one or even a series of yes/no referenda. We argued that these, or similar mechanisms, are needed immediately because there is not, as yet, a full public appreciation of the dangers posed to Confederation by a number of current trends—only *one* of which is exemplified by Québec separatism.

While some of the recommendations made in the brief have not been implemented—such as the creation of a Parliamentary Commission or the establishment of the Constitutional Conventions and Workshops—a surprising number of similar activities have been begun. Research into the technical aspects of Confederation has been commissioned. The federal government has instituted a program—known as Hospitality Canada—which promotes the exchange of young people between regions—and similar projects are under way under private auspices. The equivalent of "Canada Forums" have spontaneously sprung up across the nation. In addition, existing groups and social institutions such as labour unions, business groups, churches, schools, and universities have turned part of their attention from their normal activities to discussions of Canadian unity.

We sincerely hope that our readers will find the time to join in these types of activities. It is for this reason that we provide the following list of groups. For more up-to-date information, the reader might wish to contact either: the Canadian Unity Information Office, Ottawa, K1A 0M5, Canada, telephone (613) 593-6886; or the Task Force on Canadian Unity, P.O. Box 1338, Station "B", Ottawa, K1P 5R4, Canada, telephone (613) 995-3511.

ORGANIZATIONS WITH OBJECTIVES OR ACTIVITIES RELATED TO CANADIAN UNITY

ALBERTA

Canada West Foundation
Box 1030
Calgary, Alberta
T2P 1T4

Objective: To promote the role of the western provinces within a united Canada.

Unified Canada Movement
Box 4941
South Edmonton, Alberta

Objective: To pursue the cause of unity by all peaceful means.

BRITISH COLUMBIA

Canada United
3866 Regent Avenue
North Vancouver, B.C.
V7N 2C4

Objective: To promote Canadian unity in British Columbia.

Chuck Connaghan
President's Office
University of British Columbia
Vancouver, B.C.
V6T 1W5

Objective: To maintain a united Canada.

National Unity Committee of the Vancouver Board of Trade
815 West Hastings
Vancouver, B.C.
V6C 1B4

Objectives: To inform members of the Board of Trade in the Vancouver area of the issues at stake in Canadian unity.
To communicate directly and exchange views with other like groups across the country. To promote unity in Canada.

Save Canada Committee
Box 218
Port Alberni, B.C.
V9Y 7M7

Objectives: To promote unity in Canada, an appreciation of Canada, and greater understanding of its many cultures.

> Westerners for Canadian Unity
> 1075 West Georgia Street
> 17th Floor
> Vancouver, B.C.
> V6C 3C9

Objective: To promote the establishment of similar groups across British Columbia.

MANITOBA

> G. S. Baines
> University of Manitoba
> Continuing Education Division
> Winnipeg, Manitoba

Objective: To promote travel in Canada and thereby learn about the different cultures which exist in Canada.

> Citizenship Council of Manitoba
> 65 Redwood Avenue
> Winnipeg, Manitoba
> R2W 5J5

Objectives: To assist immigrants entering Canada, to help establish good relations among the various ethnic groups in Manitoba, and to make them known to the general public.

> Rotary Club of Winnipeg
> Room 1020
> Fort Garry Hotel
> 222 Broadway
> Winnipeg, Manitoba
> R3C OR3

Objective: To contact all Rotary Clubs in Québec in order to encourage inter-provincial exchanges among members.

NOVA SCOTIA

> Fédération Acadienne de la Nouvelle-Écosse
> 6074 Lady Hammond Road
> Suite 307
> Halifax, N.S.
> B3K 2R7

Objective: To encourage the development of the Acadian communities and of a united Canada.

ONTARIO

Alliance Française
1633 Riverside Drive
Ottawa, Ontario
KIG OE5

Objective: To promote better understanding between Francophones and Anglophones in Canada.

Association de la presse francophone hors Québec
1404-1 Nicholas Street
Ottawa, Ontario
KIN 7B7

Objectives: To help Francophone newspapers outside Québec to survive. To provide information in French to Francophones living outside Québec.

Association of Canadian Clubs
Box 654
Station "N"
Ottawa, Ontario
KIP 5P7

Objective: To promote a sense of Canadian citizenship and unity.

"Canada, My Country" Committee
Chamber of Commerce, Brantford
120 Market Street
Brantford, Ontario
N3T 3A2

Objective: To discuss the problem of national unity that is facing Canada and attempt to develop a consensus towards a national will to promote the benefit of Confederation for all Canadians.

Canada Jaycees (National Headquarters)
39 Leacock Way
Kanata, Ontario
K2K ITI

Objective: To promote Canadianism and community services.

Canadian Parents for French
Box 8470
Ottawa, Ontario
KIG 3H6

Objectives: To promote the best possible type of French language opportunities. To assist in ensuring that each Canadian child has the opportunity to acquire as great a knowledge of the French language and culture as he or she is willing and able to attain. To establish and maintain effective communication between concerned parents and educational and governmental authorities concerned with the provision of French language opportunities.

Canadian Polish Congress
255 Roncesvalles Ave.
Toronto, Ontario
M6R 2N4

Objectives: To promote the welfare of Canadians of Polish origin, and Canadian patriotism and unity.

Canadian Progress Club (National Office)
67 Yonge Street
Suite 532
Toronto, Ontario
M5E 1J8

Objectives: To aid and assist those in need and foster goodwill throughout Canada. To aid in uniting all the people of Canada and to show by leadership and example the pride of being a Canadian.

Bill Charlton
1 James Street S.
Hamilton, Ontario
L8P 4R5

Objective: To promote Canadian unity and to review the Constitution.

Committee for an Independent Canada
46 Elgin Street
Suite 48
Ottawa, Ontario
K1P 5K6

Objective: To achieve an independent Canada.

Destiny Canada
York University
4700 Keele Street
Downsview, Ontario
M3J 1P3

Objective: To provide a forum where individual Canadians—particularly those Canadians who might not have an opportunity to articulate their opinions—may express their views on the future of Canada.

> Fédération des jeunes Canadiens-Français
> 1404-1 Nicholas Street
> Ottawa, Ontario
> KIN 7B7

Objective: To serve as a spokesman for Francophone youth associations outside Québec.

> Federation France-Canada
> 1551 Featherston Drive
> Ottawa, Ontario
> KIH 6P2

Objective: To promote French language and culture in Canada.

> Forum For Young Canadians
> 262 Mariposa Avenue
> Ottawa, Ontario
> KIM 0T2

Objective: To bring students together from all parts of Canada for study of governmental process in action.

> National Association of Friendship Centres
> 200 Cooper Street
> Suite 3
> Ottawa, Ontario
> K2P 0G1

Objective: To provide an umbrella service on a national level for native peoples, including general co-ordinating, communication, liaison, lobbying, and urban adjustment.

> National Council of Women
> 270 MacLaren Street
> Room 20
> Ottawa, Ontario
> K2P 0M3

Objectives: To carry out work for the betterment of the family and the nation. To research social problems and recommend changes to government leaders.

National Discovery Foundation
Box CP522
Ottawa, Ontario
K1P 5P6

National Survival Institute
2175 Victoria Park Avenue
Scarborough, Ontario
M1R 1V6
Objectives: To alert the general public to problems in the areas
of energy, food, human settlements, and population; and to seek
ways to ensure that there will be food, energy, and other necessities for everyone.

National Voluntary Organizations
Box 2477
Station "D"
Ottawa, Ontario
K1P 5W7
Objectives: To develop a stronger basis of common interest and
understanding between national unity organizations. To estab-
lish effective mechanisms for liaison and understanding between
National Voluntary Organizations and the federal government.

Non-Partisan Committee for Canadian Unity
Through Diversity
125 Rusholme Road
Toronto, Ontario
M6H 2Y6
Objectives: To be a service organization providing educational,
bibliographic, and discussion material to the grass-roots Canadian unity groups. To engage in research and communication
designs to link together Canadian unity groups as well as the
technical aspects of Canadian unity such as communication,
transportation, macro-economics, and energy policy.

One Canada Campaign
Box 116
Mississauga, Ontario
L5J 3A8
Objectives: To inform Anglophones of the depth of the French

fact. To contribute to the debate on national unity.

Option Canada (Guelph)
Trafalgar Square
Box 954
Guelph, Ontario
NIR 6M6

Objectives: To encourage dialogue in the community and create a greater understanding of national problems, and to inspire interest in Canadian unity.

Toronto Legal Fund for French-Speaking Pilots
Box 540
Station "Q"
Toronto, Ontario
M4T 2M5

Objective: To support legal action for "Les Gens de l'air", and to protect their rights.

U-Can
RR No. 1
South Mountain, Ontario
KOE 1WO

Objective: To promote Canadian unity.

United Canada Movement
1285 Matheson Blvd.
Mississauga, Ontario
L4W 1RI

Objective: To work towards and promote the cause of Canadian unity.

Unity Canada
21 Jamestown Crescent
Rexdale, Ontario
M9V 3M6

Objective: To display to the people of Canada the benefits of unity under Confederation by dealing with the issues that divide the country, while displaying the benefits of social peace, Confederation, and federalism.

Unity Train Foundation
Box 522
Station "B"
Ottawa, Ontario
KIP 5P6

Objectives: To provide an opportunity for the Canadian people to become more familiar with the people and provinces which make up this country by providing a visible link among the regions; to foster a better understanding of the diverse nature of this country, and greater awareness of the realities with which Canadians live.

University of Toronto President's Special Committee
c/o Bill Saywell
Innis College
2 Sussex Avenue
Toronto, Ontario
M5S 1J5

Objective: To reassess Confederation.

QUÉBEC

Association canadienne d'éducation de langue française
980 St. Louis
Sillery, Québec
G1S 1C7

Objective: To promote French language and culture in the field of education in Canada.

Canadian Chamber of Commerce
1080 Beaver Hall Hill
Montréal, Québec
H2Z 1T2

Objective: To improve the economic, social, and political environment in Canada.

Citizen Impact
c/o National Council of Jewish Women
5775 Victoria Avenue
Montréal, Québec
H3W 2R4

Objective: To serve as a vehicle for the expression of concern regarding the Québec referendum, Canadian unity, and the quality of life (human rights) in Québec.

Commitment Canada
200 Davignon
Cowansville, Québec
J2K 1N9

Objectives: To encourage and assist as many Canadians as possible to make a visible demonstration of their pride in Canada. To facilitate contacts between Canadians in different parts of the country, either directly through travel-related projects, or indirectly through communication links of Commitment Canada or project publicity.

Conseil du civisme de Montréal
10025 l'Acadie Blvd.
Montréal, Québec
H9N 1L6

Objective: To promote a sense of civic responsibility and closer co-operation among all ethnic groups.

Co-ordinating Committee for a United Canada
Place Ville Marie 1
Suite 1411
Montréal, Québec
H3B 2B2

Objectives: To maintain a calendar to avoid confusion in planning events among the various groups. To organize a speaker's bureau. To provide volunteers. To do research.

Council for Canadian Unity
1470 Peel
Suite 925
Montréal, Québec
H3A 1T1

Objectives: To emphasize the benefits of national unity, encourage greater dialogue and understanding among Canadians, and engender a pride in our country by the promotion of various social and educational programs and research.

Decision Canada
Place Ville Marie 1
Room 1411
Montréal, Québec
H3B 2B2

Objective: To inform the Québec population of the necessity to decide that Québec's future is with Canada.

Gamma Study by McGill University
1001 Sherbrooke Street W.
Montréal, Québec
H3G 1G5
Objective: To provide technological, social, and economic forecasting for Canada.

Positive Action Committee
Box 1120
Station "H"
Montréal, Québec
H3G 2N1
Objectives: To participate in the development of the province of Québec within Canada and bring about within the non-Francophone community a forum for such participation.

Programme d'échange des étudiants du Québec
1117 St. Catherine Street W.
Suite 52
Montréal, Québec
H3B 1H9
Objective: To promote cultural exchanges in the province of Québec.

Québec-Canada
Box 56
Station "H"
Montréal, Québec
H3G 2K5
Objective: Québec-Canada is non-partisan association of Québec residents whose objective is to keep Québec within Canada by preparing for the referendum on independence.

Québec Chamber of Commerce
500 St. François Xavier
Montréal, Québec
H2Y 2T5
Objective: To encourage co-operation and promotion between companies and businessmen in Québec.

Ralli-Canada!
9637 Côte de Liesse
Dorval, Québec
H9P 1A3

Objective: To work towards a united Québec in a Canada in which all Canadians are equal.

SASKATCHEWAN

Centre d'étude bilingue
(Bilingual Centre)
College West
Room 218
University of Regina
Regina, Saskatchewan
S4S 0A2

Objective: To promote understanding between English- and French-speaking groups.

NOTES ON CONTRIBUTORS

MILTON ACORN is a poet, born in Charlottetown, Prince Edward Island, and now living in Toronto. In 1970 he won the unique Canadian Poet's Award granted by his peers.

GREGORY G. BAUM received his BA from McMaster University, his MA from Ohio State University, and his DTh from the University of Fribourg, Switzerland. He is presently teaching in the religious studies department of St. Michael's College, University of Toronto.

S. D. BERKOWITZ is Assistant Professor, Department of Sociology and New College, and Research Associate at the Institute for Policy Analysis at the University of Toronto. He is a specialist in studies of corporate and institutional structure.

TERESA BERKOWITZ (BA Saskatchewan) is a Toronto sculptor and writer. She has been a researcher and psychological counsellor at the Swift Current Mental Health Centre in Saskatchewan.

ERNEST CHANG is a physician, computer scientist, and researcher on health.

JEAN CHRÉTIEN, MP, PC, is the Member of Parliament for Shawinigan–St. Maurice, Minister of Finance, former President of the Treasury Board, former Minister of Industry, Trade, and Commerce, and former Minister of Indian and Northern Affairs.

JUNE CORMAN is a graduate student in the Department of Sociology at the University of Toronto and a Canada Council Pre-doctoral Fellow.

JAN DUKSZTA is a psychiatrist and MPP. He is the NDP Health Critic in the Ontario Legislative Assembly.

DAVIDSON DUNTON was co-chairman of the Royal Commission on Bilingualism and Biculturalism. He is Professor and Director of the Institute of Canadian Studies at Carleton University and co-chairman of the national unity group, Contact Canada.

LAWRENCE F. FELT is Chairman of the Department of Sociology

at Memorial University. He has worked extensively with anti-poverty groups in Montreal, Toronto, and Newfoundland.

EUGENE FORSEY (Senator) was born in Newfoundland and educated in Ottawa, Montreal, and Oxford. He is a former trade union official and university teacher and the author of *The Royal Power of Dissolution of Parliament* (1943) and *Freedom and Order* (1974). He was called to the Senate in October 1970.

ROYCE FRITH (Senator) is a QC and former legal advisor to the Commissioner of Official Languages. He was President of the Ontario Liberal Association in 1959-60 and a member of the Royal Commission on Bilingualism and Biculturalism in the 1960s. He was called to the Senate in April 1977.

F. KENNETH HARE is Director of the Institute for Environmental Studies at the University of Toronto. For many years, while at McGill University, he worked on surveys of northern Québec and Labrador.

JOHN HARNEY was born in Québec City and educated at Queen's University, Kingston. Formerly New Democratic MP for Scarborough West, he is now a member of the Humanities Department, Atkinson College, York University, Toronto.

EDWARD HARVEY is a Professor of Sociology at the Ontario Institute for Studies in Education and the University of Toronto. He is the author of *Education Systems and the Labour Market*, a recent study of post-secondary graduates in Ontario.

JOHN F. KINZEL is Special Advisor to the Minister of Finance, Government of Saskatchewan. He has worked extensively with federal and provincial government agencies concerned with resource development. He was editor of the *Proceedings* of the Resources for Tomorrow Conference and has written widely in the area of resource management.

MAURICE LAMONTAGNE (Senator) is a member of the Club of Rome, a Fellow of the Royal Society of Canada, and Chairman of the Senate Special Committee on Science Policy.

ROBERT K. LOGAN is a futurist, Associate Professor of Physics at the University of Toronto, member of the Canadian Association of the Club of Rome, founder of the Club of Gnu, and Chairman of the Policy and Research Committee, Liberal Party of Canada (Ontario). He is co-author, with Marshall McLuhan, of two forthcoming books: *Library Without Walls: The Future of Information Science*, and *Alphabet: Mother of Invention*. He is also the editor of *The Way Ahead for Canada*.

H. MARSHALL MCLUHAN is Marshall McLuhan, author of *The Gutenberg Galaxy* and *Understanding Media*, and Director of the Centre for Culture and Technology, University of Toronto.

GALE MOORE is bio-medical book selector, University of Toronto Library, and Associate Instructor, Faculty of Library Science, University of Toronto. She is an information consultant concerned with communication and learning.

CLAUDE MORIN (BA, Laval University, MSW, Columbia) was born in Montmorency near Québec City. From 1956 to 1963 he was a Professor in the Faculty of Social Sciences of Laval University. He is now Québec Minister of Intergovernmental Affairs and a member of the Priorities Committee of the Québec Council of Ministers.

BARRINGTON NEVITT is a telecommunications engineer, educator, author, consultant, and the former Director of Innovation and Management Training, Ontario Development Corporation.

ANTHONY SCOTT is Professor of Economics, University of British Columbia. He is a Fellow of the Royal Society of Canada, and has published widely in the field of political economy.

LORNE TEPPERMAN is Associate Professor of Sociology at the University of Toronto. Author of *Social Mobility in Canada* and *Crime Control: The Urge Toward Authority*, Professor Tepperman has written numerous papers and is completing a co-authored book, *Canada's Political Culture*.

LEONARD WAVERMAN is Associate Professor of Economics and Research Associate at the Institute for Policy Analysis, University of Toronto. He is the author of numerous articles and books on energy resources.